Date Due

The Beginnings
of the American People
and Nation

BY

MARY G. KELTY

*Formerly Supervisor of History and the Social Studies in the Train-
ing Department and Instructor in the Teaching of History
State Teachers College, Oshkosh, Wisconsin*

GINN AND COMPANY
BOSTON · NEW YORK · CHICAGO · LONDON
ATLANTA · DALLAS · COLUMBUS · SAN FRANCISCO

𝕿𝖍𝖊 𝕬𝖙𝖍𝖊𝖓𝖆𝖚𝖒 𝕻𝖗𝖊𝖘𝖘

GINN AND COMPANY · PRO-
PRIETORS · BOSTON · U.S.A.

Introduction for Teachers

This book and its companion volume, *The Growth of the American People and Nation*, contain material from the field of American history which is adapted to the interests and capacities of children in the middle grades of the elementary school. Although material for use in these grades has long been in existence, its selection, organization, and gradation have been little affected by the recent fundamental changes in educational principles and procedure. In her *Teaching American History in the Middle Grades of the Elementary School* (Ginn and Company, 1928) Miss Kelty has presented the theory and the technique which have been evolved by modern experimentation. This book will be of great service to teachers, but success in improving the teaching of history depends largely on the materials conveniently available for use by the children.

The following educational principles and practices have served as standards in the preparation of *The Beginnings of the American People and Nation*.

1. *Emphasis should be laid on silent reading.* Recently an insistent demand has arisen for factual materials for use during the silent-reading period. Materials from the content subjects, but adapted to the interests and capacities of young children, are urgently needed. The stories contained in these volumes are offered to meet such a demand. They may be used in the history period and in some of the silent-reading periods.

2. *History in the intermediate grades should be read rather than studied.* To furnish vicarious experience, history should be read freely and fluently. Laborious study and much memorizing do not attain the objectives for intermediate-grade history. Texts which are skeleton summaries are not suitable. Material chosen should be full of romance, adventure, and colorful detail. It should provide an atmosphere of reality, awaken interest, and aid in building up concepts.

3. *Books for children should be written in a tested vocabulary.* Recent studies show that children's difficulties with history are due partly to the vocabulary and partly to a lack of understanding of the abstract topics dealt with. The second of these factors is treated below under 4. Vocabulary difficulties themselves are of two distinct types. One consists of the technical terms necessary to the subject matter. This cannot be avoided. The technical expressions in history used in this book have been taken from the list of minimal-essential terms in Miss Kelty's book for teachers. They are purposely included in the narrative and are repeated often to insure understanding. Eighty such terms are used.

The other difficulty presented to children is that of the author's own vocabulary, which is his medium in telling the story and explaining the technical terms mentioned above. To insure clarity, the basic vocabulary of this volume is included within the first 1500 words of the Thorndike Word List plus 526 additional words whose use was desirable in order to portray the interesting details of the narrative. The vocabulary has been checked also by the Graded Word List prepared by Dr. B. R. Buckingham and Dr. E. W. Dolch.

4. *Concepts should be developed before they are named.* One of the greatest obstacles to comprehension is the use of abstract terms or topics for which the children's experiences furnish no basis. Great care has been taken throughout these stories to develop the concepts fully before naming them. Examples of this principle are found on page 23 in connection with the word "siege" and on pages 206 and 285 in connection with the words "representative" and "town meeting."

5. *The number of minimal essentials, such as proper names and dates, should be limited.* The proper names and the dates used in these stories are limited to the list given in *Teaching American History in the Middle Grades of the Elementary School.* Those chosen are mentioned repeatedly, are strongly stressed in the stories, and are included in the test exercises.

6. *Adequate emphasis should be placed on the social and economic phases of history.* Adequate attention has been given to the social and economic phases of history in selecting the content of the stories. The number of military and political leaders has been limited to the irreducible minimum, and entire units of social and economic materials new to elementary texts have been included, especially in the fifth-grade work.

7. *Children should be supplied with an abundance of self-testing exercises.* To assist children in checking their own comprehension of the historically significant phases of the stories, self-testing exercises and questions are provided. These serve as study guides.

8. *The visual appeal should be intelligently utilized.* The pictures and maps in the volume have been chosen for the purpose of aiding the child to visualize events. Connection with the story is established by means of legends beneath the pictures and by map-study directions embodied in the narrative. The visual aids thus become an essential part of the content.

9. *Materials of instruction should be organized as units.* Grouping materials of instruction into coherent units is rapidly becoming the accepted practice. For more than a decade progressive school systems have been seeking the unit organization of subjects. Several modern texts in history now offer such an organization, and doubtless the use of texts arranged according to the older practices will soon be the exception.

10. *Textbook material should be subjected to experimental verification.* Before publication these stories were used for four years in history classes of the training department of the State Teachers College, Oshkosh, Wisconsin; in Bloomsburg, Pennsylvania, for one year; and in the public schools of Wilmette, Illinois, for two years. Through such experimental classroom use, difficulties in sentence structure and lack of clearness in presentation were detected and remedied by the author. It is therefore reasonable to conclude, after such experimental use and verification, that these stories are adapted to the interests and capacities of intermediate-grade children.

R. M. TRYON

Contents

The Beginnings of the
American People and Nation

To the Boys and Girls who are about to read This Book

If you like to read stories, you will like this book. The stories tell of the discovery of our country and how ships were wrecked and men lost for years in the wilderness, trying to explore its coasts and rivers. Some of the later stories tell about the beginnings of our nation.

Perhaps your father and mother will be interested to have you tell them about these great events which happened so many years ago. As you read the stories, keep in mind that you may not have the book before you when you want to tell the stories.

Many boys and girls have read these stories. They found them easy to read. The stories are written just as I would tell them if I were talking to you. You will not have to stop and think about the meaning of the words. I have given you the names of only a few persons and places, so that you may the more easily remember them.

Somewhere in almost all the stories there is a picture which will interest you. Of course you know that photography was invented long after the events took place which are told about in this book. For that reason most of the pictures are drawn by people who imagined, as well as they could, how the places and the people looked. The picture is followed by a question which you may not be able to answer until you have read the story. There are also several maps to help you to locate the places mentioned. Perhaps your teacher will show you these places on the large wall map at the front of the room.

Now we are ready to begin reading. First, read the story all the way through. Do not try to remember everything that is told. Just get the story. Afterwards see if you can answer the questions at the end. If you cannot, turn back in the story and find the answers. Some exercises and games are placed after the questions. I believe you will enjoy them.

THE AUTHOR

Unit One

Why Men wanted to find a Short Route to the East

||||||||||||||||||||||||||||||||||||||||||||||||||||||||||||||||||||||||||||||||||||||||||||||||||||||||||||||||||||||||||||||||||||||||||

TITLES OF STORIES

Unit One

Why Men wanted to find a Short Route to the East

Suppose that we had to go without ice in the summer time. Meat would spoil, would it not? The only way in which we could keep it would be to cover it with spices. How gladly, then, would we spend our money for spices! If we could not buy any in our own country, do you think that we would send for some from the lands where spices grow? This story tells how men from the West first reached the spice lands.

ONE OF THE GREATEST JOURNEYS THAT EVER WAS MADE

Do you like to hear your father or your mother tell stories? And did you ever stop to think that the children about whom you read in your history books liked to hear *their* fathers and mothers tell stories? They listened with as much delight as you do.

No one ever listened more eagerly than young Marco Polo, who lived in Venice long ago. His father and uncle had traveled to China and had seen more wonderful sights than anyone in Venice. Marco never tired of hearing about the strange people among whom they had lived and the long journeys they had made.

The Polos go to India and China

Marco's father and uncle were traders; their business was buying and selling spices. No one knew just where the spices came from. It was a country far to the east; some said it was an island. Long before Marco was born his father had once met other traders who said they came from the spice lands. He had decided to go back with them and see for himself just what kind of country it was.

So Marco's father and uncle had set out. They were not the first white men who had ever gone to China and India. Some good men of the church had traveled there long before, but no one knew much about their journey.

The Polos set out by an overland route, for the journey had never yet been made by sea. Most of the way they had to ride on the backs of camels. It was a long, hard journey; but they had made up their minds to reach the land of spices, perfumes, and silks, and they kept on.

When they reached China the king was very kind to them. He asked many questions about the West, made them rich presents, and when they left gave them a piece of gold with strange writing on it. Any

The Polos leaving Venice
Why do the people all seem sad?

man who saw the gold piece would know that they
were friends of the king and would help them. Before
they left, the king made them promise that they would
return some day and would bring to him teachers
from their own land.

Marco Polo goes with his Father and Uncle

When Marco heard that his father and uncle were
going back to China, he was greatly excited. He
wanted so much to go with them! His father was
troubled; he thought the boy was too young to endure
such hardships. But Marco had been lonely at home

since his mother died, and he begged so hard that at last his father gave his consent. Marco might go with them.

Two years went by before all the necessary business was attended to; by that time Marco was seventeen years old. Only two teachers had been found who dared to make so long a journey and to face its many dangers.

At last father, uncle, the two teachers, and Marco set forth, little dreaming that it would be twenty-four years before some of them would again see their homes.

The journey began in one of the fine large ships that Marco had so often watched at home. After sailing many days they came to a land which the people of Venice had known for hundreds of years. There they left the ship and took the overland route, riding on the backs of camels. In this way they traveled a thousand days, or, in other words, about three years.

When the two teachers saw how long and hard the trip was to be, they were discouraged and returned home. The Polo family went on alone.

They went first through a country of mountains. In summer many cows were feeding there, but in winter it was so cold that no living thing could be seen. The people who lived close by said that Noah's Ark was resting on top of one of the mountains, but no one had ever been able to climb high enough to see it.

In the next country they saw a great well of oil such as people use for burning, and then they came to the land where silk was made. From that time on, in almost every house they passed, the people were busy making silk.

These people were different from any that Marco had ever known. They were of a yellow color and were small and thin. But they were able to make many very beautiful things which the people of Venice could not: silks of all kinds, beautiful little figures of wood, and articles of gold and silver — for there seemed to be plenty of these precious metals. The people also made swords of steel so fine and strong that they could be bent round like a circle without breaking. The way did not seem long to Marco, since he was always seeing new and strange sights.

In the land they reached next were mountains of salt, from which the people cut pieces to use in cooking. Other mountains were full of rubies, all of which the king kept for himself. No one else dared to take even one.

All this time the road had been going up and up until it reached a region so high that it was called the "Roof of the World." It was a very cold place; so our travelers hurried on, and came, after a long time, to a great plain. This plain was a desert, across which they journeyed for twelve days without seeing any growing thing or any house. Even in the desert it was yet so cold and high that fire would not burn brightly nor give out much heat.

Marco Polo in China

This country was ruled by the king of China. Marco was much interested in seeing how different the houses were from his own. They were somewhat like Indian wigwams, but round at the top. When a family moved, the house was put on wheels. Some houses were large enough to hold a thousand people. The people had learned one thing which we sometimes think was discovered in our own times. They made milk into a paste, which looked very strange to the Polo family. Today we call this paste condensed milk.

The end of the journey was at last in sight. They had reached the place they were seeking. The great king of the country was living in his summer palace, so to the palace our travelers went. They first saw a wall sixteen miles around. Inside were rivers, and a beautiful park full of strange animals. In the center of the park was a shining white-stone palace, the rooms of which were lined with gold and painted with pictures of men and animals and flowers.

The great king received the travelers very kindly and was glad to see that they had kept their promise to return. He was sorry that the teachers had gone back, but was pleased with Marco, whom he had not seen before. The father and the uncle entered the service of the great king. They told him how business was carried on in Venice and gave him new ideas about how to make war. In return he allowed them to trade, and soon they became rich.

Marco was a bright boy. In a short time he learned many of the languages of the Far East, and the manner of writing, and the way in which the people worked and lived. The great king sent him with messages to far parts of the country. When Marco returned he not only reported the business on which he had been sent but also told about the manners and ways of the people and the strange sights he had seen. The great king delighted in hearing such stories and learned to love Marco.

For seventeen years the Polos remained at the court of the great king. Marco was always in his service, going on long journeys to the north, the west, and the south. Sometimes he was gone six months at a time. So it came to pass that he knew more about China than any other man, more even than the great king himself.

The Return Home

When seventeen years had gone by, Marco's father and uncle began to grow old. They had gathered a great amount of money and, being tired of the riches of the court, began to think of returning home. Each time they spoke of it to the great king he seemed sorry. "I do not want you to leave me," he would answer.

They would never have been allowed to leave if the great king had had his way. But the king of a country far to the south wanted a wife and sent men to China asking that a lady of the court might come to marry him. The great king agreed. He prepared to send the lady and, with her, many gifts. Then this question came up: By what route should he send her on so long a journey? Not overland, because there were many wars in those parts. Then he must send her by sea. His men were not good sailors, but the Polo family could sail ships very well. There was nothing for the great king to do but to send the three Polos back with her. It was then about the year 1300.

You may be sure that the Polos were glad to go, even though the king had treated them so kindly. They wanted to return home and to see their old friends.

They started from the city from which most of the pepper came, and sailed in a fine ship for more than two years before they came to the country where they were to leave the lady. No white men had ever before taken that journey. At one time they had to stay for months on an island of man-eaters.

After leaving the lady with her husband, they sold their ship and traveled once more on the backs of camels. After another long journey they reached Venice, having been away from home twenty-four years.

No one in Venice knew them. Many of their friends were dead, and the others could not believe that these two old men and the middle-aged man could be the Polos. You should know too that Marco and his father and uncle had dressed in very poor clothes on the journey, so that no one would think they were rich and try to harm them.

This is the way they proved that they were indeed the Polo family. They gave a party to which they invited all their friends. When the guests were about to sit down to dinner, the three Polos came forth in red silk clothing wonderful to see. After a little while they went back to their rooms and came out in red satin. Later in the meal they changed again and came forth in red velvet. By this time their friends were almost ready to believe.

The Polos showing their jewels

Can you find the three Polos in the picture?

After the meal was over, the Polos brought out the old clothes in which they had returned home. They opened all the seams and took from them great numbers of precious stones of all colors and sizes — rubies and diamonds and pearls and many more. All the riches that the great king had given them they had traded for precious stones. Such a great pile poured out on the table quite took their friends' breath away! They said: "You are indeed the Polos. We will honor you for your great deeds by making you officers of our city."

Marco Polo's Book

For some time our travelers lived in peace and plenty and told their wonderful stories to all. But Venice, their fair city, had a great enemy, with whom she was generally fighting. Soon a new war began, and Marco Polo was made captain of a ship. His ship was taken, and Marco was cast into prison. There he had to remain for a year.

How long the days seemed! There was nothing to do; so Marco spent much of his time in thinking about the wonderful adventures he had had and in telling the other prisoners about them. After a while the people in the enemy's city heard that there was a great traveler in the prison, and many of them came to see him. Marco Polo grew very tired of telling his story over and over again; and at last one of the other prisoners said to him: "Why not write your wonderful adventures in a book? Then people could read the book, and you would not have to tell your story so often." It seemed a good idea; but since there was no printing at that time, the writing would have to be done by hand.

Marco answered: "You are a much better writer than I am. I will tell you the whole story, and you can write as I talk." The other prisoner agreed, and in this way was written *The Book of Sir Marco Polo*.

In the book Marco told the story that you have read here, and much more. He told of a palace in which the steps were of gold and silver, the floor was of silver, and the roof was of gold. He told of the wonderful roads over which a traveler could make a ten days' journey in two days; of the largest river in the world, which the people called Son of the Ocean; of towns in which all strangers had to live outside the walls. He told of a "snake" whose body was as big as a barrel. What did he mean?[1] He told of burning "black stones." What were they?[2]

The book was copied many times and read in other lands. Most people did not believe it, and it is true that the stories were changed somewhat when Marco told them over and over again to his friends. But the stories of gold and silver, of spices and perfumes, and of great numbers of precious stones made a few wish to go to China. They kept saying to each other: "Let us go to the strange lands Marco Polo has told about. Then we too will see the wonderful sights and will become rich."

Thus Marco Polo made many people interested in the Far East. We shall see later what his book led some of them to do.

Thinking It Over

Did you understand what the story told you? Test yourself by the questions given below. Can you answer them? If not, turn to the story and find the answers. They will help you to do the next exercise.

1. Can you find the sentence which tells how Marco's father and uncle traveled to China the first time?

2. Why did the king make Marco's father and uncle promise to return to China?

[1] An alligator.
[2] Coal; unknown to southern Europe at that time.

3. By what route did the Polos return home the second time?

4. When the Polo family reached home why did no one know them?

5. What did Marco Polo's book make people want to do?

Something to do

In the story you read certain names and dates which are missing in the following sentences. On a piece of paper make a list of the words which you think should be used in place of the blanks. Show the list to your teacher.

1. The man whose book told about the Far East was
_____.

2. He was born in the city of _____.

3. He traveled for seventeen years in _____.

4. He returned home in about the year _____.

Here are some new words used in the story. Choose the right words for the blanks in the following sentences:

Far East   **overland**   **route**

1. India and China were called the _____ _____.

2. The path, or road, over which people travel is a
_____.

3. A route which passes over land rather than over the sea is an _____ route.

Marco Polo's story made people very eager to find a way to go to China.

Hundreds of years ago people in Europe did not use soap or glass or carpets or beautiful dyes. From whom do you suppose they learned that mattresses would make their beds more comfortable? This story will tell you.

WHAT MEN FROM THE WEST LEARNED IN THE HOLY LAND

Which day of all the year do children like best? Most will answer "Christmas." Why does Christmas come on the twenty-fifth of December? Because Jesus was born on that day; so we keep it as a holiday.

We are interested not only in the day when Jesus was born but also in the places where he lived. The town where he was born, the church which he attended, the lake on which he sailed, and the grave in which he lay are very dear to all of us. We call that land the Holy Land.

Journeys to the Holy Land

For many years after Jesus died, people from all over the world came to visit the Holy Land. Because they had to travel far they were called *pilgrims*. They would wander around the holy places and perhaps pick up a stone from Jesus' grave or take a leaf from a tree near his workshop. These they carried home.

The king who ruled the country did not belong to the same church as the pilgrims, so he made them pay a tax to enter his lands. But the pilgrims were glad to pay it so that they might visit their Lord's home.

19

In time even far-away Venice heard of the Holy Land. You must remember that Venice was a great trading city. Its townsmen therefore not only went to see the village where Jesus lived, but they also began to trade with the natives of the country. Some stayed and set up shops. The traders from Venice would bring slaves, wool, and iron. Traders from the Far East would bring silks and spices. Then they would exchange goods. In this way Venice grew richer than ever.

For many years the two classes of people, pilgrims and traders, continued to travel to the East. They found the way long, the road very hard to follow, the tax heavy, and the dangers great; but the pilgrims felt paid for all their trouble when they saw the Holy City, and the traders made so much money that they too were satisfied.

The Turks conquer the Holy Land

After a time, however, a great change took place. The Holy Land was conquered by a fierce and terrible people, the Turks, whose lands stretched from China to the Mediterranean Sea. The Turks cared nothing for holy places: they cast down the churches, they robbed and killed the pilgrims, and they drove the traders out of their lands.

The Christians in all countries of the world grew angry. They began to say to one another: "The Holy Land is no longer safe. Shall our pilgrims be treated thus? Shall we allow the terrible Turks to spoil the city of Jesus? Can we bear to have our holy

The Christians' first sight of Jerusalem

Can you tell why it was so hard for the Christians to cross this
hot country?

places in the hands of strangers?" And they all answered: "No. We will make war upon them. We
will gather the greatest army that ever was seen, and
fall upon the Turks like a destroying wind. God wills
it!" And from the farthest corners of the Christian
countries came back the cry "God wills it!"

People became so excited that on all the roads, in
public places, and in their homes they could talk of
nothing else. There was to be war against the Turks.
The holy places were to belong once more to the
Christians! Each man who would promise to go received from the church a red cross, which he sewed on

his left arm. Because the holy war was for the sake of the cross, it was called a *crusade*, which means "for the cross."

Men, women, and children, all were ready to go. Some went for love of the holy places, some for love of adventure or travel, some to win for themselves the lands of the Turks, and some to trade in the country after the Christians had conquered it. Many started off without supplies of food or money. They had no idea how far away the Holy Land was, and at each new town they would ask, "Is this Jerusalem?" Long before their journey was ended, many died by the way.

The Crusades

Late in the spring the main army was ready. There were so many that they could not all go at once, but were divided into five sections. All the long journey had to be made overland, since not enough ships could be found to carry the people. The Crusaders climbed slowly over the rocks of the mountains in the winter; they journeyed for days at a time in cold rain in the spring; they passed over burning waste land in the summer. Men, women, and horses died for want of water in the heat of the July sun, because they did not know how to carry water in skins as the natives did. They sometimes had to use sheep and goats to carry their baggage. The Turks followed at a distance, shooting their arrows at the sick, the weak, or any that could not keep up with the army. Those were terrible days for the Crusaders!

When they saw the first city of the Turks a great shout went up. They were glad to fight at last, after having come so far. The battle was won with ease. The second city, however, was much larger and stronger. Many great battles were fought around it, but neither side won. The Christians then decided to draw up their army around the city and let no one go in or out until the city was given up. So when the Turks had used up all the food and water in the city and could get no more, they had to choose between going hungry and giving up their city. They chose to give it to the Christians. In this way the second city was won. When an army wins a city in this way, we say they win it by a *siege*.

After meeting such good fortune the Christians forgot their hard journey and pressed on to the Holy City. They reached it three years after they had left home. Placing their army around the walls, they again made a siege. They built machines which threw great stones against the walls; they climbed up and shot arrows down into the city. The Turks from the walls shot at the Christians and poured fire down upon them. So many were killed on both sides that the dead lay in great piles.

At last, however, the Turks were beaten and the Christians entered the city. The first crusade was over. The Holy Land was won.

The Crusaders decided that they must have a king to rule the country. They chose a great and good man, but he refused to take the name "king." He said, "In the same city where Jesus died on the cross, shall

I wear a crown of gold?" He remained in the country, however, and ruled it. Most of the Crusaders went back to their homes in Europe, but some stayed and lived in the Holy Land the rest of their lives.

Trade Grows Up

When the war was over, the natives and the Christians became friendly. The people from the West found out that those of the East knew many things which they themselves did not. They learned how to raise lemons, oranges, plums, watermelons, rice, and, best of all, sugar cane. They learned to use ginger and such spices as pepper and cloves. They learned that they could color their clothing by the use of dyes, that silk was much more beautiful than wool, and that glass could be used for dishes. They found that carpets added to the comfort of a room and that mattresses made beds softer. They learned the use of soap, and began to bathe more often. The men began to shave. They used windmills to pump water. They had never known any of these things at home, for life in the West was very simple.

Once the Christian ruler sent some of his soldiers with a message to the king of the Turks. The soldiers passed between marble doors, under golden roofs, and over beautiful floors. They wondered greatly at the sight, since in the West there was nothing to compare with it. There were marble bowls for fish. Strange birds flew about in the rooms. Suddenly a silk curtain covered with pearls rose and showed the king on a golden throne. The soldiers remembered these wonderful sights as long as they lived.

You may be sure that the Christians liked the new ideas. When they went back to Europe many of them took seeds of the new plants with them, and at home, in the West, taught their neighbors the new ways of living. Thus the West learned from the East.

The traders of Venice had built many ships to help to carry the Crusaders to the Holy Land, so they could very well spare a few for the Eastern trade. They began to make regular trips each year, taking with them slaves, wool, iron, and leather. In every Christian city of the Holy Land they had a market in which they sold their goods. They bought from the natives or from camel trains out of the Far East the goods for which they had come. In this way a great trade grew up between the East and the West. It was the stories of these traders that had made Marco Polo's father wish to go to China.

End of the Crusades

For a time all went well. Then the Christian nobles began to grow jealous of one another; each wanted to be king, and none would help another. So the Turks began to conquer the land again, little by little, town by town. A second crusade from the West failed to help. Still the Christian nobles would not work together. There could be only one result. Jerusalem was taken again by the Turks, and in a short time all the Holy Land was again held by the enemy.

The news was a great blow to the West. After much hard work a third crusade was made ready. A few of the towns in the Holy Land were taken; but again the Christian kings quarreled among themselves, and the crusade failed.

A fourth crusade was started, but the army did not even reach Jerusalem. Instead they stopped and fought against the great Christian city of Constantinople. They robbed the homes of the people, and even went into their churches and carried off their holy treasures. The fact that these people too were Christians made no difference. Christians were now fighting against Christians instead of against Turks.

After that the men of the West lost heart. Four more crusades were begun; but the great leaders did not take part in them, for they had come to believe that the Holy Land could never be taken and held by Christians from the West. Once a band of children started out, hoping that the Lord would help them to succeed where older people had failed. But they never reached the Holy Land; some of them met a sad death at sea, and others were sold as slaves.

The West became interested in other questions; and no matter how hard the churchmen tried, they could never again lead an army to the holy wars. However, there were still many pilgrims who wished to visit the Holy Land. They learned that they could make the journey, just as they had before the Crusades began, if they were willing to pay a tax to the Turks. They decided that paying a small sum in this way was easier than making war.

The people of Europe could not be happy, however, without the goods of the East which they had learned to use while on the Crusades. So trade continued, even after the Holy Land had been lost.

You may see, then, that in one way the Crusades and Marco Polo's journey had the same effect: they both made the people of the West want the goods of the East.

A Memory Test

I. Can you answer the following questions? If not, turn to the story and find the answers. You will need to use the facts soon.

1. How did the Turks treat pilgrims who went to the Holy Land?

2. Why did Christians go on the Crusades? Give four reasons.

3. Can you tell some things that Christians learned from the people in the Holy Land?

4. Why were the Turks able to take the Holy Land again?

5. In what way did the Crusades and Marco Polo's journey have the same effect?

II. Fill these blanks with words used in the story. Make a list of the right words and show it to your teacher.

1. The _ _ _ _ _ _ _ took the Holy Land from the Christians.

2. The great body of water between Europe and the Holy Land is the _ _ _ _ _ _ _ _ _ _ _ _ _ _.

3. The great city of _ _ _ _ _ _ _ was attacked in the fourth crusade.

III. The following new words were used in the story. Can you put each one in the right blank in these sentences? Add the right words to your list.

pilgrims   capture   crusade
siege   conquers

1. An army makes a _____ when it will not let any-one into or out of a town. Its purpose is to force the townspeople to give up the town.

2. An army _____ an enemy when it beats him so badly that he must do just as he is told.

3. A _____ is a war for a holy cause.

4. _____ are people who travel to holy places.

5. To _____ a person or place is to take him or it by war.

The Crusades were fought to win back the Holy Land.

The men who went on the Crusades learned to like the products of the East and wanted to trade with the East.

Do you always walk down the same streets in coming to school? By how many different ways could you come? There were three ways for the men from the West to reach the East. Find out by reading the story what these three routes were.

MAIN TRADE ROUTES TO THE EAST

You would perhaps like to know how people traveled to the East in order to trade. There were three main trade routes: the middle, the northern, and the southern.

The Middle Trade Route

The middle route was the oldest. It had been used for hundreds of years. Ships started from Europe, where they were loaded with woolen and linen cloth, hides, and metal. These things may not seem very important to you, but in the East the people did not have them and were willing to pay high prices for them.

The ships crossed the Mediterranean Sea and came to Asia. There all the goods were removed from the ships and loaded on the backs of camels. Some of the goods would be torn or broken, some would get wet, some would be lost; and it cost a great deal of time and money to change from the ships to the camels.

What a sight the caravan was! Picture to yourself a long line of camels, sometimes fifty, sometimes five hundred, sometimes even a thousand. A long rope led from the first camel to the second, another rope from the second camel to the third, and so on. All were thus tied together. The leader's harness was of red leather with little bells which rang when he walked. When all was ready a man on horseback led the way, for camels are very stupid. The caravan started early in the morning, rested awhile at noon, and then went on again until late at night. If the camels were very heavily loaded they could travel only about two miles an hour.

Travel by caravan was very slow. The reason why the middle route was the best was because camels were used only a little way. After a while a river was reached. The camels stopped, the goods were unloaded and again put into ships, and the ships sailed down the river to the sea. Then they went on to India.

This is as far as the people from the West generally went, but some of the natives of India went on to China.

The traders brought back so many goods to the West that we can hardly name them all. The chief product was spices: nutmegs, cinnamon bark, cloves, ginger, and, most important of all, the pepper berry. In Europe even kings thought themselves fortunate if they could season their food with pepper, and they paid the high prices gladly.

There were also brought back from the Far East precious stones that were little known in Europe: diamonds, rubies, pearls, and others whose very names the people of the West did not know. These were sold to rich men for rings and chains and sometimes to the churches for use in their services.

There were also sweet-smelling woods, from which pretty boxes and chairs were made. Drugs and per-

A caravan unloading

What goods are probably in the bags on the camels' backs?

fumes were sold. The traders brought rich cloths of silk and cotton and gold to cover the bare walls of the houses in Europe, and heavy rugs to place on the cold floors.

We must not forget to speak of the dishes. They were much more beautiful than any which the people of the West had seen before. Rich people would not buy any dishes except those that came from the East. Even today we call our finer dishes "china."

Dishes of glass, fine metal-work, and a beautiful blue dye called indigo, as well as a red dye, were carried to Europe. Perhaps the best of all, however, was sugar.

That was what everybody wanted; but it was so costly that none except the rich could buy it.

You may have noticed that none of the articles in the list of Eastern goods was really necessary. People in Europe could have lived without them, but not so pleasantly. Their food was coarse, their clothing was plain, and their houses were bare. Things that were beautiful or rare or hard to make had to be brought from the East. The East was far ahead of the West in such matters.

To sum up what has been said, the middle trade route was more important than any other because it was shorter. Ships came across the Mediterranean Sea, a little part of Asia was crossed by caravan, and then men sailed down the river straight to India. (Find the middle trade route on the map on page 33.)

You may wonder why any other trade route was ever used if the middle route was so good. But the fierce Turks captured the part of Asia over which the caravans traveled. To be sure, they did not say that no caravans could pass that way, but they taxed the travelers heavily, robbed some, and killed many. It no longer paid to carry goods over the middle route, and business there was ruined.

Genoa's Route in the North

Genoa had a route which was called the northern trade route. Her ships went by sea to the greatest city in the world. If you have thought Genoa and Venice great, you must know that they were only little villages compared with Constantinople. It was said that the

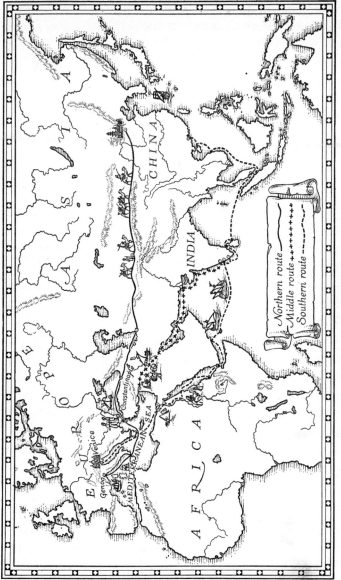

Early trade routes to the East

people there were as many as the sands of the sea, and the buildings as many as the stars in the sky. This, of course, was not exactly true, but Constantinople was a very great city.

In Constantinople the traders from Genoa left their ships and began the long caravan journey which lasted a hundred days, through snow and heat, until they came to China. (Find the northern trade route on the map on page 33.)

They could not trade in such common goods as carpets or dishes. What they carried had to be small in size but great in value. What would it be? Precious stones and silk. From the trade in precious stones and silk, Genoa became one of the greatest cities in Europe. Its trade route was much newer than the middle route, but it had already made almost as much money. Genoa would allow no other city to trade over this path.

But the same thing happened that had put an end to the middle route. The Turks went out against Constantinople year after year, always in greater numbers than before. At last, though its soldiers were brave and strong, it could hold out no longer. Constantinople was taken by the Turks in 1453.

As long as the trade had been good, Genoa was prosperous, even though there had been for years a great deal of trouble between the people and the ruling class. These troubles had been growing more and more frequent, however, so that when the trade route was closed and her business destroyed, the city was ruined. Her ships lay idle and rotting, grass grew in her streets, and her shops fell to pieces. All Genoa became poor.

Venice's Route in the South

Marco Polo's book had made many people of Venice eager to trade with the East. At first they went by the middle route, but they did not like to make the journey by caravan across Asia to the great river.

Instead they began going across the Mediterranean Sea to the great river of Africa. They sailed up this river until they came to a place near another sea which led into the ocean. There they unloaded their ships and took to caravans. The distance they had to travel on camels was shorter this way than by the middle route, though the whole journey was longer.

When the travelers reached the ocean, they found other ships. In them they sailed to India and China. This water route belonged to Venice; she would not let other cities go that way. (Find the southern trade route on the map on page 33.)

Since the traders from Venice did not have to travel so far by caravan, they could carry home more of the heavy goods, such as carpets, sugar, spices, and metals. And in India they could buy rubies and pearls.

Goods for which the people of Europe paid so high a price were very cheap in the East. The people of Venice could buy them for very little, but it cost a great deal of money to carry them home. Goods that were bought in India were sold in Africa for three times their cost, and by the time they reached Europe they were sold for five times their cost. The southern route was not so old as the middle route, but it had made a great deal of money for Venice.

Did the Turks capture this route also? At the time our story begins they had not yet conquered the lands around it, but they were very near. Day by day they kept pressing closer. Every journey that the traders made they expected would be their last.

So, little by little, Venice's trade was dying also. In a few years more the Turks would own all the land in Asia, and the trade routes would be no more.

Could no ships go to the East, then, by any route — northern, middle, or southern? Yes, a few ships a year did go through; but the Turks would tax them heavily, and the men all knew that they might be killed.

Never again could much trade with the East be carried on until someone should find a new route. The only route that could be used should go all the way by water, so that the merchants could keep out of the way of the Turks and the goods need not be loaded and unloaded so many times.

At the time of which we are reading no one knew of such a route. It looked as if all trade with the East must come to an end.

A Practice Exercise

I. Ask yourself the following questions. If you can answer all of them, choose one to ask your neighbor. You may judge whether he answers correctly.

1. Can you name some goods that were carried from the West to the East?

2. Where did the middle trade route go? Find it on the map.

3. Can you name some goods that were brought back from the East to the West?

4. Where did the northern trade route go? What city used it?

5. Where did the southern trade route go? What city used it?

6. Why did everyone want to find an all-water route to the East?

Sentences to Finish

II. In the story you will find the words which belong in the blanks below. Four are names of places, and one is a date. Write the correct words in a list and show your list to the teacher.

1. The people of the West went as far as _____ by the middle trade route.

2. The northern trade route belonged to _____.

3. The continent in which the people of the West lived is _____.

4. The continent in which India and China are located is _____.

5. Constantinople was captured by the Turks in the year _____.

III. These new words were used in the story. Put each one in the right blank below. Add these words to your list, arranged in the right order.

trade route	products	East
caravan	water route	West

1. Asia was called the _____.

2. Europe was called the _____.

3. A train of camels is a _ _ _ _ _ _ _.

4. Any road or path used for trading is a _ _ _ _ _ _ _ _ _ _ _ _ _.

5. A route that goes by water is a _ _ _ _ _ _ _ _ _ _ _ _ _.

6. Goods raised or made in a country are its _ _ _ _ _ _ _.

People traded with the East by three main trade routes. What were they?

It cost a great deal of money to change from land routes to sea routes.

Everybody wanted to find a route entirely by water.

Why did people want to travel to the Far East by sea rather than by land? Ask your teacher to point out Portugal and India on the globe. Plan how you might go from Portugal to India entirely by water; then read the story, and find out whether your route was the one really used.

HOW AN ALL–WATER ROUTE WAS FOUND

Many people wished for an all-sea route to China and India, but no one knew how to begin to search for it. After many years the question was answered in the little country of Portugal. Portugal had taken little part in the Crusades, but soldiers going and returning had stopped there with their tales of the East and of the great need for a new route.

Prince Henry the Navigator

In that land lived John, called the King of Good Memory, with his five strong sons. Four of the boys were interested in games, in court life, and in war, as were most youths of their age. One, however, was very different. Prince Henry was thoughtful and grave, spending most of his time in study. Many fine offers to take charge of armies were made him, but he refused. When he became a man he left his father's court and built, far out by the sea, a tower in which to study the stars.

In this place he spent most of his time for forty years, thinking out plans for discovering a new route to the

East, drawing maps, making finer instruments than sailors had ever used before, sending out ships, and hearing the reports of the captains when they returned. He had no wife nor children, but gave all his time to study. He was kind to all who came to him for help. His motto was, "Desire to do Well."

His tower was very close to Africa, as you may see on the map. At that time nobody knew how large Africa was. The part which had been visited by traders was only the northern edge. To be sure, caravans carrying gold and ivory and slaves came from the deserts farther south, but no one knew just where they came from, and no white man dared to find out.

Prince Henry's Plan

The great question on which Prince Henry was working was this: Could a ship sail around Africa and then go on to India? The wisest men of the day said that it could not be done — that Africa had no end. Their idea was discouraging to the prince, who hoped to find a route on which there would be no fear of being robbed, no slow caravan journeys, and no Turks or Arabs to share the gains.

The more he studied the question, the more he believed that such a route could be found. It would require many men, many ships, and a great deal of money. The prince therefore set to work to train seamen and to teach captains the art of sailing. It was wiser for Prince Henry to teach many men how to carry out his idea than himself to set out on the journey.

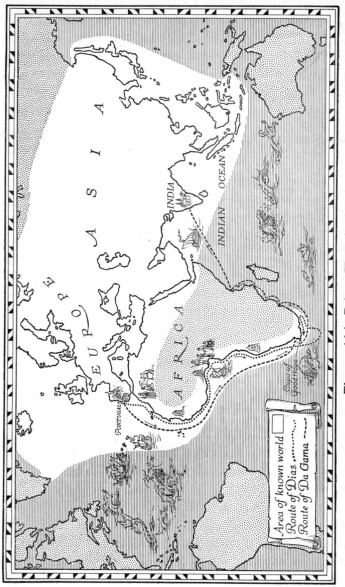

The world in Prince Henry's time

He built a town around his tower, "the prince's town," washed on three sides by the ocean. To this place he invited every good map-maker, every skilled maker of instruments, every wise man, every man who could build ships well, and every great traveler and sea captain that he could find. These men formed a school to teach sailors and shipbuilders, and soon the sailors and ships of Portugal became the best in the world. One of Prince Henry's older brothers was a great traveler. Once he brought home a large map showing the trade routes to the East.

Prince Henry then began to send out ships every year to try to sail around Africa. They had orders to discover and trade. When they returned they told about the part of the coast they had seen, and Prince Henry added it to his maps. Thus, year after year, the ships crept a little farther south.

Difficulties in carrying out the Plan

The work, however, was not easy. Although the captains had been trained, their men knew little about the real size and shape of the earth. They believed all the wild tales which had long been told about the ocean. None of them had ever sailed far out to sea, and did not know what was to be found there. Terrible stories were told. Some said that any white man who sailed far south would be turned black; that there were whirlpools to pull the ships under the waves; that the sun poured down fire; that the seas were boiling; that great animals would rise and destroy them; that the giant hand of the Evil One was raised above the waters to seize any man who came near; that they would sail downhill and never be able to come up again. Because so many evil things were believed about the ocean, it was called the "Green Sea of Darkness." God made the earth, they thought, but not the sea.

How discouraged Prince Henry must have been! Then his people began to object to having so much money wasted in the search. They whispered that the prince must be mad. His father and brothers, however, believed in him and gave him money when all his own had been spent. It must have been a bitter time for Prince Henry. For ten years little advance was made.

The Advance down the Coast

When Prince Henry first sent out his ships they returned with the story of a coast of hot white sand stretching out mile after mile. Sometimes the brown Arab natives would come down to the sea and trade with the sailors in gold and ivory and salt, but such trade amounted to little.

After some years they found a few islands, but on searching through his old books Prince Henry learned that they had been known long ago and forgotten again. He sent people to live in them, and towns began to grow up, but they were of little help in finding a route to India.

Many times the sailors would remember the stories about the Green Sea of Darkness and would return home without finding any new lands at all. Then Henry would become angry and would send them back, telling them not to dare to come home without news.

In this manner, slowly and painfully, the search continued. After sixteen years the captains reported that the desert had been passed and that plants and trees were now to be seen along the coast. They said, "So sweet was the smell from the shore that it was as if one passed by some fine fruit garden." Continuing still farther south, they came upon natives very different from the Arabs. These people were black in color and large and strong. The men of Portugal seized some of them and carried them home to sell as slaves.

Then people began to look upon Prince Henry's work very differently. They began to think he was a wise man, for had he not found a land from which they could get slaves? Many ships went out to the new lands to seize the black men.

Some of the slave-traders sailed still farther south and came to a land where the natives had gold. The natives were not sure whether the strange ships were birds or fishes. They were greatly surprised at seeing that the men of Portugal had white skins. When they found that the white men wanted to trade, they were glad to sell gold dust and slaves in exchange for horses.

After that Prince Henry never had any trouble in finding sailors. Everyone was eager to go to the south and get slaves and gold. In only a few years, more than nine hundred slaves had been brought back. The route, however, belonged only to Prince Henry. No one might go that way without his consent.

The people in Portugal were satisfied, because they

A temple in India

This building shows the wealth of India

had a rich trade. The country grew great and powerful. Prince Henry, however, had another purpose. He wished to find out the shape of the world, to make men feel at home in it, to take away the fear of unknown seas, and to sail around the continent of Africa. Therefore he still continued to send out ships, directing each captain to build a stone tower six feet high at the farthest point he reached. Then the next one would know that he must go farther yet if he was to find anything new. Henry's orders were to sail south and "not wait anywhere for other matters."

After many years Prince Henry died. He had not

yet succeeded in sailing around Africa, but he had prepared maps and trained many men. After his death his friends said: "Let us continue the work of our master and teacher. What he would want us to do is to send out more sailors and to keep up the search for the route around Africa." (Show on the map on page 41 how much of Africa was known in Prince Henry's time.)

The Southern End of Africa

Prince Henry had already done the hardest part. The sailors now found it easy to advance farther down the coast of Africa. One of them, named Dias, the third in his family to spend his life in traveling, set sail with two small ships. He sailed for thirteen months, far past the last stone tower. Then a great storm came up, and for days Dias was blown farther and yet farther south. When the storm was over he found himself in a very cold place, so he turned northward again. He sailed and sailed without coming to any land; and then when he did see it, the land was west of him instead of east. Not understanding this at all, the sailors demanded that he turn back.

Sadly Dias started for home. After several days of sailing, however, he saw in front of him a great stretch of rock with the open sea beyond. At once the truth burst upon him. He had reached the end of Africa and had sailed around it. Shouts of joy went up from the men! They were quite sure then that they could sail on to India, but instead they hurried home to tell the king the great news.

You may be sure that all Portugal was happy. How people wished that Prince Henry might have lived to see that day!

When Dias told the king of the great rock he had seen, he called it the Cape of Storms. "Not so," replied the king. "We will call it the Cape of Good Hope, because now we have a good hope of reaching India by an all-sea route." (Point out Dias's route on the map on page 41.)

India is reached by an All-Sea Route

As soon as he could the king sent out another captain, whose name was Vasco da Gama, with four fine vessels. Vasco da Gama knew from Dias's route just where he should go. He struck boldly out into the ocean instead of following the shore as all the others had done. He reached the Cape of Good Hope and sailed around it; but his men feared to go farther, and he had a great deal of trouble. He kept on, however, and began to search out the eastern coast of Africa.

At one of the towns an Arab guide was obtained who showed Da Gama how to sail directly to India. Da Gama arrived there in 1498 and set up a stone tower as usual to show people who should come afterwards where he had landed. Portugal's great purpose had at last been carried out.

At first the natives looked upon Da Gama as an enemy, but later they decided to trade with him. Loaded with the products of the East, he returned home. The "good hope" had become a fact. Da Gama was

Vasco da Gama at the court of a prince of India

What do you suppose Vasco da Gama is trying to persuade the prince
to do? (From a painting by José Velloso Salgado)

received in Portugal with the highest honors, and soon
gained great wealth.   In his old age he was made ruler
over the land he had found.   (Point out Vasco da Gama's
route on the map on page 41.)

Portugal had done what every country had wished
to do: she had reached India by an all-sea route and
had built up a great trade with the natives.   Every year
she sent out ships and received in return a great amount
of costly goods.

The Mediterranean Sea no longer carried the world's
trade.   Trade moved over to the Atlantic Ocean, and

Portugal was for a time the most important trading country of Europe.

To whom should the greatest honor be given? Vasco da Gama was the first man to sail directly to India; Dias was the first man to find that ships could sail around Africa. But the idea was Prince Henry's. It was he who had kept his purpose throughout fifty years, had driven fear out of men's minds, and had set an example to all later discoverers. More than by any other one man, the great age of discovery was brought on by Prince Henry the Navigator.

Looking Backward

Do you know the main points in the story of Prince Henry? Test yourself by answering these questions. When you can answer all of them you are ready for the next exercise.

1. What was the great question on which Prince Henry was working?

2. Of what were his men afraid?

3. Why did finding black men make his people change their minds about sending out ships?

4. What did Dias find out?

5. What did Vasco da Gama do years later?

Using New Words

This time you may make some sentences yourself. In the story all the following words are to be found. Make a sentence for every word in the list. The class will decide whether or not your sentences are right.

Names of Persons	*Date*
1. Prince Henry	8. 1498: Vasco da Gama
2. Dias	reached India
3. Vasco da Gama	

Names of Places	*Words*
4. Africa	9. navigator
5. Portugal	10. continent
6. Cape of Storms	11. all-sea route
7. Cape of Good Hope	12. Sea of Darkness

The Portuguese were the first people to reach India by an all-sea route.

Then trade shifted from the Mediterranean Sea to the Atlantic Ocean.

Have you ever been lost? How might anyone find his way if he were lost in the woods or at sea? Here is a story that will tell you.

HOW SAILING WAS MADE SAFER

Let us suppose that you were living five hundred years ago. You very much wished to go to sea and become a sailor, but you knew nothing about ships.

You decided to go down to the shore and find out how to begin. You climbed the ladder to a ship which was waiting for its load, and walked along the deck until you met the captain. You asked him if you might look around the ship, and he said you might.

The Compass

You walked forward and found a sort of box on a table. It had a glass cover through which could be seen a round card like the face of a clock. A hand, or needle, pointed to the letter *N*. At the right was the letter *E*, at the bottom the letter *S*, and at the left the letter *W*.

You knew what that was. It was a compass. You had often heard sailors talking about it. They said that in the old days the only way to tell where a ship was going, if it was out of sight of land, was by the stars. Every captain knew the stars well, and by looking at them could tell whether he was going north or south.

But sometimes the night was cloudy, and no stars could be seen. Then how would the sailors know where to go? At sea all places look the same.

The compass had come to be used to settle that very question. Long ago people knew about magnets, and after a while someone had a new idea about how to use them. He took a thin needle of magnet-iron, put it on a cork, and set it in a bowl of water. The needle turned around very fast for a while and then settled in a line pointing directly to the north.

Someone else then put the needle in a box instead of in water, and placed it so that it could move freely and point always to the north. Under it was put a card like a clockface. Sailors have used the compass ever since; if they wish to know in what direction to go, they need only to look at it.

No one knows who first invented the compass. Some say it was the Chinese and some say the Arabs. When people in Europe first began to hear of it they were afraid that there was some magic about it.

When the cities of Genoa and Venice began to use it, however, the rest of the world followed, and ship captains found it a great help. Each of Prince Henry's captains had a compass; Vasco da Gama had one on his great voyage. With its help men dared to strike out boldly into the sea and to go on long ocean journeys to find distant lands. It helped to make sailing safer.

Today our great ships would not dare to leave port without their compasses. High up, at the front of the ship, is a room from which the ship is steered. And the most important article in that room is the compass.

Maps, Globes, and Charts

Having seen the compass, you went into the captain's cabin, a small room lighted by candles, to look at other things of interest to sailors.

The first thing that caught your eye was a large globe made of paper. On it was a map of the world. Wise men knew that the earth is round and that they could best show it by a globe. But most people five hundred years ago thought that the world was flat.

Then you went over to a table where there were many maps — some carved on stone, some made of bronze, and some of little pieces of marble put together so as to show land and water. Some of the finest were made on sheepskin. They were very beautiful, and showed every body of land and water plainly. The land was of one color and the water, another. There was Europe; there, Asia; there, Africa; and the ocean around all of them.

But what were these large sheets of paper? They were somewhat like maps, and yet there were on them many lines and figures never seen on maps. The figures told how deep the water was. Captains needed to know this so that they would not sail their ships in places where there was not enough water.

Other marks showed where there were sharp rocks that would dash the ships to pieces. Other marks showed sand bars. Some of the figures told how far away from land a ship was, and others showed where there was a strong current which would carry ships out of their path.

You learned that these papers were not called sailing directions, as you thought they should be, but *sailing charts*.   Seamen of Italy made them.

With a compass, a globe, maps, and sailing charts, no captain needed to fear making a journey, even though it were to a land he had never seen before.

Shipbuilding

Then you took a walk around the ship to see how it was built.

The floor on which you were walking was the *deck*, and the great black space down below was the *hold*. You looked down the stairway, but it was so dark that you could see little except bags and boxes.   These contained the goods that were brought from the Indies. You could smell all sorts of strange sweet smells which you did not know.

The three large poles holding up the sails were the *masts*.   Long before this time ships had only one mast and therefore could not carry much sail.   The three sets of sails that you saw could make this ship go very fast.   You also learned that the ship easily carried a crew of fifty men.

You were pleased to see that the sails were painted with pretty pictures.   High up on the mast was a place that looked like a house in a tree.   This was the crow's nest.   Men stood there to watch far off for land or for any sign of danger.

The raised part of the deck at each end was the quarter-deck.   You saw several big guns there.

This ship was a very large one, measuring more than a hundred feet. It was about twice as long as it was wide.

There were many laws to make sailing safe, and no ship might set sail until city officers had looked it over carefully to see that everything was right.

A Wonderful New Invention — Printing

On your way home, while you were thinking about the wonderful things you had seen, you came upon a large crowd of people standing in the muddy streets in front of a small shop. Someone told you that inside was a great invention made by a man named John Gutenberg. It was a machine that would print.

You had often seen men carve a letter on a little block of wood, thus: M. They would ink the letter, put it down on paper, and it would leave a mark. Then they would do the same with another letter, and still another, until they had printed all that they wanted to say. That was *block printing*.

At last you had a chance to enter the shop. A man whom John Gutenberg himself had taught how to print showed you the new and quicker way. In the middle of the room stood a great table covered with rows of little boxes. In them were many letters made of lead, dozens of *a's* in one, dozens of *b's* in another, and so on — some capital letters and some small.

The man took some of the letters and placed them in a little metal groove and fastened them in; then he put some thick black ink on them, pressed a piece of

John Gutenberg's press

Can you tell what each man in the picture is doing?

white paper upon them, took off the paper, and showed it to you. The line of type looked like this:

John Gutenberg was the inventor of a new way of printing.

He printed the whole line at once in a book instead of making one letter at a time, as had to be done in block printing. After he was through with this line, he threw all the little letters back into the boxes again, so that he could use some of the same letters over for the next line. A little later he had enough letters so that he could print a whole page at once. Of course he could then print much more quickly.

You learned that this method of printing was called printing from *movable type*.

How much easier it was, and how much faster books could be made in the new way! Because they could be made so much more quickly, they could also be sold more cheaply. Before this time books had cost so much that only rich people could buy them. In libraries, the books were chained to the desks. But after men had learned to print with movable type books became cheaper, and poor people could buy them too.

Now, whenever a man found a new land, he could write about it in a book for all to read. Whenever anyone made a new invention, he could let everyone know about it in the same way. New ideas would spread very fast, and the world would not be the same as it had been before, because of the invention of an easier way of printing.

Searching for Sentences

First find the sentences in the book which answer all the following questions. Then choose a question and ask one of your classmates to find the sentences in the book which answer it.

1. For what is a compass used?

2. Why is a globe used to represent the earth?

3. For what is a sailing chart used?

4. What is the hold of a ship? What are the masts?

5. What is block printing? What is printing with movable type?

6. Why was the invention of printing important?

A Missing-Word Test

In the story you will find the words needed to complete these sentences.   Put each word in the right blank. Exchange papers with a classmate and correct each other's work as the teacher reads the right answers.

1. _____ _____ invented printing with movable type.

2. A man who makes something that has never been made by anyone else is an _____.

3. The _____ tells sailors the direction in which they are going.

4. Anything made by an inventor is an _____.

5. _____ _____ is made up of letters that can be used again and again for printing.

Before the invention of the compass, sailors were afraid to sail out of sight of land.

The compass showed in what direction they were sailing.   Then men did not fear the sea so much.

The invention of printing made it easier to print books. Then new ideas could spread faster.

You probably have learned that Columbus discovered America. How did he happen to be sailing so far out in the western ocean? Did he say to himself, "I think I will go out and discover America"? Of course not. Read the story and find the reason why Columbus was sailing so far to the west.

A NEW IDEA

While Prince Henry's men were creeping down the coast of Africa, and before the old trade routes had been given up, a small boy might have been seen almost any pleasant afternoon in Genoa, watching the ships come in. Probably he loved to see a vessel fold its sails and rest at the end of its long journey. He loved to see the boxes of linens, the rolls of silk, and the bags of sugar loaded into little boats and brought ashore. He loved the strong smell of spices. And, best of all, he loved to hear sailors tell of the strange lands they had visited and the wonderful adventures they had had. Very early in life he decided to be a sailor.

The boy's home was a tall, narrow house, with other tall houses crowding close on both sides. There was no yard. He would not enter on the first floor, for that was where his father kept the shop in which he combed wool all day.

Christopher Columbus would climb the stairs to the second story instead. There he would find his mother and his three younger brothers and sisters, and would tell of the interesting things he had seen during the day.

Christopher went to school only a little while because his parents were poor. He was a strong lad both in body and mind, and soon learned his father's trade. At the age of fourteen he began to learn to sail. For years he was a sailor in the Mediterranean Sea and in the Atlantic Ocean. He sailed down the coast of Africa and perhaps as far north as Iceland.

In the meantime he was studying. He learned a great deal about geography and he learned some history. He read many books of travel, and probably one of them was Marco Polo's book.

Columbus in Portugal

We are not surprised to learn that when the boy became a man he wished to go to Portugal. Prince Henry had made that country the center of all knowledge about sailing. Since Columbus (as we shall now begin to call him) was more interested in sailing than in anything else in the world, he went to Portugal. One of his brothers was already living there; he had seen the return of Dias from his great voyage to the Cape of Storms.

This brother had learned the art of making sailing charts, and it was probably from him that Columbus learned it also. When he was not working he used to go every day to the church. Every day he saw there a beautiful young lady whose father had been one of Prince Henry's seamen and governor of one of the new-found islands. Day after day they saw each other. At last they fell in love and were married.

What Columbus planned to do

Columbus spent part of the time with his young wife on her father's island. It was there that their son was born. His wife's father left her some old sailing charts which interested Columbus; he studied them carefully. He was always reading and studying maps and charts and books. If he did not agree with the writer, he sometimes wrote his own ideas in the margins of the books. Sometimes he took long voyages to far-away lands, and he always listened eagerly to the tales of sailors.

Some of the stories seemed strange to Columbus — stories that told of plants, of carved wood, and even of the dead bodies of strange-looking people being washed up on the shore from out of the west. His own brother-in-law had seen some of these things. Where could they have come from?

Columbus had learned from his books that the earth is round. Marco Polo had said that there was a sea east of Asia. The more Columbus thought about it, the more surely he believed that the ocean he could see from his door, the Atlantic, must be the same sea that washed Asia on the other side of the earth. How easy then to sail directly west from Portugal and reach Asia by the back door! Columbus believed it would not be very far to the Indies — perhaps not more than four thousand miles. (Show on the map on page 61 how Columbus planned to go.)

He wrote a letter to one of the wisest men of the time, describing his plan and asking if it were not a good one. The wise man wrote back that the idea was quite sound; that it would be an easy matter to sail west and reach Asia. He sent a map to guide the journey, and said: "You will find great countries and meet great princes. There are plenty of precious stones, and the people will receive you gladly."

Columbus was now filled with his great idea. He went to different countries, trying to get men and money to carry out his plan. For twenty years that one idea drove him on; he could not be happy except when working for it. It seemed simple enough. All that was needed was to get ships, supplies, and men, and the promise of some king that he would protect them.

Full of hope, Columbus went first to the king of Portugal. He probably said something like this: "You have been wasting years in trying to reach the Indies by sailing around Africa. You have not yet been able to do so. I have a much better plan. I am sure that we can sail directly west from Portugal, and that within four thousand miles we shall reach the Spice Islands."

The king thought the idea was very foolish. "Nobody knows what is in the western ocean," he replied. "Many men have tried to find out, and all have failed. I do not believe your idea will work."

Columbus answered: "For many years you, and Prince Henry before you, have been trying to sail around Africa. You have not succeeded. I am sure you will succeed if you try the western route. You will then be able to make all the Eastern people Christians, and you will find great riches."

The king was not sure what to do, so he called a council of his wisest men and laid the matter before them. They said that he ought not to listen to Columbus.

He was not quite satisfied, so he called another council, and said: "This sailor asks for only three ships and supplies for a year. That is not much."

After long thought they answered, "The cost would not be much, but the whole plan is foolish."

To make sure, they secretly sent out a ship of their own to sail west and see if it could reach the Indies. The vessel set sail; but a great storm arose, and the crew became afraid and returned. "There is no land there," they said.

So the king of Portugal did not help Columbus, and the work of years had come to nothing. Many men would have given up, but not Columbus. The churchmen said, "The Bible says that the earth is flat, so, of course, you cannot sail around it." Other people said: "Why, we can *see* that the earth is flat. Anyone who thinks he can sail around it is crazy." They began to laugh at Columbus and tap their heads when they saw him coming. Thus seven years went by.

No matter how others laughed at him, Columbus was sure he was right. He had courage and will power such as few men have ever had before or since. He spent the best years of his life in carrying out his one idea.

The Search for Aid in Spain

When there was no longer any hope in Portugal Columbus decided to go to Spain. His wife had long since died, so he took his young son with him. Footsore, tired, and hungry, they arrived in Spain.

At once Columbus set out for the *royal court* to lay

his plans before the king and the queen. Everyone told him that it was useless. Spain was then carrying on a great war, and the rulers would have no time even to listen.

Columbus paid no attention, but set out on foot. After a time the boy grew tired and hungry, so they stopped at a convent for food and drink. The priest who was in charge of the convent became interested in them, and Columbus told him his story.

The priest then called in a wise doctor, and the doctor called in a friend who was a great seaman. Together they studied Columbus's charts while he told them all about his plan. How pleased he must have been! For years he had not been able to get anyone even to listen to him!

These men decided to help him all they could. They gave him a letter to the court, and kept his little son with them at the convent while Columbus went on his way.

Columbus started out hopefully, sure that this time he would win. But he found the court greatly excited because they were getting ready for another battle. It was just as he had been told that it would be. He could get no one to listen to him.

Once more, most men would have gone home and would never have tried again. But not Columbus! He rented rooms in the city, earned his living by making charts, and talked of his plan to everyone he met. Little by little he became known throughout the city. Some of the nobles heard the story and believed in him, and at last he was allowed to go before King Ferdinand and Queen Isabella!

You may imagine how happy he was. He bought new clothes, and very carefully thought over just what he would say to make the king and the queen believe in his plan. They listened to his story and then called a council of the wisest men in the country. Again Columbus had to tell his plan, show his charts, and answer questions. The wise men decided that the idea was only the dream of a dreamer. The churchmen told him that he was wicked, because the Bible said that the earth had *corners*; so it could not be round. The nobles asked him how he could sail uphill on the return voyage, and how the men on the other side of the earth could walk with their heads hanging down. Columbus answered all their questions, but they had already made up their minds that he was wrong, and so they did not listen.

They did not really refuse his plan, but they said they would think it over. For four years they met once in a while to talk about it. During this time Columbus followed the court about from place to place, always talking about reaching the Indies by sailing west.

After four years the council at last gave their opinion. The plan was impossible! How Columbus's heart sank! He turned then to the nobles of Spain, but they dared not help him.

He had been working for more than ten years and had failed everywhere. His money was gone; he was so deeply in debt that even his maps and charts had been taken away from him, and he had to sell books in order to earn a living, but he still believed that he should find a way.

Columbus before Queen Isabella

Which of the people seem to believe in Columbus, and which do not?
(From a painting by Brozik in the Metropolitan Museum of Art,
New York)

Seven more years went by. Columbus tried to get aid from Genoa and Venice, but failed. His brother, who lived in Portugal, made a long journey to England to lay the plan before the king there, but the king was not interested. Then he went to France, but thus far had met with no success. Columbus, poor, tired, and sad, but still firmly believing in his idea of a western route, decided at last to leave Spain. Where should he go? Perhaps to France to join his brother.

On his way he stopped at the convent to see his son, now almost grown up. The priest was sorry to hear that Columbus had failed. He called in his neighbor the great seaman, talked with some sailors who had seen signs of land in the west, and then wrote a letter to Queen Isabella, asking her to give Columbus another hearing. At this time Spain had won the war, and the country was at peace.

The queen sent for Columbus and once more called together her wise men. This time she told them that they were not to consider whether the idea was foolish or good, but to decide how it could be carried out. Columbus showed them that the risk was small for so great a gain, and at last they agreed. Then, with success almost in sight, Columbus asked so much for himself that the council was angry. "What a bold man!" they must have said. "He expects far too much."

For Columbus had demanded that he, and his children after him, should rule, under the king, all the new lands that he might discover, and that he should have one tenth of all the gain that came from them. The council offered him less, but he would not accept it.

Help at Last

Seventeen years of work seemed to have come to nothing; so, turning slowly away, quite heartbroken, he began the journey back to the convent. After he had started, the queen's taxgatherer said to her: "My queen, I believe that a great mistake has been made. The ships for which this man asked would not cost a great amount. I can furnish the money. And if he should happen to find the riches of the Indies, you would gain a great deal."

Ships of Columbus
From a painting by M. Zeno Diemer

Queen Isabella had for some time been almost ready to believe in Columbus. She said: "I am going to settle this matter. I am queen, and whether or not the council thinks it is right, I will furnish the money. Send for Columbus and tell him he may have what he asks."

By that time Columbus was six miles away. A servant was sent out to ask him to return. Can you imagine how he felt? After all those years of failure and heartbreak, of waiting and disappointment, he had at last won. He was to be allowed to carry out his idea.

The queen did not have to give him the money, after all. King Ferdinand ordered a little town on the seacoast to furnish two ships and enough men to sail them. The great seaman who had been Columbus's friend at the convent furnished another ship, which he commanded himself.

An hour before sunrise on the third of August, 1492, seamen and officers and servants gathered at the shore. There were less than a hundred in all. Three little ships, the *Santa Maria*, the *Niña*, and the *Pinta*, were waiting out in the bay. The largest of them, the *Santa Maria*, was only about eighty feet long. The crew was frightened; most of them had been forced to serve against their will, and they thought that they were going to certain death. Some were seeking adventure; some wanted part of the great hills of gold of which they had heard; some were prisoners who had been set free upon promising that they would go. All were terribly afraid of the Green Sea of Darkness.

The townspeople came down to see them off, some cheering, some weeping. Columbus's son was there to bid his father good-by. He had been given a place as page at the court.

Then there was a sudden stillness. A priest from the church blessed the ships and the seamen. Sails were set, anchors raised, and the three vessels moved slowly out to sea. One of the most important journeys in the history of the world had begun.

In the largest ship, looking forward to the west, stood the man who had risked his own life and the lives of all the crew for an idea. How would it turn out? He must not fail.

Test Yourself

I. Can you answer all these questions without look-ing back in the story? If you can, your score is 6. If you needed to look back for one answer, your score is 5. What is *your* score?

1. What did Columbus learn in Portugal?
2. What was Columbus's great idea?
3. Why did he need help in carrying it out?
4. From what countries did he ask for aid?
5. What did Columbus ask for himself?
6. What did Spain finally give him?

II. Can you finish the following sentences? Write the complete sentences and show them to your teacher.

1. Ferdinand was
2. Isabella was
3. Columbus was the man who
4. Atlantic is the name of
5. The Indies were
6. France was the country
7. Spain was the country
8. A royal court is
9. A sailing chart is

Wise men had long known that the earth is round.

Columbus was the first man who had the courage to try to sail around it.

Unit Two

How the Nations tried to get Wealth from the New World

ıı

Unit Two

How the Nations tried to get Wealth from the New World

You have just learned that Columbus was trying to reach India. What did he expect to find there? Do you suppose that he found what he wanted? How could anyone succeed and fail at the same time? The story will tell you how Columbus did that very thing.

SUCCESS AND FAILURE OF COLUMBUS

As the shores of Spain faded from view behind them, and the ships reached the open sea, Columbus must have been very happy. After twenty years of trying and failing and trying again, at last he had three good ships and their crews, the queen believed in him, and he was on the way to test his idea. It must have seemed too good to be true!

Trouble during the Voyage

But trouble came very soon.   Columbus and his men
had been at sea but a few days when a part of one of
the ships broke down.   They repaired it, but the next
day it was broken again.   The sailors had been forced to
serve against their will.   Had they broken something so
that they might have to return to Spain? No one knew.

Columbus decided that they would have to stop at
the nearest island while the ship was being repaired.
The Canary Islands were supposed to be almost in a
straight line with the Indies, so they would not lose
much time by stopping there.

They remained at the Canary Islands for some weeks.
When all was ready another start was made.   Day after
day they sailed through calm seas with an east wind
always blowing.   There were no storms.   They found
no strange animals ready to eat them, they found no
boiling water, and they did not fall off the edge of the
earth.   Still the men were afraid.   If the wind always
blew from the east, how would they be able to sail back
against it?   They were crossing strange waters where man
had never been before. Almost anything might happen.

To quiet their fears, Columbus kept two records of
the distance that they went each day.   On his own
record he wrote the full number of miles; on the record
he showed to the crew he wrote a smaller number, so
that they might not know how far they had traveled.

After a time they came to a great sea covered thickly
with seaweed.   The men were sure that the ships could
never pass through it, that they would be caught and

Columbus on the *Santa Maria*

From a painting by Stanley M. Arthurs

held there, and never could get free. They begged Columbus to turn back, but he commanded them never to speak to him of such a thing again. He had set out to reach the Indies, and to the Indies he would go, no matter what happened.

Days went slowly by. Columbus himself was troubled, for they had sailed far past the place where he had expected to find land. Still he kept on. The crew whispered among themselves. They would kill Columbus; they would throw him into the sea and return to Spain. They planned a *mutiny*. But no one dared to begin.

A month went by. Then one day the lookout up in the crow's nest called eagerly, "Land! land!" All rushed gladly to the side, but the land was only a bank of clouds, and their hearts sank lower than ever.

The voyage had now lasted almost two months. The crew sat about like dead men; they had given themselves up for lost. Even Columbus was full of doubt, but he would not turn back.

The Discovery of America

Then things began to happen. The men saw some land birds flying before them. They saw some logs, a carved stick, and a bush with fruit on it floating on the waves. Where could these things have come from? Everyone felt new courage.

At last, one night, Columbus saw a dancing light in the dark. Could it be a fire? Soon afterwards came a joyful shout from the man in the lookout, "Land!

land!" This time there was no mistake. Land could be seen plainly lying low in the distance before them. You may be sure that there was little sleep on board that night.

The next morning Columbus dressed himself in his best red-velvet cape and took his sword in one hand and the flag of Spain in the other. The captains of the two smaller ships carried green banners with the letters *F* (for Ferdinand) and *I* (for Isabella). They all climbed down into small boats and were rowed ashore. There they bent and kissed the earth and gave thanks to God for having brought them safe to land. Columbus drew his sword, lifted up the flag of Spain, and took possession of the land in the name of Ferdinand and Isabella.

The natives soon came crowding about them, surprised at their white skins and their beards and the clothes they wore. For the natives wore no clothes at all. They were strong, active people with coarse black hair and with red-brown skin painted in bright colors. They carried spears and traveled in canoes, which could hold as many as fifty men. They wore rings and necklaces of gold. The gold interested Columbus most. When he asked the natives where it came from, they pointed toward the south. So he gave them presents and prepared to sail south. Thinking that they were the people of India, he called them Indians; and Indians they have been called ever since, even though the name was a wrong one.

Columbus reached this land on October 12, 1492. Though he did not know it, he had discovered a new world — a world separated from both Europe and Asia

by great oceans.   If he had known what he had discovered he might not have been so well pleased, because
what he wanted to find was a short route to the Indies.

However, he felt sure that he had touched one of the
islands off the coast of India, and so he decided to sail
south to the mainland, where the gold must be.   As he
advanced he passed many little islands covered with
palm trees and saw strange flowers and fruits, and birds
and fish, and savage people, but no spice trees and no
great cities.   He was surprised, but not discouraged.

On he sailed, past other islands, until he reached
Cuba.   This island lay stretched out so far, as he coasted
along its shore day after day, that he was sure he had
at last reached the mainland.

He sent two of his chief men, loaded with presents,
to carry a letter to the great king that Marco Polo had
told about.   But these men could find no king, no
court, and no great cities — nothing but the rude huts
of savages.   When they returned to Columbus they
could only say that they had failed.   Still they had seen
interesting sights; they had seen the natives roll great
leaves, put them into their mouths, set fire to them,
and blow out the smoke. They had seen great nets
in which people slept. These were hammocks. The
Spaniards had never seen anything like that before.

The ships then sailed on and discovered another
island, so large that Columbus called it the Spanish
Island, in honor of Spain.   A short time afterwards
one of his ships, the *Pinta*, deserted so that its captain
might seek gold for himself.   The *Santa Maria* was
wrecked on the coast, and only the little *Niña* was left.

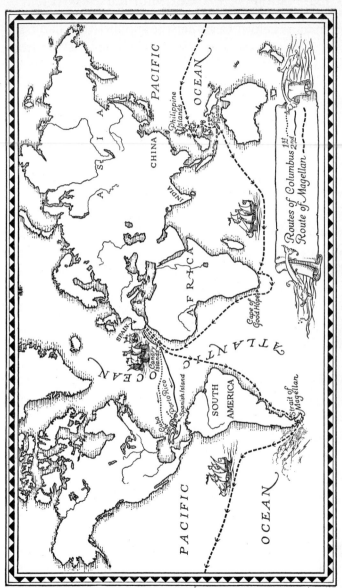

Routes of Columbus and Magellan

The Indians helped to gather the supplies that had been saved from the wrecked vessel and to build a fort from its wood.

The Return Home

Columbus knew that it was time to return home. Not all the men could sail in the tiny *Niña*; forty-four were willing to stay in the fort until Columbus could bring more men and supplies from Spain. He told them to learn the native language, to be friendly with the Indians, and to explore all along the coast.

Taking ten of the Indians with him to show to the king and queen, he and the rest of the crew set sail for Spain. The *Niña* ran into a great storm which lasted for weeks. Columbus, fearing that they might sink, wrote out the whole story of his voyage and put it into a barrel which he threw into the sea. He hoped that some ship which was passing might see it and pick it up.

But the *Niña* at last reached the coast of Europe. Portugal was the first land seen. Columbus put in at its largest city for a rest. Great crowds came to his vessel; the water around it was black with small boats in which people came out to see the discoverer of the Indies, for that was what Columbus himself thought he had found. The king of Portugal invited him for a visit. How well Columbus must have remembered the time when a king of this same country had scorned him and the crowds had laughed!

Then he went on to Spain, to the city from which he had set sail eight months before. The whole town turned out to see him, and a great line of people marched

Columbus's return

Can you point out different things which Columbus brought back with
him? (From a painting by Balaca)

to the church to thank God for his return. How different it all was from his setting out months before!

Columbus was eager to see the king and the queen,
so he hurried to the court. Every city that he passed
was glad to honor him; he was treated as a great man,
and everyone was talking of his great discovery.

It was a month before he was received at court,
where Ferdinand and Isabella sat upon a throne in a
great tent, surrounded by all the high nobles of the
land. Columbus stopped at the foot of the throne, but
they made him come up and sit by them. He told all
of his story — of the voyage outward, of the cares and
fears, and of the discovery of land on October 12, 1492.

He made his ten painted Indians appear before them. He showed forty bright-colored parrots, and he gave the king and queen all the gold that he had found. While Columbus was talking everyone was very quiet, for fear of losing a word. It was a great moment for the man who only a year before had wandered on foot through Europe begging for help.

His story was printed, and people in far-away lands read it. His name was known in distant places. It was not what he had brought back with him that was so wonderful — caravans from the East had brought far richer goods. It was the supposed finding of an all-sea route to the Indies that interested people everywhere.

If Columbus had known that all America stood in his way, and that still another ocean lay between it and the Indies, he might have given up his idea of reaching the East by a western route. But he was sure in his own mind that he had reached islands lying off the coast of Asia; he lived and died firmly believing that. The name *West Indies*, which we use today for all the islands that he discovered, is another record of Columbus's mistake.

No matter how sad his life had been before, the spring and summer of the next year must have been very happy. The king and the queen treated him as a friend, the nobles were eager to walk and talk with him, and wherever he went crowds gathered about him and shouted his name. He was the greatest man in Spain. (On the map on page 81 find Columbus's first voyage.)

Gifts of the Old World to the New

Columbus began at once to plan another voyage. This time everyone was eager to go. He held out high hopes to them — hopes of palaces of gold, shiploads of spices, and all the precious stones they could carry. It is no wonder that more men wanted to go with him than he could possibly take.

He was going to found a colony and to begin a New Spain. The king and queen gave him five times as much money as he had the first time. He had seventeen ships and fifteen hundred men. Some of the men were soldiers, some were men of the church, some were nobles, and some were workmen of different kinds. There were no women. He was now going to take back to their homes the Indians that he had brought to show to the queen.

He also had horses, sheep, cattle, young trees, and slips for grapevines. He had goats and chickens, seeds of oranges and lemons, and sugar cane and other plants — gifts of the Old World to the New.

The ships set sail; and before Columbus and his men arrived at the Spanish Island they discovered another very beautiful island, one which the United States owns today (Porto Rico).

When they reached the place where Columbus had left the forty-four men, they fired guns to let their countrymen know that they were coming. There was no answer. All was silent as the grave. Full of fear for their friends, they landed quickly and went to where the fort had been. No one was there. Afterwards the

Indians told them that some had died and some had gone far away. They had never been seen since.

Columbus decided to found his new colony on the northern coast. On reaching there the men cut down trees, laid out streets, and began public buildings, a church, and a fort. They called their town Isabella. But the work was so heavy, and the change from their former ways of living was so great, that most of the people fell sick. Columbus himself lay ill for five months.

He then sent twelve of the ships back to Spain for more supplies, more workmen, and more horses. With them he sent some Indians to be sold as slaves. This was a great mistake on his part, because it made enemies of the Indians.

Knowing that what Spain wanted was gold, Columbus tried hard to mine it; but his own men could not stand the hard work, and the Indians would not come near him, fearing to be made slaves.

Because of the hard work and because so many were sick, the colonists soon lost courage. They planned to seize the rest of the ships and sail home. But Columbus took the ships and sailed through the surrounding seas, finding still more islands.

His brother, whom he left as ruler of the colony, had a very hard time. The gentlemen would not work, and the natives made war upon the settlement. The Spaniards, with their guns and great dogs, killed a large number of the natives.

When peace was made the Indians were forced to agree to pay a certain amount of gold or cotton every three months. There was not enough gold in all the island to pay so much, so they ran away to the mountains, where many of them died. At the end of three years only one third of the Indians in the island were still alive.

By that time things were in such a bad way that Columbus had to return to Spain for help. Much had been done; but very little gold had been found — nothing to compare with the accounts in Marco Polo's stories. If Columbus had had supplies enough he would have tried to sail on around the world, instead of re- turning as he had come; but supplies were very few, so he had to go back to Spain the shortest way.

When he arrived he found himself no longer a great man. People knew that he had found strange lands; but little gold had been secured, and a great deal of money had been spent. So they lost interest in him. (On the map on page 81 find Columbus's second voyage.)

Getting Ready

When you have answered the following questions, you have learned your history lesson. You will then be ready for the matching game on page 88.

1. For whom did Columbus take possession of the land he discovered?

2. Why did he call the natives "Indians"?

3. What did Columbus think he had found?

4. Why were the people of Spain not satisfied with his discoveries?

5. What had Columbus discovered?

A Matching Game

In the right-hand column below are groups of words describing the words in the left-hand column, but in a different order. When your teacher asks you, be ready to say which word-group in the right-hand column describes each of the numbered words in the left-hand column.

1. The Indians were	the year in which Columbus discovered America.
2. The Indies were	to find something the world has not known before.
3. Spain was	the country which helped Columbus.
4. The Canary Islands were	a person who finds something that the world has not known before.
5. 1492 was	where Columbus's ships had stopped for repairs.
6. Discovery means	followers refuse to obey their leaders.
7. A discoverer is	the countries of the Far East.
8. To discover means	the finding of things new to the world.
9. A mutiny is when	the natives of America.

Columbus discovered America in 1492.

He never knew that it was a "new world"; he thought it was the Indies.

Do you know anyone who has traveled all the way around the world? Is such a trip hard to make nowadays? Why did it require great courage in the year 1500? This story will tell you about the first man who ever sailed around the world.

SAILING AROUND THE WORLD

One morning there was a great stir about the court of the young king of Spain. Pages were hurrying to and fro, and nobles had already begun to gather in the hall. Something was about to happen.

The king was ready to listen to the story of a sailor from Portugal. All the court had heard of this sailor and wished to be present when he came before the throne. The story was connected in some way with a westward voyage. Ever since the time of Columbus that had been a subject in which men were greatly interested.

Magellan before the King of Spain

The king of Spain was about to come into his court. A loud sound of horns was heard; all the nobles bowed down and took off their hats; and the boy king, only eighteen years old, passed down between two lines of people and mounted the throne. He was a grandson of Ferdinand and Isabella.

After he was seated he gave a signal, and a short man with black eyes, firm lips, and a full beard came forward.   This man was not tall, but he had great strength and a will that had never been conquered. His name was Magellan.

Magellan came near the throne and, holding up a globe that he had brought from Portugal, explained the route he wished to take.   He thought that he might sail to the south around Columbus's land, and that he would then be very near to India.   This route would be very different from that of Portugal and so would cause no trouble between the two countries.

After hearing Magellan's story the king of Spain decided that he would help him, that he would fit out some ships at his own cost, and that he would not send any other sailors the same way for ten years.

There was a long delay, but at last all was ready. There were five ships, old and almost worn out, supplies for two years, and two hundred and seventy men from different parts of Europe, Asia, and Africa.   Magellan was to receive one twentieth of the profits and was to be the governor of any new lands that he should find. Among the goods with which they were to trade were colored cloth, red capes, looking-glasses, knives, combs, and thousands of little bells.

Trouble from the Beginning

Trouble began at once.   The king of Portugal was very angry because Magellan was going to try to find the Indies.   He thought they belonged to him because Vasco da Gama had reached India first by an all-sea route.   He sent men to kill Magellan, but they could not. Then he ordered his captains in the East to be sure to capture the ships as soon as they should arrive.

The Spaniards in Magellan's own vessels did not like him. They said: "Why should a man from Portugal be put over us? We ought to sail under captains from our own country." Everything seemed to be against him.

He set sail in 1519 with five ships and with four captains besides himself, but there was only one of them whom he could trust. The voyage had hardly begun when his wife's father sent a fast ship after him to give this warning: "I have heard that your captains are going to kill you. You must be very careful."

It was fortunate that one of the men who went on the voyage went only "to see the world," as he said, for he kept a record of everything that happened. From his record the story that you are reading was written.

First the ships stopped at the Canary Islands; then they followed the coast of Africa, where they ran into a belt of calms. For three weeks there was no wind to fill their sails. Then there was a month of such storms that the ships nearly turned over.

Food and water became scarce. The captain of one of the vessels came to Magellan to complain. Magellan, remembering the warning that his wife's father had sent, immediately put him in irons. It was well that he had been warned. After that the captains were more careful.

Two months later the ships reached the continent of South America, where they found food, fresh water, and fruits.   Before they arrived it had been very dry, but as soon as they came it rained.   The natives therefore thought they were gods, who had brought the rain, and were kind to them.   They gave Magellan's men five or six chickens for one fishhook, two geese for a comb, a full basket of fruit for a little bell, and for a looking-glass they gave fish enough to feed ten men.

As Magellan sailed along the coast, expecting every day to reach the end of the land, he came to a great body of water.   Was it a river?   Was it a strait which led to another ocean?   It took three weeks to find out that it was only a river.

Magellan and his men went on down the coast, and soon fierce winter storms attacked them.   Magellan stopped his ships, landed, and told the men to get ready for a six months' stay.   They must spend the winter there.

The men saw that the land was bare, that there were few people living in it, and that they should have very little to eat, so they decided to mutiny.   They were far from home, their ships were old, and they did not believe that there was any strait through which they could pass to the other side of this land.

Magellan spoke to them of their duty as Spaniards and of the great riches they would find if they kept on, but nothing moved them.   Three of the ships chose new captains and prepared to return to Spain.   Two remained loyal.

What should the brave leader do?   If he did not act quickly it would be too late.   He sent two little boatloads of loyal sailors to one of the ships which had refused to follow him. These loyal sailors had guns and knives under their coats. The crew did not think that so few could do them any harm, so they let them come on board. But the loyal sailors struck down the captain, fought fiercely, and in a short time had possession of the ship.

Magellan then had three ships against two. He moved to the mouth of the harbor and would not let the others out. They had to obey him; the mutiny was over. He punished the leaders, and the rest were glad to follow him once more.

The winter days passed slowly. Some of the *natives* came to visit the travelers. They were so tall that the Spaniards looked like little boys beside them. Their feet were bound about with many furs, so the men called them "Big Feet." During the winter one ship was wrecked while on an exploring trip, so only four ships were left.

Finding the Strait of Magellan

Spring came at last. How glad everyone was to prepare for action again! They set up a large cross to show that they took possession of the land for Spain; then they sailed away. After two months they came to a narrow stretch of water which seemed to run far up into the land. Did it lead to an ocean on the other side? The water was salt water; it was deep. Magellan sent two ships to find out where it led. Soon the ships returned. They had found a great ocean beyond. Magellan had waited so long for this news that when it came he wept for joy.

The Strait of Magellan

Notice how barren and forbidding the land looks. (Photograph from Ewing Galloway)

A council was held. Most of the captains wished to return to Spain with the news, since their supplies were running low. But Magellan had promised the king that he would find the Indies. He said, "I will not go back, even if I have to eat the leather off the ship's yards." He would not let anyone say the word *return*.

They all started through the narrow strait. Far to the south they had seen lights of many fires, so they called that land the Land of Fire. As they sailed on, steep mountain walls covered with snow shut them in on both sides. Terrible winds blew above them; black water rose and fell beneath them. For thirty-eight days, full of fear and wonder, they sailed on. Then they passed the last rock and came out into the open sea. Today we call that narrow stretch of water the Strait of Magellan.

When they reached the ocean on the other side one ship was missing. Magellan feared that it was lost, but it was not. The crew had put the captain in irons and had sailed back to Spain, where they told the king that Magellan had wrecked all the other ships.

The three ships that were left found themselves on a calm and pleasant ocean, so peaceful that they called it the Pacific. Before that it had been known as the South Sea.

The Greatest Voyage the World has ever Known

Magellan and his men coasted north for a while along the shore of South America, and then struck boldly out to sea, knowing nothing of what was before them. If they had known, even Magellan's strong heart must have failed him, for they faced far greater troubles than those of Columbus's first voyage.

Three months passed before they saw even an island, and that was only a pile of rocks. The ocean seemed to have no end. Already they had traveled twice as far as Columbus; and although they did not know it, they still had five thousand miles before them.

All that was left of their food was in small pieces full of little worms. The drinking-water was thick and yellow. They ate sawdust; they ate rats, but there were not even rats enough. Magellan's words came true: at last they took the leather off the ships' yards, dragged it through the sea at the end of a rope to make it softer, and then ate it.

Sickness broke out. The sailors' mouths were badly swollen; they were weak from lack of food, and many died. "I think that never again will men attempt such a voyage," one of them wrote. They had to keep on, for to go back so long a way was certain death.

At last they saw land — large green islands, where they found fruit, meat, and, best of all, water. The natives had no bows and arrows and did them no harm, but tried to steal from them; so they called these lands the Islands of Thieves.

Ten days later they came to the islands which were afterwards called the Philippines in honor of King Philip of Spain. The United States owns them today. There they met traders from China; they had passed through the unknown parts of the sea and were near the Spice Islands. Some of the sailors had visited these waters before by the route around Africa. Magellan's *circumnavigation* of the globe was almost ended. (On the map on page 81 find Magellan's route.)

They gave the natives presents of bells, combs, and looking-glasses, and received in return fish and wine and the first bananas they had ever seen.

They made some of the natives Christians. Magellan and the chief promised that they would live as brothers. These people had no guns and so asked the Spaniards to help them in war against a neighboring tribe. If Magellan wanted to trade with them and wanted to trade with their neighbors also, he must first show them how strong the Spaniards were.

Magellan and his men

From a painting by Fred C. Yohn

Trusting in his guns, Magellan went. In the battle which followed, forty-eight Spaniards with guns were attacked by thousands of natives. There could be only one result: the Spaniards were driven back to their ships. Magellan was killed in the fight — killed when he had almost reached the end of his long voyage and before he could receive the honors waiting for him in Spain!

Circumnavigation of the Globe Completed

The Spaniards by this time numbered only one hundred and fifteen. One of their ships was quite worn out; so they burned it, and sailed to the Spice Islands in the two which were left. There they took on a great load of cloves and started for home.

Then one of the two ships was found to be leaking and could not go on. The last of the ships, the little *Victoria*, with forty-seven men, continued alone on the long voyage around the Cape of Good Hope. Again supplies gave out; again the crew became sick. There were islands belonging to Portugal at which they might have found food along the way, but when a few of the Spaniards went ashore they were made prisoners.

At last, three years after they had left home and thirty years after Columbus had first set out, the brave little *Victoria* sailed slowly into a Spanish port with eighteen men on board. The year was 1522. The hardest voyage in the history of the world was over. It had proved to everyone that the world is round, that there is more water than land on the earth's surface, and that America is a separate *continent*. The *Victoria* brought home twenty-six tons of cloves, which more than paid the cost of all the five ships that had set out together. The wrecks of the other ships lay scattered about all the seven seas. And of the nearly two hundred men who had set out three years before, only eighteen were left in the *Victoria's* crew.

But the man who should have received all the honor for this was lying in a distant land among savage people. The idea had been his; his brave heart had kept all at the task until the great ocean had been crossed. To him belongs the honor of first sailing around the earth. In the Philippines today a statue of the hero looks out over the place where the battle occurred.

Since Magellan was dead, the next honors went to the captain of the *Victoria*. The king gave him a globe with this sentence written on it: "You first sailed around me."

To Test your Memory

The answers to these questions were given in the story. You will need to know them in order to play the game on the next page.

1. Why did Magellan sail so far to the south?

2. What was Magellan's plan?

3. The Strait of Magellan led from what ocean to what ocean?

4. Why did Magellan call the ocean west of South America the Pacific?

5. Why were the islands he found called the Philippines?

6. What did Magellan's men do after his death?

Choices to Make

From each of the following groups, choose the part that completes the sentence and makes a true statement.

1. Magellan circumnavigated the globe in

1820–1823   1519–1522   1492–1495

2. The Strait of Magellan is at the southern end of

South America   North America   Asia

3. Any people who are born in a certain land are called its

foreigners   Indians   natives

4. The islands in which Magellan was killed are called the

Canary Islands   British Isles   Philippines

5. The first man to sail around the world was

Vasco da Gama   Columbus   Magellan

6. Sailing around the world is called

circumnavigation   mutiny   discovery

7. The ocean west of South America is the

Atlantic   Pacific   Indian

8. A very large body of land is called a

country   island   continent

Magellan was the first man to circumnavigate the globe. He proved that South America was a separate continent. He did not discover the Pacific Ocean, but he named it.

Why did the Spaniards want to reach the Indies? If they could find another country as rich or even richer, would they be satisfied? Do you know whether there was any such country?

A COUNTRY AS RICH AS THE INDIES

Little gold had yet been discovered in the New World. Columbus and Magellan had seen strange lands and had told wonderful tales of the natives, but they had found little gold! Only Vasco da Gama had brought wealth to Europe. Spain had received no riches from her colonies overseas.

A young man in Spain named Cortez, who had heard much talk about these voyages, began to dream of the far-away lands. He was a happy, fun-loving boy, always running into danger, always getting himself into trouble, but in some way always getting out again. His father, a captain in the army, had decided that since his son's health was not good he should go to school and study law.

To school young Cortez went. But he had heard so many stories about battles and travels that he took little interest in study; so when he was nineteen years old he went out to the Spanish Island to seek his fortune. There he was given a large amount of land and many Indian slaves to work it. For a time he was a successful farmer, but his heart was not in the work. The life was too calm and peaceful.

Then came a fight between the Indians and the Spaniards. Cortez felt when he led his men into battle that his chance had now come. He fought so well that he was made an officer.

Cortez in Cuba

The governor had taken notice of this young man who was so brave and cool and whose men would follow him anywhere. As a result, Cortez was sent to Cuba and helped to conquer the Indians there.

Then he spent a number of years working his own gold mines and raising cattle. He became a rich man. Once, indeed, the governor lost faith in him and put him in prison, but he soon took him out and made him chief judge of a large city. By that time he was thirty-three years old, not very tall, with dark eyes and hair and a short beard. He was very strong and a good soldier.

After a time news came from the west. Sailors who had gone there had discovered another land greater in size than any of the islands. And along its shores they had found pearls.

The governor of Cuba at once made up his mind to send out a party to trade with the natives. Everyone wanted to go. Who would be chosen as leader? That position was the one thing in the world that Cortez wanted most. He asked for the command and offered to share the expense. The governor considered the matter for a long time, but at length he decided that he could not find a better leader in the whole island. So he chose Cortez, and together they began to prepare for the voyage. Cortez put all his money into the expedition.

After a while the governor began to feel doubts. Could he trust this man? Perhaps when the party landed in the strange country he would take it for his own and never come back. Perhaps it would be better to take the command away from Cortez.

Sailing for Mexico

Word of these doubts reached Cortez, and he made haste to sail before the governor should have time to change his mind. Letters were sent after him ordering him to return, but no one dared to stop him. His ships sailed on, westward across the Gulf of Mexico.

There were eleven ships, six hundred men, many weapons, and much ammunition. There were sixteen horses, and two hundred slaves who were to do the work. As they neared the shore a change began to come over Cortez. He no longer thought of the fun and adventure that lay before him; he became grave, and studied out his plans carefully.

At an island very near to the mainland they picked up a Spaniard whose ship had been wrecked eight years before. Since that time he had lived among the Indians; he knew their language well, so he was a great help to Cortez.

At last the land of Mexico rose up out of the sea before them. Cortez, carrying his flag of black velvet and gold with a red cross amid flames of blue and white, went ashore and took possession of all the land for Spain. The year was 1519.

News soon spread among the natives that strange towers or "waterhouses" with wings were walking toward them over the sea. (What were they? [1]) Still stranger was an animal which had four legs below, two legs higher up, and one head in front and another on top. (What was it? [2]) The Indians had never seen a horse nor a man riding a horse. They were surprised at the "shining shirts," at the sticks which sent forth fire and thunder, and at the white faces of the strangers. They came down to the shores in great crowds to see these sights.

A hot battle was fought, but bows and arrows and spears and stones were no match for guns. The Spaniards won, not because they were braver but because they were better armed.

When the natives made peace they gave Cortez twenty young women. One of these proved to be of greater value than many soldiers; for she could understand all the Indian languages, and many times she told the Spaniards about the plans of their enemies. She could serve them as an *interpreter*.

Before leaving the town Cortez threw down the idols which were in the temples and put up the cross in their place, but he tried to be kind to the natives. Having found little gold along the coast, he decided to go farther into the heart of the country.

[1] The ships.
[2] Horse with rider. The Indians thought of them as "being all one animal."

All this time the king of the Aztec Indians in Mexico had not been able to decide what to do. Years before, so the story ran, a fair god had lived in the land. After teaching the people the arts of peace he had sailed away into the sunrise, promising that some day he would return. After many years, out of the sunrise had come these white-faced strangers. Had the fair god sent them? If so, the king ought not to harm them. But if they were enemies, he ought to send his army against them. Which should he do?

He sent some of his servants to ask the strangers what they wanted. They replied that they had come to see the king. In fear, he tried to buy them off — to give them rich gifts and beg them to go away.

Among his presents were gold and precious stones, ten great rolls of cotton cloth embroidered with tiny colored feathers, feather fans covered with gold and pearls, gold bars, collars with golden bells hanging from them, little fish made of gold and silver, books of picture-writing, and a great round piece of gold as large as a wagon wheel. With these beautiful things he sent word that the strangers must leave the country at once.

Do you suppose Cortez was willing to leave after he had seen all this wealth? He was more than ever determined to go on. He showed the king's servants his men and horses, and made his great guns roar for them so that they might feel his power. They drew pictures of his camp to show their master. Then he sent them back with the presents he had brought for the king. These were poor enough: a great armchair, a red cap, many beads, and articles of cut glass. The king would not have cared, however, if only he had been able to drive the strangers away.

Instead, the Spaniards began to lay out a town; they made a new government for themselves and gave to Cortez the right to conquer and settle Mexico. He wrote to the king of Spain for his consent to this plan, but did not wait for an answer. Every day he made long marches so that his men might grow used to hard work.

Then he did a bold thing: he sank all his ships but one. Now his men could not go back even if they wanted to. They would have to conquer the Aztecs, as the Indians were called, or die. Some of his followers complained among themselves. Cortez cried out: "There is one ship left. It could not carry all of us back to Cuba, but it could take a few. I now set that ship aside for the cowards. Will all cowards, who want to go home, step forward?"

Not a man moved. No one was willing to be thought a coward. "Very well, then," said Cortez; "all brave men will set out with me to Mexico City. There the wealth of the Indies awaits us."

The First March on Mexico City

Cortez and his men set out on their march inland with six cannon and fifteen horses, passing now through swamps and then through woods so thick that they had to cut their way. The king sent his servants a second time and a third time, ordering them to go back, but they kept on.

The natives did not try to stop them, but treated them kindly and even furnished men to carry their loads. Some of the Indians would have been glad to change from the rule of the Aztec king to any other, because the Aztec rulers were very cruel and offered up to their gods prisoners still alive.

On their march the Spaniards met a very fierce tribe which the Aztecs had never been able to conquer. Cortez sent them a letter asking that his men might be allowed to pass in peace on their way to Mexico.

The reply was a rain of arrows and spears. Again a great battle took place. The Indians fought very fiercely. They tried to take their prisoners alive so that they might offer them up to their gods. But again they were no match for men who fought with thunder and lightning, as they called the Spaniards' guns. Only one or two Spaniards were killed. These Cortez buried at night, so that the Indians might still think that they were gods.

This fierce tribe of natives, since it could not hold its own against Cortez, offered to go with him and help him to conquer the Aztecs. Cortez was glad indeed to accept this aid, and went on with an army much larger than before.

The Aztec king tried once more to make the Spaniards go back to their own land by offering them rich gifts. But the richer the presents, the more eager were the men to go on to the *capital city* from which the wealth came.

They advanced to the first city of the king's own territory, expecting a battle, but to their surprise they

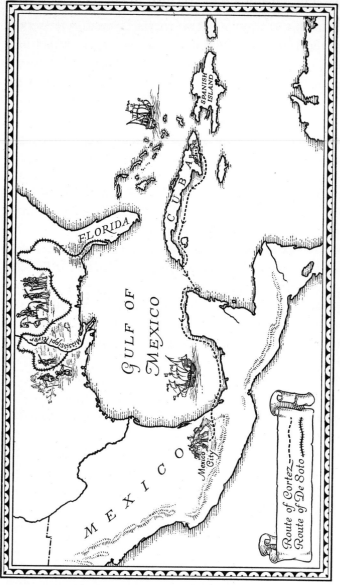

Routes of Cortez and De Soto

were received kindly.   The Indian woman who served as interpreter went about in the city and learned of a plan to attack the Spaniards and kill them all. She told Cortez, so he made ready, placing his guns in the streets.

When the chiefs came to see him the next day he told them he knew what they had planned. They were much surprised and went away, telling the others that the wonderful Spaniard could read men's minds.

From that time on the white men passed through town after town safely, the Indians looking upon them with fear, although they were only a little handful of Spaniards among thousands of enemies.

After some weeks they reached the top of a great range of mountains and, looking down, saw a lake with an island in the center. On the island was the great city of Mexico, joined to the mainland by five long bridges. The houses were of red stone covered with a white coating which shone like silver in the sun. The low, flat roofs were made into flower gardens. It was a city of wonders. How eagerly the Spaniards looked at it! They thought that at last they had arrived at one of Marco Polo's cities of gold. (On the map on page 107 find the route of Cortez.)

The Aztec king did not know what to do. Were the strangers gods? Their horses were not, for his people had killed and eaten some of them. But in every battle the white men had conquered his soldiers. If they should be gods it would not do to make enemies of them.

While he was trying to decide, the Spaniards came marching on. The king at last decided not to fight. He dressed himself in his finest robes, came out to meet

The soldiers of Cortez seize the king of the Aztecs

Does the picture show why the Spaniards were able to conquer
the Indians?

them, and invited them into Mexico City. There he
gave them one of his own palaces to live in. In a secret
room they found treasure piled from the floor to the roof.

Cortez knew that his men were not safe. At any
moment the whole city might attack them, make them
prisoners, and offer them alive to the terrible gods. To
prevent such an attack, one day when the Aztec king
came on a visit Cortez seized him and held him as a
prisoner. Then, if the people should make war on him,
he would threaten to kill the king. The Indians did not
know what to do with their leader gone, so they did
nothing.

All this time the Spaniards were sending out men to look for gold mines. They made the Aztecs bring them great wagonloads of treasure. In Mexico City they threw down the wooden gods from the temples and put up the cross, and did not allow men to be offered up alive. Cortez showed that he was a good business man and could rule a city.

Cortez called to the Coast

Then came bad news. The governor of Cuba had been angry because Cortez had not obeyed his orders to return. He was now sending eighteen ships and twelve hundred soldiers to bring him back to the island.

Cortez could think of only one thing to do. Leaving some of his men in the capital city in charge of one of his officers, he hurried down to the coast, attacked the governor's army at night, and won a battle. The next day he showed the army the gold and treasure that he had found in Mexico, and almost all of them came over to his side. He returned to Mexico City with four times as many men as he had when he had left it.

When he reached the city he found things in a very bad condition. The officer whom he had left in charge had been afraid that the Aztecs were plotting against him and had attacked them while they were having a feast, killing six hundred of them.

The Aztecs had risen in anger. They had held a council, had chosen a new king, and had attacked the Spaniards with fury. When Cortez arrived he made the former king, who was still his prisoner, stand on the wall and try to quiet his people. But now that they had a new king, they would not listen to the old one. They threw stones at him and hurt him so badly that he died soon after.

Mexico City Lost

Cortez knew that if he remained in the city he could no longer get food. He should have to leave. So that night, carrying whatever gold and precious stones they could, the Spaniards slipped quietly away during a cold rain. All went well until they came to the bridge. It had been taken away!

At that moment there was a sudden noise. A woman screamed. The great drums in the temple began to beat, armed men gathered in the street, and others began coming in boats from all directions.

It was a dreadful night for the Spaniards. To this day they call it "the night of sadness." All that they could do was to try to reach the farther shore across a broad stretch of water.

The next morning, when Cortez counted his army, he found that of fifteen hundred and fifty Spaniards only five hundred were alive, of eighty horses only twenty remained, and of six thousand of his Indian friends only two thousand had escaped. No cannon had been saved. They were at the bottom of the lake. And, worst of all, forty Spaniards had been taken prisoners. Across the water he saw them offered alive in the temples.

The Spaniards fought their way back to the country of their Indian friends, weak, hungry, and discouraged. Cortez became ill from his wounds and almost died.

The Second Conquest of Mexico City

Did Cortez give up the conquest of Mexico? No, indeed! As soon as he was well again he sent to the Spanish Island for help. He built boats in many separate parts, which could be carried on the backs of men and animals. For months he worked, and at the end of that time he had gathered a thousand men, eighty-six horses, a dozen cannon, and several thousand Indians.

On Christmas Day he began a second attack. As he neared Mexico City many Indians came over to his side, so that his army grew still stronger. At the shore of the lake he put his boats together. The bridges should not conquer him this time.

The Aztecs fought fiercely. They knew that their homes and their country would be lost forever if the Spaniards won again. They threw stones from the roofs, they shot a rain of arrows, they killed the horses, and they sank some of the boats.

Cortez decided to lay siege to the city. No food was allowed to go into it and no person to come away from it. For eight months the Aztecs held out. By that time their food was gone. There was no fresh water. Many houses had been burned. Death and ruin were on all sides.

At last the city gave itself up. The fight was over, and Mexico City was won. Cortez had done what few men could have succeeded in doing.

He quickly tore down the old town and built up a new Spanish city. Churches took the place of the Aztec temples. Horses and cows were brought in. The plants of the home land — sugar cane, oranges, and lemons — were made to grow.

The Spaniards made their own guns and powder and continued the war in other parts of the country until all Mexico was under the power of Spain.

Cortez sent men out in all directions to explore the land. Some even went as far north as California. The Spaniards were very proud of their conquest. They had found more gold than they had ever dreamed of. The long search for riches had ended. The Indies were no longer needed.

" *Prove It* "

You probably think that you understand the story you have just read. Prove it to yourself by answering the following questions.

1. What was the story about the fair god?

2. How did Cortez prevent his men from going back home?

3. Why did Cortez leave the city of Mexico the first time?

4. What happened while he was gone?

5. How did Cortez finally succeed in taking the city of Mexico?

6. Why were the Spaniards pleased with the conquest of Mexico?

Using New Words

In the story you found several new words. They are used in the sentences given on page 114. Complete the sentences, and call on someone in the class to decide whether or not your sentences are right.

1. Cortez was
2. The Aztecs were
3. The Gulf of Mexico is
4. Mexico is a
5. Mexico City was the
6. A capital city is the city where
7. The conquest of a country means
8. An interpreter is a person who

Cortez conquered Mexico.

Spain became very rich because of the wealth in her new lands.

Mexico belonged to Spain until about a hundred years ago.

Why do you suppose that a man's friends might bury him in a river? Read the story and find out whether you guessed the reason.

A GRAVE IN A DEEP RIVER

One morning in late spring the shores of Florida saw a strange sight. Nine great Spanish vessels had appeared at sunrise. They lay out in the bay, with folded sails. Over and around them worked six hundred busy men.

Into the small boats at the sides of the ships they carried down cannon, firearms, armor, forges for working iron, and great loads of iron collars and chains. What do you suppose the collars and chains were to be used for? For the Indians whom the Spaniards hoped to capture as slaves.

As the small boats began to make for the shore the water round about was dashed into foam, and black figures appeared everywhere in the waves. These were horses which had been brought for the conquest. Of the two hundred and thirteen horses landed on this spring morning, some were to go all the long bitter way with their masters for three years.

What could those other animals be? They were much too small for horses. Pigs! A whole army of pigs, to furnish fresh meat for the explorers. On the decks of the ships could be seen fierce bloodhounds to help catch Indians who might try to escape. The force

115

was much better supplied than that which had conquered Mexico a *score of years* [1] before.

The boats landed, and the leader, "a stern man of few words," stepped forth. Around him were his followers, dressed in shining armor and in robes of silk. He gave orders to his men.

Who was this leader? What was his name? Why had he come to the land in which other Spaniards had found sorrow and death?

De Soto's Early Life

The name of this leader was De Soto. He too had been born in Spain, of a family noble but poor. His birth was only four years after Columbus's first voyage, and from his earliest youth he had heard of the Indies.

When he was still young he had come to the New World and had done so well that he had been made a captain. Later he had been chosen to help in the conquest of a country farther south, a country as rich as Mexico. With twelve brave leaders he had fought the natives and had received about $300,000 as his share of a great roomful of gold which they had found.

Then he had gone home to Spain, had bought a great house, and had many servants to wait on him. His name was known all over the land. He was rich enough to lend money to the king, and a great nobleman's daughter had been proud to marry him.

Into this easy life had come news of a land north of Mexico, a land unknown to Spain. Was it also full of

[1] Twenty years.

gold? Might a band of men land in Florida and, by marching west, find riches?

At this news De Soto gave up his pleasant ways of living, his ease, and his riches. He asked the king for permission to explore and conquer Florida, promising to pay all the expenses himself.

The king was very glad to accept so good an offer. He made De Soto governor of Cuba, so that he might get help from there, but he ordered that half of all treasure found in the new lands should be kept for himself.

There was great excitement among the nobles of Spain. Had not the followers of Cortez become rich? De Soto could have had thousands of men, many of them willing to pay their own expenses. Some had sold their houses, their shops, and all that they had, in order to raise money enough to buy horses and arms. Some priests had left their churches. Many soldiers had come from Portugal. De Soto directed them all to meet him on a certain day, when he would choose those whom he would take.

When the day came they were all there. The men of Portugal were dressed in strong armor, but the nobles of Spain were dressed only in silk. De Soto was angry. He sent the Spaniards home, to return the next day prepared for work. The next day, since there was not room in his ships for all of them, he chose only six hundred, the best of the company.

In nine ships they set out, as if on a holiday. Some of them had their wives with them. In Cuba they were greeted with feasts and merrymaking. While De Soto was busy gathering horses, pigs, and slaves there, he sent a ship forward to Florida to find a harbor.

The ship returned with news of a good landing place. So De Soto, leaving his young wife in Cuba, set out with his men, his horses, his dogs and pigs, his arms and armor, to seek a still greater fortune in Florida.

Marching through Florida

We have seen how the landing was made. Soon afterwards De Soto sent the ships back to Cuba for supplies. His men then had no chance to change their minds and go back; they had to go forward.

The Indians looked with great surprise at the silken banners, the shining armor, the prancing horses, the sounding horns. But they had heard about the white men and knew how they treated Indians, so they quickly deserted their towns. When the Spaniards advanced, only empty houses rewarded their eager search.

Sometimes at night the Indians would make a fierce attack, and Spaniards and horses would be wounded. By day there were swamps and thick woods to cross, with secret paths known only to the Indians. Many of the Spaniards fell ill; and they found no gold.

They caught a few Indians and made slaves of them. These were led in chains, with iron collars about their necks.

The expedition pushed on. After a while they met a white man who had been taken captive by the natives years before. He had learned their languages and could act as interpreter, but he knew of no gold and of no great cities. The country, he said, had only trees and animals and savages.

At this the Spaniards begged De Soto to return to Cuba, but he would not. "I will not go back until I have seen with my own eyes that the land is poor," he replied.

The Spaniards continued to wander about during all the winter. Whenever they reached the home of a new tribe, they would capture the chief and make him furnish food and provide natives to carry their loads. As these natives were poorly dressed and loaded with irons, many of them died during the winter. The next time that their food supply was low, the soldiers caught and ate the dogs that they found in the Indian villages. They had to eat them without salt, since their supply had been used up, and the natives had none. They did not know how to hunt the wild animals of the forest, and they did not dare to separate from one another for fear of attack.

When spring came they heard of a country ruled over by a great queen. There was plenty of yellow metal there, the Indians said. But on reaching the queen's country they found that the yellow metal was only copper. How their hearts sank! They seized three hundred and fifty pounds of pearls, but all the pearls were very small. Having found no riches there, the Spaniards went on to a country farther west. In return for the queen's having received them kindly, they made her a prisoner; but one day, on the march, she fortunately escaped and carried most of her pearls with her.

The Great River

For some time De Soto had heard of a great river to the west, a river called by the Indians the Mississippi. He decided to find it.   After a long and hard journey the Spaniards came out of the woods and stood upon its banks.   They were the first white men who had ever seen it.[1]

It was broad, deep, and swift — so broad that if a man were standing on the other side, one could not be sure whether or not he was a man; so swift that trunks of trees and great branches were carried down by its waters.   It was very muddy.   Could they ever cross it?

News of the terrible white men had gone before them. Indians from the other side of the river rowed across to see how many the strangers were, but were careful not to land.

With great labor the Spaniards built four flatboats strong enough to carry horses.   This work took a month. Then one day, before sunrise, they began taking across four horses at a time in each boat.   After five hours of work all had reached the other side.

There they found traveling even harder than before. They marched for a long time in water sometimes up to their knees and sometimes up to their waists.   There were thick forests, but no precious stones and no gold.

On their journey they came to a country where grapes, plums, and nuts grew in great plenty.   The natives had not heard of the cruel strangers, so they did not run away.   They thought De Soto was a child of the sun and

---

[1] Except at its mouth in the Gulf.

De Soto discovers the Mississippi

Can you see why it was so hard to travel along the bank? (From a
painting by Stanley M. Arthurs)

brought out their blind people for him to cure. They gave him fish and taught his followers how to catch rabbits.

Three years had passed since the Spaniards left Cuba. Two hundred and fifty men had died, and a hundred and fifty horses. All who remained were glad to sit quietly and rest. The men made clothes for themselves from the skins of wild animals. They found salt, which they had been without for more than a year. The horses liked to eat the leaves of the corn, and grew fat. Each man made a log house for himself and his Indian slaves, and there they spent three months of the winter. Deep snow kept them from exploring farther.

When spring came they learned from the Indians that the country farther north was poor and that no gold nor precious stones were to be found.

Worn out by his wanderings, De Soto decided that he would have to return to the sea, build some ships, and go back for help to *New Spain*, which was the name that had been given to Mexico.

The Spaniards turned their faces southward. There were many deep rivers to cross; they tore down the natives' houses to make bridges. Thick woods blocked their way. Their interpreter died, and they could not learn in what direction the sea lay. Sickness came upon them in the lowlands.

When De Soto sent word to a native chief to come to him, the chief replied, "If you are a child of the sun, dry up this river, and I will believe." And he would not come.

At last De Soto himself fell ill. Knowing that he was about to die, he called his officers before him and told them he was sorry for all the evils he had brought upon them. He appointed a new leader as captain general and charged him to take the men back safely to New Spain.

Then the brave explorer died — in a wild land, with no comforts, and with little chance that his young wife would ever learn of his death. His search for gold had led him over vast stretches of our continent, in the most difficult exploration in our country's history.

The new leader buried De Soto secretly near the camp, for the Indians still believed him to be a child of the sun, who could not die. They saw the loose ground, however, and talked among themselves. So the leader took the body up, folded it in many cloths, rowed out to the middle of the river at night, and lowered his quiet burden into the waters. Thus De Soto found a lonely grave in the river that he had discovered. His wife did not hear the news until many months later; soon afterwards she also died.

De Soto's men sold all his belongings — five slaves, three horses, and a hundred pigs. They told the natives that the child of the sun had gone to heaven. (On the map on page 107 find De Soto's route.)

The Return to New Spain

Then the Spaniards began the long journey home. First they traveled inland for many days until they came to a country where no food could be found.

Then they came back to the river and spent six months in building seven rough ships. They cut down the trees with a large saw which they had carried with them all the long years. Only one man knew anything about building ships; he directed the rest. They made ropes from the bark of trees, and nails from the iron collars and chains of the slaves. They made barrels to hold fresh water, robbed the Indian villages to get corn, and killed the horses and dogs for meat. And, last of all, they set free their five hundred Indian slaves.

With no chart and no compass the ships started down the river. Sailing for sixteen days and often attacked by fierce Indians, they reached the sea. With great difficulty they followed the coast westward and came finally to New Spain.

Their high hopes had died. In the land which they had explored they had found only fierce Indians and want and suffering. From that time on, for many years, no attempts were made to settle in Florida nor along the Mississippi River.

Getting Ready

To get ready for the choose-one test, answer these questions to yourself:

1. What things did De Soto take with him to Florida?
2. How did De Soto treat the Indians?
3. What river did De Soto discover?
4. Why did his men bury him in the river?
5. How did his men reach New Spain?

A Choose-One Test

Choose one answer from each set below. Write the correct answer on a piece of paper and show it to your teacher.

1. To explore means

    to make a trip through lands known before
    to search through a new country in order to learn about it
    to travel by sea

2. A score of years means

    thirty years   ten years   twenty years

3. Wandering through countries that men have not known before is called

    exploration   settlement   invention

4. The discoverer of the Mississippi River was

    De Soto   Magellan   Cortez

5. The person who makes an exploration is an

    inventor   overseer   explorer

6. The largest river discovered in North America was the

    Hudson   Mississippi   St. Lawrence

De Soto discovered the Mississippi River.

His journey was "the most remarkable exploring expedition in the history of North America."

Spain did not settle the region around the river because there was no gold there.

From what country were most of the explorers about whom we have been reading? Why might England feel that she too ought to send out explorers? Do you think that the title of this story is correct in calling discovery and exploration a game?

ENGLAND ENTERS THE GAME

While Spain and Portugal had discovered new lands England had done nothing. You remember that the king of England had refused to help Columbus's brother. He must have been sorry afterwards.

Spain used her wealth from the New World to buy greater quantities of goods from England. So while Spain was spending her money, England was growing richer. Spain's power began to fail while England's was increasing.

One of the English king's friends said to him, "If you touch the king of Spain in the Indies, you touch the apple of his eye." He meant that the New World was the place Spain prized most highly.

John Cabot's First Voyage

The English king at last decided to let someone sail into the west for England; and the man who obtained leave to do so was John Cabot, a native of Columbus's own city of Genoa. Very early Cabot had learned the art of sailing and had gone to Venice to help in carrying on trade with the East.

He was a good sailor; his very name means John the Captain. Once, in the East, he had met a caravan laden with spices. He asked the people about the distant lands from which they came and listened carefully to their answers. From that time on he was eager to make a voyage to China.

Years went by. On his journeys Cabot traveled as far north as Iceland. At last he settled in a great trading city in England. One of the merchants of this city had as many as eight hundred seamen sailing for him. They all brought back interesting stories of strange lands.

Cabot's old dream of the East came back to him. Taking a map and a globe, he went to the king and asked to be allowed to make the voyage which Columbus had made and to reach the East by sailing west.

The king was willing to listen. Cabot told his plan, and the king believed that he could carry it out. So a letter was given to him, which said that he and his three sons were "to sail to all parts, countries, and seas of the east, west, or north." They might have five ships, if they wished, and as many men as they could get, but they would have to pay all the expenses themselves. They were to find any islands or countries which up to this time had been unknown to Christian nations and were to set up the English flag and conquer all such countries for the king.

You will notice that they were not to sail south. The king did not want at that time to touch the Spanish colonies and get into trouble with Spain. His fleet was not yet great enough to fight Spain.

So in 1497, five years after the first voyage of Columbus, John Cabot set sail from England one spring morning at sunrise.   He had only one ship and eighteen men, but the men were good sailors and were used to the storms of the Atlantic.

The Discovery of the Mainland of North America

After two months they reached a new land which no white men, except perhaps the Northmen,[1] had ever seen.   It was the *mainland* of North America.   The country was wild, with great dark forests, poor soil, rocky shores, and deep bays leading far inland.   They saw no natives, but found some traps set, which showed that people must live near.   Was this an island off the coast of China? No one knew.

John Cabot landed, raised the flag of England with its red cross, and claimed the country for the English king.   Then, because his provisions were almost gone, and there was nothing but fish to eat there, he hurried home to tell the king the news.

The king was pleased.   He thought that his sailors had reached the Indies, and the voyage had cost him nothing.   So he gave Cabot a little present of fifty dollars for having found the "new island."   It was not a great sum, but it showed that he appreciated Cabot's work.   Every year afterwards Cabot was to receive one hundred dollars.

[1] The account of Cabot comes after that of the Spanish explorers for convenience of arrangement, although chronologically it is earlier. Since it is earlier, there is in fact no contradiction here of what was written about De Soto.

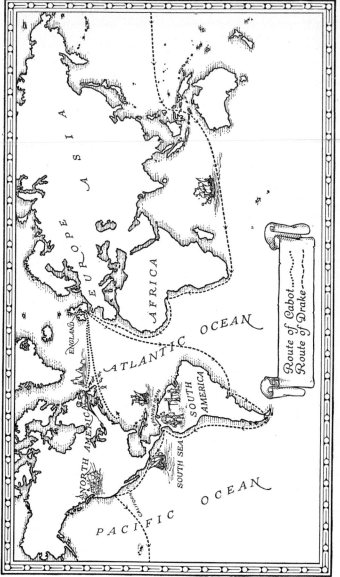

Routes of Cabot and Drake

The English people wanted to hear all about the voyage. Cabot, being foreign-born and poor, would not have been believed if his men (who were all English) had not told the same story; but, since they did, he was treated as a great man. "The English called him a great admiral. He dressed in silk; they paid him great honor; and everyone ran after him like mad."

The Spanish king was angry, for he claimed that all the islands of the Indies belonged to him; but the king of England did not care for that.

The Cabots' Second Voyage

Cabot knew that the time to make a second voyage was while people were still excited about the first. He gained the king's consent to go again. This time he was given five ships, enough food for a year, and some prisoners to help found a colony. And a year after he had returned from his first voyage he and his son set out again to find the seven golden cities of the Indies about which he had heard so many stories.

After a two months' voyage they reached the new land and sailed northward until they came to "huge heaps of ice swimming on the sea." Because of the cold they turned southward again, and after a time found the sea so full of fish that they said the ships could hardly sail on. Some of the fish were as long as a man and weighed a hundred pounds. The Cabots were also interested in watching some bears which came down to the water's edge and pulled out fish with their claws.

The Cabots leaving England

Which one is John Cabot? (From a painting by Ernest Board, in the Bristol Art Gallery, Bristol, England)

They saw some natives who wore the skins of animals for clothing and who were as proud of them as we are of our finest silks. They caught three of the savages and took them home to Europe. Someone who saw them in England wrote that they were "clothed in beasts' skins and did eat raw flesh and spoke such speech that no man could understand them."

The Cabots tried to start a colony in the land that they had found, but they had so much trouble with the prisoners they had taken with them as seamen that they gave it up. No spices were to be found anywhere.

On the way home John Cabot disappeared; we hear no more about him. Perhaps he died and was buried at sea. We only know that his son returned and told about the discoveries and great deeds of his father as if he had done them himself.   (On the map on page 129 find the route of the Cabots.)

Results of the Voyages

England was disappointed in the new land.   It was not the Indies, and so the Cabots' voyage was looked upon as a failure.   No trade could be secured.   The land did not seem to be worth much.   But one thing was sure: it was a good place for fishing, and English ships went there every year and came back loaded with fish. These fishing grounds were a mine of wealth, for at that time all Europe fasted on Fridays and holy days.   Fifty English ships spent two months in America every year.

The voyages of the Cabots were soon almost forgotten, but many years afterwards England found that the new land which they had discovered was valuable, and wished to lay claim to it.   Then she remembered, and claimed all of North America because John Cabot had been the first white man to reach its shores.   So a voyage which had been thought a failure gave England her *claim* to a continent.

Testing Yourself

How well do you remember the most important parts of the story?   Test yourself by the following questions. You will need these facts soon.

1. Why did Spain grow poorer?   Why did England grow richer?

2. What did Cabot find on his first voyage?

3. What did Cabot and his son find on their second voyage?

4. What did England think of the newly discovered land? Did Englishmen use it?

5. Why did England remember the Cabots' voyages later?

Filling Blanks

Write the correct words in a list and number them as the sentences are numbered. Show your list to the teacher. All these words were used in the story.

1. The year in which John Cabot discovered North America was _ _ _ _ _ _ _.

2. The parts of a new country which each nation called its own were the _ _ _ _ _ _ _ of that nation.

3. The nation which claimed the eastern coast of North America was _ _ _ _ _ _ _.

4. Land on a continent rather than on an island is called the _ _ _ _ _ _ _.

5. The name of the Englishman who discovered North America was _ _ _ _ _ _ _ _ _ _ _ _ _.

6. The land which England claimed in the New World was in _ _ _ _ _ _ _ _ _ _ _ _ _.

John Cabot discovered the mainland of North America in 1497.

Because of his voyages England later claimed all the eastern coast of North America.

What kind of person must a man have been to be called a dragon? From what country do you suppose he came? After you have read the story, tell whether you think Drake ought to have burned Spanish towns.

THE DRAGON THAT STRUCK FEAR INTO SPANISH HEARTS

One young Englishman had been filled with hate for all things Spanish by his experiences in battle with them. Usually the Spaniards had won. Day after day Francis Drake planned how England might even up her score.

How Drake learned Sailing

Francis Drake came of a family of seamen. As a child he had lived in an old ship that could no longer be used for sailing, and he had learned to know all the changes of the sea. When he was ten years old his father had hired him out to a captain on a vessel that traded along the coast. It was hard work, and Drake was very small, but he kept at it. After many years his master died and left him the ship. In this way he won his start in life.

Soon after this he began sailing to the New World. On one of his early voyages he burned and took the treasure of a great city on the Spanish Island, for at that time Englishmen thought it was right to take anything that belonged to Spain. This was called *sacking* the

134

city. Then, in the sea near the *Spanish Main*, or northern coast of South America, he captured a Spanish treasure ship so heavily loaded with silver that his own vessel could not carry it all and he had to bury most of it in a secret place on shore.

Drake's Fifth Voyage

The most interesting of Drake's earlier voyages was the fifth, the one in which he tried to capture a Spanish treasure fleet. The English queen dared not help him, because England and Spain were then at peace, but she did not stop him. He told no one but her about his plans.

First he went to his secret harbor where he had buried the Spanish silver, but the Spaniards had found the place, and the silver was gone. He then planned to capture one of the mule trains that the Spaniards used to carry their treasure to the coast, but to find them it would be necessary to go inland. No Englishman had ever before tried to do this, but Drake did not know what fear meant. With his little band he soon reached the town where the silver was stored. His plan was to make an attack the next morning, but the men could not wait. While it was still dark they made a rush. Bells rang, horns blew, drums beat, and the Spaniards, surprised, defended themselves as best they could.

The Englishmen fought their way into the treasure house and found three hundred tons of silver, but they could not carry it away. They were looking for the storehouse where the precious stones were kept when their leader, who had been wounded, fainted from loss of blood. So, in good order, they went back to their ship.

From that time on the Spaniards called Drake the Dragon. Mothers made their children obey by telling them that the Dragon would get them.

After this adventure the party had to wait five months because of the rains. Then their native guides led them through deep forests until they came to a tall tree from whose top, they said, could be seen two oceans.

Drake climbed up and saw at his left hand the Pacific, and at his right the Atlantic. He looked longingly at the Pacific and promised himself that some day, if he lived, he would sail a ship on its waters.

The party struggled on until they came upon the path from the mines. There they hid in the grass for a long time. But at last they heard bits of Spanish song one night, and the sound of the little bells on the mules' necks. The treasure train was coming out to meet the ships.

The Englishmen jumped from their hiding places in the dark and attacked fiercely. They wore white shirts over their coats, so that they could tell their friends from their enemies. Before morning the Spaniards had fled and had left more silver than the ships could carry away. Drake divided it among his men.

The king of Spain was so angry that he offered the sum of $200,000 to anyone who could kill the Dragon. He ordered his planters in the New World to hang every Englishman they could lay their hands upon, and told his sailors to sink every English ship that they met.

The Great Voyage

After his return Drake spent five years reading books, studying charts and globes, and questioning seamen as to how he might reach the Pacific coast of America. His plan now was to secure the Spanish treasure from that side.

The only way seemed to be far to the south, through the Strait of Magellan, but this passage was so dangerous that no one had been able to sail through it since the great voyage made by Magellan six *decades* [1] before. Many had tried it, but all had failed. Drake believed that he could do it.

At last all was ready. Drake's ship was called the *Golden Hind*. It was furnished like a palace. The dishes for the table were all of pure silver, and at every meal there was music. His clothes smelled of perfume which the queen herself had given him. Drake was greatly respected by his men. Whenever he met any of his crew, they stood with their hats off. No one spoke until he spoke.

While the *Golden Hind* was still sailing the Atlantic, Drake held a great council and explained to his men why he was going to attack Spanish ships when England and Spain were not at war. One reason was that the Spaniards had attacked an English fleet in Mexico during a time of peace. The second reason was that Spain had often captured English seamen and put them in prison or killed them if they did not obey orders. The third was that the king of Spain was planning secretly to kill the English queen and to take possession of England.

[1] A decade is ten years.

They sailed down the coast of South America for several months.   Near the place where Magellan's captains had tried to desert him they ran into a very bad storm.   The sailors thought that the natives had raised this storm by magic.

Up the Western Coast of South America

After seventeen terrible days in the Strait of Magellan the Pacific Ocean lay before them.   They had been away from home more than a year, and not a whisper of their coming had reached the Spaniards.

Making maps of the land as they passed it, the little company sailed up the western coast of South America. Soon they saw a Spanish ship.   The Spaniards, thinking that none but Spanish ships could find their way into this ocean, brought up wine and beat on their drums a welcome to the strangers.   It was a great surprise to them when Drake's men boarded the vessel and drove them below decks.

Two thousand jars of wine were found and a great quantity of gold and precious stones.   One great cross of gold set with green stones was a foot high.

Drake set all the prisoners free, put some of his men in charge of the Spanish ship, and started north again. The Spaniards sent word up the coast, warning all the towns to be on the watch for him; but his ship went faster than the news.

As he journeyed on, one day, he saw a Spaniard on the shore, fast asleep, with thirteen bars of silver beside him.   Drake took the silver and did not even wake the

Drake captures the treasure ship
Which is the Spanish ship? What causes the smoke?

man. At another time he captured a train of animals
with half a ton of silver ; and, again, he found a hundred
pounds of silver guarded by only one negro.

Then he began to hear stories of a great Spanish
treasure ship which was called "the chiefest glory of
the whole South Sea." She had left a harbor two weeks
before, but Drake was sure that he could catch her.

On his way he seized four other rich vessels, but took
little interest in them. He offered a golden chain to the
man who should first see the treasure ship. The one to
whom this good fortune came was little Jack Drake,
his page.

The Spanish vessel, not having heard of any danger from the English, waited for the *Golden Hind* to come up.

"Who are you?" asked her captain.

"Strike your sail, or I will send you to the bottom," came the reply, ringing across the water.

The surprised captain answered, "Come on board and do it if you can."

A rain of shot and arrows followed. The English ship had many guns, and the Spaniards had few; so in a short time the Spanish sailors were driven below decks. The ship was put in charge of English sailors, and the two ships sailed together for some distance before Drake dared take time to search his prize.

Great treasures were found, including thirteen large boxes of gold pieces, eighty pounds of pure gold and precious stones, and twenty-six tons of silver. Drake set his prisoners free, gave a gift to each one, put them in their ship again, and let them return home.

By this time his own ship was so heavy with silver that he could fight no more battles. He would have to go back to England. What route should he take? If he went back the way he had come, he knew that all the Spaniards would be on the watch for him. There was wild excitement in all Spanish America; armed ships were already looking for him in all directions. They did not want him to return to England with the news that the South Sea was no longer a Spanish ocean but was free to the English as well.

Trying to find a New Way Home

Drake therefore decided to keep on sailing northward to see if he could not find a way through America to the east and thence home. He reached the Pacific coast of North America, finding on the way a ship with more gold and, better yet, a chart of the way to sail to China and around the Cape of Good Hope. That chart was of great value to him.

Farther north the country was very cold. Rain changed to snow as it fell; the ropes of the ship were like iron rods; meat froze as it was taken off the fire. This would never do. He must turn south again.

So he turned south and soon came to the coast which we now call California. The natives received him as a god and made him king. He accepted the country in the name of Queen Elizabeth of England, and called it New Albion, which means New England; for he hoped that colonies might soon be founded there. To show that it belonged to England, he set up a metal plate with the queen's name upon it. (Find Drake's route on the map on page 129.)

Sailing Home around the World

Not having found any strait by which he could pass through North America, Drake decided to return home by sailing around the earth, as Magellan had done. In a month his vessel was ready, supplies were gathered, and the long journey was begun.

Near the Philippines he met thieves, just as Magellan had done. By this time he had only fifty-six men left, so he hurried on to the Spice Islands, where he traded some of his silver for spices.

There the *Golden Hind* landed on a rock, and could get free only by throwing three tons of spices overboard. Some of the natives guided the vessel out again into the open sea.

Many other adventures followed, but at last there came a morning, three years after the ship had left home, when the signal guns on the English coast roared out a welcome.   Drake had returned.   He had sailed around the world.   In the hold of his vessel was such treasure as no one had ever dreamed of.   Even the common sailors were rich beyond measure.

The queen did not quite know what to do.   Should she receive him, or should she treat him as a pirate? But the tales of his treasures were too interesting. She sent for him.

With loads of gold and silver and spices and precious stones, Drake appeared at court.   The queen was greatly pleased with his story, which she made him tell over and over again.   She wore the largest of his precious stones in her crown.   She kept him with her most of the time; she talked with him "as often as nine times a day"; she took the greater part of his treasure and put it in her tower.

One night she took dinner with him on board his ship. After the dinner she made him kneel before her and, striking his shoulder with a golden sword, said, "I bid thee rise, *Sir* Francis Drake."   In this way she *conferred knighthood* on the brave sailor.

Sir Francis Drake gave many presents to the nobles, a few of whom would not accept his gifts because they

feared his deeds would bring on war with Spain.   But
the common people loved him and never tired of telling
his adventures.

The king of Spain sent word to Queen Elizabeth that
Drake was a pirate and should be hanged.   In reply the
queen asked him to prove it.   If the king could prove it,
she would have the treasure returned.   But the treasure
never went back to Spain.

Years later, when the *Golden Hind* had become so
old that it could no longer be used, it was broken up
and a chair was made from some of its wood.   The
chair can still be seen today in England.

Sir Francis Drake had done much for his country.
He had shown Englishmen that they need no longer be
afraid of Spain, that they could hold their own against
her, and that they should put their trust in ships.   But
his voyages had made the Spaniards hate the English
even more than they had done before.   Spain felt that
she must teach England a lesson.   War soon broke out
between the two nations, and Drake had all he could do
to lead the English fleet to victory.

Helping Yourself

The following questions are to help you find out
whether you know the story.   If there are some that
you do not know, look up the answers before you try
the next exercise.

1. What did Drake try to do on his fifth voyage?

2. What was Drake's latest plan to seize the Spaniards'
gold?

3. Drake told his men why he attacked Spain when Spain and England were at peace. Can you give his three reasons?

4. What did his crew do as they sailed up the western coast of South America?

5. Why did Drake then sail around the world in order to reach England?

Selecting Words

Here is a list of words. From this list choose the word which belongs in each blank below. Write your words in a list and exchange with your neighbor. The teacher will read the right list. You may mark on your neighbor's paper those which are wrong, and he will correct them.

Names of Persons

Sir Francis Drake
English

Words

confer knighthood
decade
pirate
sack (of a city)
attack

Names of Places

Pacific coast of North America
Spanish Main

South Sea
California

Sentences

1. To _____ is to try to take a place or an army by force.

2. The natives of _____ received Drake as a god.

3. The _____ nation was constantly quarreling with Spain.

4. Queen Elizabeth decided to _____ _____ on Drake.

5. The northern coast of South America was called the
_____ _____.

6. _____ _____ _____ was called the Dragon.

7. A _____ is a man who robs ships at sea.

8. Drake spent the winter on the _____ _____
_____ _____ _____.

9. Ten years are a _____.

10. Before Magellan made his voyage the Pacific was
called the _____ _____.

11. The _____ of a city was the taking of its treasures
by an enemy.

Sir Francis Drake was the first Englishman to
circumnavigate the globe.

He made Spain angry by sacking her towns and
capturing her treasure fleets.

Where was the first home of the English nation? Where do you suppose that the second home was to be? Read the story and find out whether your guess was right.

A SECOND HOME FOR THE ENGLISH NATION

When Francis Drake returned from his voyage on the *Golden Hind*, one of those who welcomed him home was the queen's favorite, Sir Walter Raleigh. Raleigh was a tall good-looking man with thick wavy hair. His mind was keen and his tongue ready. He had left school to fight the Spaniards, and was in trouble with Spain all the rest of his life in one way or another.

First Efforts to found an English Colony

Raleigh's stepbrother believed that if England expected ever to equal Spain she too must plant colonies in the New World. To show what could be done, he prepared to found a colony on the eastern coast of North America, where the Cabots had seen so many fish.

Walter sailed with his stepbrother, but they ran into a heavy fog and into mountains of ice driven by the winds upon the sea. So they had to return to England.

At once the stepbrother began to make ready for a second voyage. Walter was eager to go also, but the queen said: "No. We cannot part with you. We cannot have you run the danger of being lost at sea. Send out a ship if you wish, but do not go yourself."

He was much disappointed, but had to obey and contented himself by fitting out a ship to send with the others. The expedition failed. Raleigh's ship came back, but his stepbrother's ship was lost with all on board.

One might think that after two such failures Raleigh would have given up the thought of a colony and would have been satisfied to enjoy the pleasures of the court. But no! he was determined to carry out his plan.

Raleigh sends out Explorers

Raleigh explained to the queen that founding colonies was the only way in which she could hold the land that the English had discovered in the New World. The new colonies would trade with the mother country and would buy all their goods from her. Thus she would gain a double advantage. Elizabeth believed that Raleigh was right. She drew up a paper which gave him permission to explore any lands not held by a Christian prince or by Christian people. He might build a fort; the land was to belong to him; but the people he took out must still have in the New World all the rights that they had had in England.

Remembering the mountains of ice that he had seen on the voyage with his stepbrother, Raleigh chose a course that lay farther south. First he sent out a ship to explore the land and bring back news as to what kind of place it was.

The explorers sailed for many days, and at last reached a shore where they said "the air was as sweet as if in the middle of a garden." They stopped at a harbor where there were so many grapes that "in all the world the like number was not to be found." In the woods were the tallest trees they had ever seen. The forests were full of deer.

They found the natives gentle and friendly. One of the sailors wrote that the Indians were "gentle, loving and faithful, very handsome and goodly; as mannerly as the people of Europe." There was much visiting between the explorers and the Indians. The Englishmen gave the chief a bright tin dish; it pleased him so much that he hung it about his neck. In return he sent them every day deer, fish, fruits, corn, beans, and peas.

The party had been sent out only to explore, not to found a colony. After a pleasant visit they took two natives with them and returned to England.

The queen was delighted with their report. She called the beautiful land Virginia, and conferred knighthood on Raleigh. From that time on he was known as *Sir* Walter Raleigh.

The First Colony returns to England

You may be sure that no time was lost in sending out a colony to Virginia. The reports had been so good that many people wished to go. The greater number, however, went with the hope of finding gold and were of little help in building homes in the New World. The queen did not let Raleigh leave England, but he put one of his friends in command and stood watching as the seven ships departed with their hundred colonists.

When the colonists reached the New World they sailed along the coast eight days before they could find a river large enough to enter. They thought that the land must be "a continent of huge and unknown greatness"; they called it the "sweetest soil under heaven." Corn, potatoes, and tobacco, none of which they had known in Europe, grew to a great size. Bears made excellent meat for them.

They built a fort and then sent the ships back to England for supplies. The Indians, who had been friendly at first, were not at all pleased when they saw the ships sail away, leaving so many men behind.

After a time some of the Englishmen, while they were visiting an Indian village, charged one of the natives with stealing a silver cup. It was not returned at once, so in order to punish the Indians the Englishmen burned their village and destroyed their standing corn. This made the Indians their enemies.

Stories had been heard of a land of gold and pearls farther up the river. A party was sent to find it, but the Indians would not help them. Their food gave out; they even had to kill and eat their dogs. No gold was found.

When the exploring party returned to the fort, they found the other colonists in great fear of the Indians. A wicked plot was agreed upon. They asked the chief for permission to visit him in his house. As they were sitting peacefully talking the English leader gave a signal, and his men at once killed all the Indians in the hut.

After that they thought they had better go back to England. They had lost only four men during the year that they had been in Virginia, but they were afraid of the Indians. Supplies were running low, and the supply ship had not come. Just then some ships appeared out at sea. Sir Francis Drake, who was going home after fighting on the Spanish Main, had stopped to see the colony of his friend Raleigh.

Drake offered to leave them supplies or to take them home in his ships, whichever they preferred. They cried, "Take us home." And Raleigh's plan had failed a third time.

They had hardly left when the supply ship came. Finding no one there, it returned. Two weeks later more ships came, with supplies to last for years, but the colony was already broken up.

The men who had lived in Virginia took home with them a full account of the new land and carried some of its plants to Raleigh — among them potatoes and tobacco. Raleigh planted the potatoes on his broad lands and taught the courtiers to smoke tobacco. The story is told that one day his servant came into the room and saw great clouds of smoke rising from his master's head. He rushed out, seized a pail of water, and dashed it into Raleigh's face, fearing that his master was on fire.

The Second Colony Disappears

Although Raleigh had lost all the money that he had put into the colony, he at once began to plan another. This time he would send families of men and women; they would build homes in the New World. They were to found a city. He furnished all the money; the queen had given nothing but her name.

Raleigh's colonists leave England

Does the picture tell you whether the colonists were well-to-do or poor? (From a painting by C. Y. Turner)

Again the ships landed in Virginia.   At first the men used the fort and the buildings that had been left by the other colony. From the beginning they had trouble with the Indians, for instead of attacking an enemy tribe they made a mistake and attacked one of the few tribes that were still friendly.

When the ship returned to England the colonists sent their governor back to ask for more supplies. He was sad at leaving his daughter and his little grand-daughter, Virginia Dare, who had been born since the colonists reached the new land and who was the first white child born in what is now the United States. But the colony was in great need of help, so he went, leaving behind him a hundred and eight settlers.

When the governor reached England he found the country at war with Spain. Raleigh had by this time spent $200,000 on his colonies, but at last raised enough more money to send two ships with supplies. No sooner had the ships left England than they were driven back by the Spaniards.

It was two years before the governor was able to return to the New World. He feared what might have happened during all this time to his daughter and his little granddaughter. As the ships neared the shore the guns roared a signal, but not a sound was heard in reply.

The governor landed and looked about. Not a soul was there. The fort looked as if the people had left in a hurry, but there was no sign that they had been in trouble. On a tree the governor found the word CROATOAN cut in the bark. Croatoan was the name of

an island close by. The ship could wait no longer;
it was ready to go on its way, and there was nothing
for the governor to do but to go with it.

Five times afterwards Raleigh is said to have sent
out ships to find his lost colony, but none ever succeeded.

Up to this time robbing Spaniards had been a much
better business for the Englishmen than trying to plant
colonies.

A Sad Old Age

Raleigh had spent all his fortune and had given years
of his life in the attempt to found an English colony.
He had failed; but he had talked and written so much
about his plan that the English people were becoming
used to the idea of founding a colony. So we may well
call him the father of the English colonies in America.

In the war with Spain he had fought bravely and had
helped the queen to make the best use of her ships.
After the war was over he had made a long voyage to
South America in search of treasure. But again he
failed. His good fortune was at an end. He was thrown
into prison and was kept there for thirteen years.
During that time he wrote a history of the world.

At the end of the thirteen years he was set free and
sent once more to find the mountains of gold behind the
Spanish Main. But again he found no gold. Worse
than that, his son was killed in an attack on a Spanish
fort.

When he returned the queen was dead, and the new
king ordered that Raleigh's head should be cut off.
As he was about to die he felt of the edge of the ax,

smiled, and said, "'Tis a sharp medicine, but a cure for all diseases." Thus the soldier, sailor, adventurer, statesman, poet, and writer of history died a ruined and broken-hearted man.

Two hundred years later the city of Raleigh, named for him, became the capital of one of our great states. What we like best to remember about him, however, is his great faith in the New World and his firm belief, "I shall yet live to see it an English nation."

Keeping your Score

I. Can you answer the following questions? If not, turn back and find the answers. When you have finished No. 6, report to your teacher how many times you had to turn back.

1. What was Raleigh's plan for the New World?

2. What did his captains report about the land that had been granted him?

3. What did the queen call the new land?

4. What happened to Raleigh's first colony? Who took the colonists home?

5. What two plants were brought back to England?

6. What happened to Raleigh's second colony?

II. If you could answer the questions, you will find these exercises easy. Fill the blanks with the right words.

1. The Englishman who wanted to plant colonies was
- - - - - - - - - - - - - -.

2. He wanted to plant them on the _ _ _ _ _ _ _ coast of
_ _ _ _ _ _ _ _ _ _ _ _ _ _.

3. The queen named the land _ _ _ _ _ _ _.

III. Here are some new words that were used in the story. Put each one in the right blank in the sentences below.

courtier   failure   found a colony

1. To begin settlement in a strange land is to _ _ _ _ _ _ _
_ _ _ _ _ _ _.

2. A person who spends much of his time in the king's court is a _ _ _ _ _ _ _.

3. Not to succeed in accomplishing your purpose is
_ _ _ _ _ _ _.

Walter Raleigh tried hard to found English colonies in
the New World.

He failed, but his idea lived on.

Could France settle in the parts of the New World that had already been taken by England and Spain? Why might she be jealous of them? Read the story and find out where France sent her explorers.

FRANCE ENTERS THE NEW WORLD

While Spain and Portugal were growing rich and powerful with the help of their colonies, France was becoming jealous. The king of France said, "Can anyone show me the will of our Father Adam in which he left all the world to Spain and Portugal?" Of course no one could.

For many years, ever since they had heard Cabot's stories about the fish in the New World, French fishermen had been sending their ships to the northeastern coast of America. Hundreds of vessels went there every year. The men would spread out their great piles of fish to dry while they searched the islands for fur-bearing animals. Thus fish, rather than gold, drew the French to our shores.

Sometimes ships from other countries came to the fishing grounds also. Each nation kept to itself; each built its own little village on the shore, where its men could get food and water. At times the different nations fought one another, but the French usually won because of their greater number.

These early fishermen discovered and made maps of many islands, about which they told their king.

Finding the Gulf

The king of France was interested. Perhaps this was his chance to build up a great trade like that of Spain and Portugal. He decided to send a party to explore the new islands, hoping to find a way through them to the Indies. Whom should he place in command? He had heard of a sailor in one of the western towns of France, a man who had followed the sea from his youth and who had already made several voyages to the fishing banks. Cartier was this man's name, and he was the one who was chosen.

On his first voyage of discovery Cartier sailed straight across the ocean from France for twenty days, meeting many storms and much floating ice, but arriving safely at one of the islands known to the fishermen.

He soon found many new islands. Off the coast of one he saw a huge white bear swimming ashore to get his dinner from the great numbers of sea birds that nested there. On another island he set up a tall wooden cross to show that France claimed it. The farther he went, the more islands he found; their shores were chiefly "rocks, as steep as any wall."

Later Cartier called the great gulf in which he had been sailing the "St. Lawrence." As he sailed up the gulf, Indians in canoes came crowding about his ship, and to frighten them away he fired guns up into the air. But he gave the chief a red hat, and they became friends. Another large cross was set up with the words "Long live the king of France," to show that France claimed this land also.

Then the same thing happened to him that had happened to many others before him. In those days of small ships and large crews it was very difficult to carry food enough for more than a few months. Cartier's supplies gave out, and winter was coming on. Taking two of the Indians with him, he returned to France.

He had not yet found a new route to the Indies, but he had seen a great gulf that might lead there and he had gained new lands for France.

Exploring the Great River

The next year the king sent Cartier with a few young nobles to explore the waters he had found, to make a colony, and to trade with the Indians. There was still hope that a northwest passage to the spice lands might be discovered. But the French sailors had said that the country around the Gulf of St. Lawrence was cold and rocky, and it was hard to get people to go there. Cartier had to take some prisoners as colonists. That was not a very wise thing to do, for prisoners do not make good colonists.

On this second voyage the weather was very stormy, as it had been on the first voyage. When they reached the Gulf of St. Lawrence the two Indians who had come back with them told of a great river to the westward. Cartier hoped that it would prove to be not a river, but a strait leading to the Indies. But he was disappointed, for as he sailed farther inland the water became less and less salt. At last it was perfectly fresh; so it was only a river. This river was called the St. Lawrence River.

Cartier discovers the St. Lawrence

To what is Cartier pointing? (From a painting by Haskell Coffin.)

© Haskell Coffin

The country was very beautiful. The leaves were red and gold, the water shone in the sun, and on both sides the banks rose straight up, far above the river. On one of these high hills near the river today lies Quebec, one of the most beautiful cities in America.

The Indians were afraid of the "winged canoes," as they called them. The chief came out to meet the white men, and when he heard that they were going still farther up the river he determined to prevent them if he could. So he dressed up some of his men to look like evil spirits and told these "spirits" to dance wildly in front of the Frenchmen. When Cartier asked who these dancers were, the chief replied that they were sent by a god farther up the river who did not like strangers. Any Indian would have been frightened at this, but Cartier only laughed and kept on.

Soon he was stopped by some great rapids. He was sure that by this time he must be near China. The rapids were later called Lachine Rapids. Today, though we know that China is thousands of miles away, we still call the rapids "Lachine," which is French for China.

Landing there, Cartier found a high island-mountain and a large Indian town, round in shape and well protected by stones. He called the island Mont-Royal. Today we call it Montreal.

When the Indians found that Cartier was friendly, they traded fish and corn for knives and beads. They even brought some sick Indians to be cured, for they thought that he was a god.

It was now late in the fall. No gold or silver had been found and no northwest passage to China. Cartier

Map of New France in Cartier's time

decided to return to a place farther down the river to spend the winter. The Frenchmen had no heavy clothing, no warm houses, and very little food. They were not used to such weather, and they suffered greatly. Then sickness broke out. At one time all but ten of the men were sick. But they learned from the Indians how to make a tea from the needles and bark of the white-pine tree, and this cured some of them.

How glad they were when the breaking up of the ice in the river told them that spring had come and that they might go home! They captured some Indians and even the chief who had been kind to them, and took them to France. Before leaving, Cartier gave the land a name; he called it New France.

The king was glad to hear that New France was so large, but he was once more disappointed at not finding a short route to the Indies. Other people were not much interested, for New France contained no gold.

The Last Attempt

Five years later another attempt was made to found a colony in New France. This time Cartier had with him another leader. They were to explore farther up the river.

They landed after a passage even stormier than before. At once the Indians wanted to know what had happened to their chief. Cartier replied that he had died in France; but the Indians blamed Cartier, and from that time on were unfriendly.

Both sides of the river were carefully explored, but there was no sign of gold. Again the supplies failed within a few months, and again the party spent a terrible winter without even any help from the natives. In the spring the few who were still living went home. Cartier was made a knight because of his services in finding the new land, but he died soon afterwards.

France continued to send out her fishing fleets, but for more than fifty years made no further attempt to found a colony in the new lands.

Testing a Friend

I. After you have studied the following questions, perhaps your teacher will let you choose a partner, and you may then ask the questions of each other.

1. Why did French people first go to the New World?

2. What did the king of France want to find there?

3. What did Cartier call the gulf and the river which he discovered?

4. On the second voyage what three things was Cartier ordered to do?

5. Did Cartier found a colony?

II. Each partner will then make sentences using the following words. Exchange your papers and correct each other's. If your partner questions your sentence, prove that it is right (or wrong) by turning back in the story. Your teacher will help you to find the right places in the book.

Names of Persons	*Names of Places*
1. Cartier	4. France
2. French (people)	5. Montreal
	6. St. Lawrence River

Word

3. attempt

Cartier discovered the St. Lawrence River and claimed all the land round about for France.

It was easy to sail up the St. Lawrence River into the new land.

This story is about the man who was called the Father of Canada. What must a man have done to win such a name as that? Did you ever hear George Washington called the Father of his Country?

THE FATHER OF NEW FRANCE

For a long time after the death of Cartier the French continued to seek in the New World only fish and furs. No colonies were founded and no cities built. The building of cities had to wait for the coming of the most famous man in the early history of New France, Samuel de Champlain.

Champlain's father and grandfather had been adventurers. At an early age he learned to sail ships and to make maps, and soon he was fighting for France both at sea and on land. The king looked upon him with favor because of his bold ideas, his brave deeds, and his strong will.

When Champlain could not find enough adventure in France, he went out to the West Indies in the service of the king of Spain. There he learned how the Spaniards founded colonies and how they managed them. After three years in the West Indies he returned and wrote the story of what he had seen and done. He even showed that it would be possible to make a canal through the place where, three hundred years later, America built the Panama Canal.

He showed so much good sense and used his eyes so

well that when the king again sent an expedition to find a northwest passage to the Indies, Champlain was sent with the party and was told to bring back a careful record of the exploration.

Making a Colony

After a voyage to New France, Champlain had helped to form one colony that failed. But we have learned that great men do not give up because of one failure. Four years later he was back in Canada as captain of a small ship. He had decided to found a city on the St. Lawrence River, far away from the English colonies and in the heart of the fur country.

The city of Quebec still stands in the place he chose. It was the first French town in the New World, and it was built at the foot of a high rock which could be easily defended against an enemy. There Champlain placed a wooden cross painted with the arms of France. To-day his own statue stands on that rock, keeping watch over his city.

During the first winter the colonists suffered terribly. Having come from the warmer country of France, they could scarcely endure the cold. Sickness again broke out, and of the twenty-eight men of the colony only eight were living when spring came.

Champlain was very busy, for he was now governor of New France. He cut down trees and planted corn. He built a fort, which the Indian women and children were allowed to enter but not the Indian men. A deep ditch was dug all around the fort, and cannon were set in many places.   Then a house was built in which the colonists might store the corn that should be raised the following summer.

All this time Champlain had been thinking about the sickness which had killed so many of his men.   He decided that it was caused by their having only salt meat to eat, so he laid out gardens and planted seeds of many kinds of plants.   When the next winter came the colonists had fresh food, and there was no sickness.

For many years Quebec took most of Champlain's time.   He gave twenty years of his life to making it safe and firm.   Almost every winter he returned to France and came back to Quebec with more supplies and more colonists.   He tried to have the colonists make homes and farms instead of only fur-trading stations.

The town grew slowly.   After twenty years it had only about a hundred people, and of these only one or two families supported themselves by farming.   The fur trade was much more interesting. So the food supplies had to be brought from France.

Searching for a Northwest Passage

Champlain's care for Quebec did not make him forget the thought of a passage to China.   Once he sent out a young Frenchman to live among the Indian tribes, to learn their language, and to find out whether they knew anything about a passage to the west.   In return he took a young Indian to France to learn the French language.   He thought that the Indian could then tell him many things that he wished to know.

Champlain choosing a place for his city

Why did Champlain choose a place at the top of this cliff? (From a painting by Stanley M. Arthurs)

The young Frenchman came back from among the Indians with an interesting story. He had seen a great ocean, he said, and on it was the wreck of an English vessel. Champlain thought it must have been the Pacific and eagerly made ready to explore it.

The way was long and dangerous. At first Champlain and his men followed a river full of falls and rapids. Because travel was so difficult they took only two canoes with four men. Every time that they came to rapids they had to stop and carry canoes, clothes, food, and guns on their shoulders over to where the river was quiet again. "It was no small matter for persons not accustomed to it," wrote Champlain. The thick forests made walking very hard.

The men would have been glad to return to Quebec, but Champlain kept on, studying the ways of the different tribes they met. As they passed from one part of the country to another they had to find new guides who could show them the way.

Whenever Champlain came to a lake or a river which he had not seen before, he claimed all the land around it for France and planted on the shores wooden crosses carved with the arms of the king.

At last they reached the place where the great ocean and the English wreck were said to have been, but there was no sign of them. Then the young man who had told the story had to tell the truth. He had seen no ship and no ocean. He had made up the story, never thinking that he would be found out. So all Champlain's work had gone for nothing, and his time and effort had been wasted.

Champlain was disappointed and angry. He now had to return to Quebec over that hard and dangerous route. But he had learned more about the country, and he was able to take back a load of furs.

The next winter he went to France again and brought back some missionaries to teach the Indians, so that, as he said, "God should first of all be served." The missionaries lived among the natives and learned their languages in order to teach them more easily.

Exploring the Great Lakes

Champlain had not finished his exploring. Two years later he set out again and went farther than before — so far that his food supplies gave out and his men had to live by hunting and fishing and picking wild fruit. Travel was as hard as ever, and the wind had blown down many tall pine trees across his path.

By this time Champlain himself had learned the Indian languages. He talked to the natives and found out the names of many of their rivers and lakes. These names he wrote on his maps. The Indians in these far-away places thought he must have fallen from the sky, for they could not believe that any white man could have traveled so far from the great river.

Then he came to the shores of the "Great Sweet Water," which we now call Lake Huron. It stretched out in all directions, farther than Champlain could see. Turning southward and following the shore about a hundred miles, he met one of the priests who had already reached this lonely place in his work of teaching and

New France in Champlain's time

preaching to the Indians. (On the map which is shown above find Champlain's route to Lake Huron.)

Champlain sent his men to explore still farther, while he studied the country. After a time the natives came begging his help in a war against some enemy tribes. He went with them farther south to another great lake, which we know as Lake Ontario. There were with him ten other Frenchmen and the friendly Indians. They met and attacked the enemy tribe, but the Indians would not obey Champlain. Each of them fought in his own way. So they were defeated. Champlain was wounded in the knee and had to be carried north in a basket.

As he was not able to walk he had to spend the winter among the Indians. He told many interesting stories about them. They painted their faces black and red. They had two meals a day; these meals were mostly corn, deer meat, and fish. The women spent the winter spinning and pounding meal; the men made nets and fished through the ice. Their clothes were made the same way year after year; they had no changes in style.

The Indians were very fond of dancing; and as soon as a dance was over they went to sleep, which they liked best of all. Their children were never punished, and were very bad. When an Indian was sick his friends would come to his house singing, dancing, beating on drums, and making a great noise. They thought the noise would drive the evil spirits away and make the sick man well, but it generally made him much worse.

Champlain's Work

When Champlain returned to Quebec he found his wheat, corn, peas, beans, and grapevines growing finely.

The colony continued to live in spite of Indians, cold, hard work, and sickness. At times France cared so little about it that she would not send supplies, but still it endured. The fur trade grew to be an important business, sometimes as many as twenty thousand skins a year being sent to France.

Champlain had founded the first French colony in America, he had discovered two of the Great Lakes, he had laid claim to a great stretch of country for France, and he had begun to raise grain and fruit.

Before he came to Canada there were no French people living in America except the few fishermen along the coast. When he died France had a firm footing in the New World. Very justly has Champlain been called the Father of New France.

Finding your Score

Answer the following questions to yourself, and then turn back in the story to prove your answers. If all five answers were right, your score is 100; if four answers were right, your score is 80; and so on.

1. What colony did Champlain found?
2. Why did he go exploring in the northwest?
3. How many of the Great Lakes did he discover?
4. What four things did he do for France?
5. Why is he called the Father of New France?

A Missing-Name Test

Supply missing names from words found in the story.

1. The name of the trade which the French carried on in America was the _ _ _ _ _ _ _.
2. The city founded by Champlain was _ _ _ _ _ _ _.
3. The Father of New France was _ _ _ _ _ _ _.
4. The country which the French settled in the New World is now known as _ _ _ _ _ _ _.
5. They called it _ _ _ _ _ _ _ _ _ _ _ _ _ _.

Champlain founded towns and explored many lakes, so he has been called the Father of New France.

What do you suppose the *Half-Moon* was? Have you ever heard of the Hudson River? Should you like to know how it got its name?

THE VOYAGE OF THE *HALF-MOON*

One morning there was great excitement in the Dutch capital; the important men of the city could be seen hurrying to the statehouse, and sailors stood on the street corners and talked of sailing to new lands.

The Dutch were going to seek a short route to the Indies. They had for many years been a nation of sailors; they had just freed themselves from the power of Spain, and had taken a great part of Portugal's trade with the Spice Islands. Now that this trade was so important to them, the route around Africa was too long. They hoped to find a passage around Europe to the north, and had offered a prize to the man who should find it first.

A great English sea captain wished to try for the prize. He was now on his way to the council to lay his plans before the chief men of the city.

Henry Hudson before the Dutch Council

This captain was of middle age and stern-looking. Already he had sailed far to the northeast, and the council asked him to tell what he had found there.

On his first voyage he had started toward Greenland and had then turned east. Once his ship had been almost wrecked by a large whale; again it had passed between two mountains of ice floating on the sea, which nearly broke it in pieces. He had been driven back by the ice and had found no passage.

Again he had set out, but had seen nothing more exciting than a great number of whales. By that time the Englishmen who were paying the cost of his voyages became discouraged. They believed that no passage to the Indies would ever be found through the north. For that reason Henry Hudson had come to Holland when the council invited him, and he was prepared to lay his plan before them.

Holland sends Hudson

The Dutch were very slow in deciding. It seemed as if Hudson would have to go back to England. While he was waiting he saw some of his countrymen come to Holland to live. They were the Pilgrims, about whom we shall read later. About that time France heard of the great captain and sent a man to hear his plans. Upon that the Dutch decided in his favor, for they did not want the French to have him. They gave Hudson a ship called the *Half-Moon*, named after a famous fort. At the bow of the vessel was the figure of a red lion with golden mane, and high overhead floated the orange, white, and blue flag of the Dutch. The ship was beautiful with its rich colors, its fine carving, and its silk flags.

When Hudson talked to the men of Holland he had to have an interpreter, for he did not understand the Dutch language. He carried with him a letter and a map from his friend, Captain John Smith.

The Northeast Passage

The orders were for the ship to find a route to the Indies by sailing around the northern part of Europe. Hudson obeyed, pushing on as far as possible, but he was soon stopped by the ice. His crew, not used to the cold of the north, refused to go any farther.

Their leader would not go home and report failure. He told the crew that they might choose whether to go northwest or south, but that they could not go back to Holland. They chose to go northwest. So although Hudson had not been ordered to explore in the New World, nevertheless he set out for America. He hoped that he might find a northwest passage through America to the Spice Islands.

The Bay at the Mouth of the River

Touching North America first in New France, the *Half-Moon* sailed southward along the coast until Hudson knew they must be near the English settlements. Then turning north again, they came to the region now known as New York. Before they could see land, they had seen dancing fires at night.

Then a great bay surrounded by a beautiful country lay before them. Hudson said, "It is a very good land to fall in with, and a pleasant land to see." The shores were covered with great oaks. The Indians were much surprised to see the white men. They thought the ship was a house of many colors floating on the waters. They came out in their canoes and seemed very glad to see the Dutchmen.

Some of the crew went fishing and caught a fish so large that it took four of them to lift it into the ship.

The Indians traded tobacco and furs for knives, beads, and axes, but most of all they wanted clothes. Their own clothing was made of the skins of deer or other furs. Their pipes were of copper. Their chief food was Indian corn, which the Dutchmen thought was very good.

Hudson had studied the bay carefully and had decided that a great stream of water must empty into it. He sent a boat full of men to explore farther. They went only a little way, and came back saying that "the land was pleasant with grass and flowers and goodly trees" and that "very sweet smells came from it." As they were returning the Indians attacked their small boat, killing one man and wounding two. From that time the white men had to be very careful.

Up the Hudson River

When Hudson had found out what he needed to know about the bay, he decided to sail up the stream that emptied into it from the north. Was it the passage to the Pacific which the world had so long been seeking? He hoped so.

On the way the ship came to a wooded island which today is the heart of New York City and is crowded with tall buildings that stretch far up toward the sky. Many canoes loaded with Indians came out to meet the ship, but, remembering what had happened, Hudson did not allow them to come on board. He bought beans and oysters from them.

Henry Hudson on the *Half-Moon*

What do the Indians want? (From a painting by Stanley M. Arthurs)

The farther up he went, the more beautiful the country seemed. He said, "The land is the finest for farming that I ever in my life set foot upon." At one place the stream was "a mile broad with very high land on both sides." The natives stood wondering on the bank and then hurried out to trade grapes and furs.

Still farther sailed the *Half-Moon*, until it was a hundred and fifty miles from the sea. There the men landed. The Indians of this region, who belonged to the Iroquois tribe, were friendly and gave a feast for them. Besides deer and birds, Hudson said that they "killed a fat dog and skinned it with great haste with shells which they got out of the water."

The stream which Hudson had hoped would lead to the Pacific had become narrower and more shallow. The ship's boat, which was sent forward to explore, came back with the sad news that the passage was only a river and that the ship could go no farther. Greatly disappointed, Hudson turned again toward the sea. At the same time Champlain was at Lake Champlain, only a few hundred miles to the north.

On the way down the river Indians came out to the ship, and since the Iroquois had been so friendly he allowed these to come on board and wander about the ship. One of them stole a pillow, two shirts, and two guns. The sailor to whom they belonged saw the Indian running away with his things and shot him. This made trouble. Canoes full of warriors attacked the ship with arrows, and many Indians were killed before they were driven off. (On the map on page 179 find Hudson's route.)

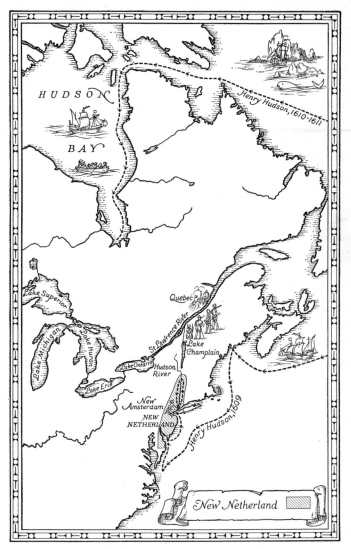

The Dutch in the New World

The Return Home

Without stopping at the West Indies, Hudson set sail straight across the ocean so that the way home might be shorter. He had spent four weeks in the new land.

The *Half-Moon* touched England first. England by this time was jealous, and since Henry Hudson was one of her citizens she did not let him return to Holland. He sent the ship forward with all his reports, but he had to remain in England in the service of his own country.

Results of the Voyage

Hudson had not found a short route to the Indies; he had shown that there was no passage through the central part of North America; but he had explored a beautiful river and had taken possession of the land around it for the Dutch. So the Dutch were now interested in the New World, in company with Spain, England, France, and Portugal.

The account of the great number of furs to be secured along the Hudson River was of special interest to the Dutch. It was not long before they set out to build up a great fur trade.

A Grave in the Ice

England was greatly excited over this voyage of Hudson's. The very next year she sent him again with orders to sail far to the north, around the continent of America. He set out in a little ship called the *Discovery*.

From the first he had trouble with his crew, many of whom were rough and lawless.

After struggling through the ice, the ship entered a great bay. Hudson felt very hopeful, even though he had been disappointed so many times. This huge body of water, he thought, must surely be a part of the Pacific. For a long time he sailed south, finding many birds and animals for food and feeling sure that this time he was going in the right direction.

But at last the end of the bay was reached! Another mistake had been made, and he would have to go back! The crew were angry. He removed some of his officers to make way for others whom he could trust. At this the crew grew angrier than ever.

Seven weeks longer Hudson sailed around the bay, searching constantly for a way through to the west. He found none. Then winter came on, the ship was frozen in, and for months the crew had to live on fish and ducks. Spring came; in June the ice broke up, and the ship started for home. Then it froze again. Their food was almost gone.

The crew had endured more than they could bear. They made Hudson a prisoner and put him, his son, and seven "poor, sick, and lame men" into an open boat with a gun, powder and bullets, an iron pot, and some meal. The small boat was set adrift, and the ship sailed home to England as fast as it could go.

Those who were left in the little boat were never seen again. No one knows what happened to them. But Hudson has left his name written large on the map of North America in Hudson Bay and the Hudson River.

Getting Ready

Answering these questions will help you to get ready for the "reminder" exercise below.

1. Why did the Dutch want to find a northeast passage?

2. Why did Hudson not go northeast as he was ordered?

3. What river did Hudson discover? What did he think it was?

4. Why did he turn back after sailing up the river one hundred and fifty miles?

5. What business did the Dutch carry on in the New World?

6. What bay did Hudson find later?

Reminders

The five groups of words given below should remind you of facts you learned in the story. Tell one fact about each. Prove your "fact" by showing the class the part of the story in which you found it.

Names of Persons	*Names of Places*
1. Henry Hudson	3. Holland
2. Dutch	4. Hudson River

Words

5. Northwest Passage

Henry Hudson discovered the Hudson River for the Dutch.

The English claimed the same land because of John Cabot's discovery years before.

Unit Three

Why English People came to live in the New World

||||||||||||||||||||||||||||||||||||||||||||||||||||||||||||||||||||||||||||||||||||||||||||||||||||||||||||||||||||||||||||||||||

TITLES OF STORIES

Unit Three

Why English People came to live in the New World

Had England once tried to found colonies in the New World? Why did it cost so much money to found a colony? This story will tell you how England tried again.

ENGLAND TRIES AGAIN

England had failed in her first attempts to plant colonies in the New World. Sir Walter Raleigh had spent a fortune and had died poor. He had worked for the glory of England, rather than to make money. But men were no longer willing to spend their fortunes with so little chance of return; they carefully counted the cost of adventures. No one would pay for a voyage which did not promise gain. For some time it seemed that England would not be able to do much in the New World.

How Settlers were Secured

Then some of England's merchants said to one another: "None of us wants to risk all his wealth in trying to found colonies, because he might lose it, as Raleigh did, but surely each one ought to be willing to risk a small amount. With a little money from each of us we would have enough to buy a ship, pay a captain, and get enough people to make several colonies. We could sell our cloth to the people who would go there to live, and perhaps the savages also could be taught to wear clothes. In return the people of the colony could sell us masts and tar for our ships, and copper, and probably silks and spices; for that western country must be very near the Indies. We could build up a great trade."

Many agreed that this was a good idea. They joined together and formed a *company*. Then other merchants in other cities did the same. Two of the companies about which we shall read were the London Company for settlement in the southern part of England's claims and another company for settlement in the northern part. Their lands lay between the lands of the Spaniards and those of the French.

Where could the members of the company find people to travel to the New World and found a colony for them? For you must not think that the merchants themselves intended to go. They called for settlers; and the call was answered by many men out of work, by some soldiers returned from the wars, and by farmers whose land in England had been taken away from them by the great nobles. A number of gentlemen of good family, too, wanted to go for the sake of adventure.

The colonists became servants of the company. Their passage was paid on the ships, they were to be clothed and given food until the first harvest, houses were to be built for them in the New World, and they were to be given farming tools, cattle, sheep, and horses. All these expenses would be paid by the company, but in return the colonists would work for the company. Whatever was raised or found in the new country belonged not to the colonists but to their masters, the English merchants. The king of England kept for himself most of the power of governing the colony.

The Voyage

By Christmas time a hundred and twenty colonists had been gathered — all men. Women and children did not seem to be wanted ; for no one at this time knew much about planting a colony, and they were afraid women and children might be in the way. Only twelve of this first group had always worked for a living ; most were gentlemen who had led an easy life, but who soon learned in the New World what hard work meant. They had heard such tales of the new lands as this : "All their pans are of pure gold, and the chains with which they chain up their streets are gold ; all the prisoners they take wear golden chains ; and for rubies and diamonds they go forth on holidays and gather them by the seashore to hang on their children's coats." Why did they believe such wild tales? Partly because the Spaniards had really found countries where there were great quantities of gold and precious stones.

One of the members of the London Company drew up for the settlers a paper with many wise rules: they should find a safe port at the mouth of some river, they should make friends with the Indians, they should build their town in a dry place, and they should be careful to eat only pure food. They were also ordered to explore the land. No man would be allowed to return to England except with the company's permission, and no man should write home any discouraging letter.

In the New World six of the colonists were to form a *council* which would decide upon laws and rules for them, but no one knew who the six would be. Their names had been put into a wooden box, which was not to be opened until they had been a day in Virginia.

The company had provided three small ships, one of the captains of which had served under Raleigh and one under Drake. The three set out on the long journey, going to the West Indies first and then sailing northward. The voyage took four months. As time went slowly by they told stories, spent hours watching the sea, and, for want of anything else to do, fell to quarreling among themselves as to who had been chosen members of the council. John Smith quarreled with many of the others and was put in irons. We shall hear more about him soon.

The ships stopped in the West Indies, and the colonists saw trees, fish, and animals that were very strange to them. Everywhere the heat was so great that they were glad to go on.

The Landing in Virginia

In the spring of the year 1607 the ships reached Virginia. The colonists found the land beautiful, and all were in high spirits.

The first night, on opening the box which contained the names of the council members, they found that John Smith was among those chosen. But the others did not allow him to take office at first.

The next day they began to explore the country, naming the great river the *James*, in honor of the king (find the James River on the map on page 190). Sailing up the river, they came to a point of land which ran far out into the water; there a large ship could come close enough to shore to be tied to the trees. They chose this place to build their town. That very night the Indians attacked them, but did little harm.

They found the Indians' ways of living very interesting. For clothing they wore the skins of wild beasts; in winter the hair was left on the skins, but in summer it was scraped off. Their bodies were painted red, so as to make them look as terrible as possible. In each ear were three great holes from which hung chains of copper. On one side of the head the hair was shaved, but on the other side it was allowed to grow long.

Their houses were built near rivers or springs. The houses were made of small trees covered with bark, and were quite warm in winter. They had fires in the houses, and there was a hole at the top for the smoke to go out. All the family slept around the fire, many of them on

English colonies in the South

the ground. In the morning all but the smallest children washed themselves in the cold water of the river.

Their food was corn, the flesh of wild animals, fish, roots, and "fine and beautiful strawberries four times bigger and better than those of England."

Boats were made of a log with the inside burned out and scraped with shells.

Their only wealth was their food supplies; there was no gold.

The Great Labor of starting a Colony

The colonists had plenty of hard work before them. If they had known how hard it would be to found a colony in a new country, they probably would not have come. They had first to unload the ship, to cut down the large trees for logs, and from these logs to build a fort, a church, a storehouse, houses for themselves, and a high fence to protect them from the Indians. Then they had to clear the fields for planting, pull out the stumps and take away the stones, protect the crops from the wild animals, pull weeds, make roads, and watch day and night for the Indians. No wonder they grew discouraged!

It was now midsummer and very hot. At first the men would not build houses; they lived in holes in the ground, in tents, and in shelters made of the branches of trees thrown together. They slept on the ground, which was so wet that many grew sick. They drank river water, which was not clean; many more grew sick and died. Almost all their food supplies had been used up on the long voyage, and whatever they bought from the Indians had to be paid for with bells, pins, needles, and pieces of glass. Soon there were no more such goods left. Then their only food was fish and oysters, with no bread.

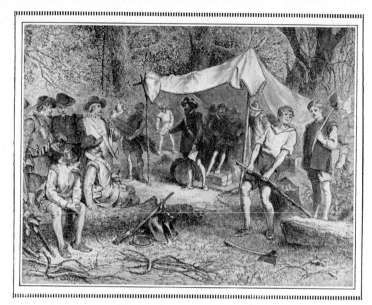

The settlers at Jamestown

Does the picture show you why little work was done? (From an old engraving)

Because of the constant danger from the Indians they had to build a fort. It was a three-cornered fort with guns at each corner. For a church they nailed a board between two trees for the Bible and prayer book, and above it placed a piece of sail for a roof. They laid out a street and places for a drill ground and a market place. The boats and houses that were built belonged to the colony as a whole, not to the men who made them.

All the supplies were placed in the storehouse; one of the colonists, the "cape merchant," had charge of them and gave each man his share of food every day.

Each man was told every morning just what to do. Sometimes he was to plow; at other times to fish, to hunt, to build, or to guard against the Indians. No man was allowed to plant his own garden; he had to spend all his time on the colony's farm. And whether or not a man did his best, he could always draw his share of the food in the storehouse. What do you suppose came of such a plan? When the men learned that they could get their share of food every day, they grew lazy. No one would work very hard, because no matter how hard he worked he got no more than those who did nothing at all. Many of the colonists became so discouraged that they would rather starve than do anything to help themselves.

The ships in which they had come were ready to return to England, but the captains dared not take them back empty for fear of the anger of the company. No gold had been found; so the settlers had to stop farming for a while and, instead, cut down trees to make boards for the ships' loads.

The First Year

During the heat and storms of that first summer the colonists had a hard time. Food supplies ran so low that each man had only one cup of wheat a day. There was much sickness; often three or four men would die in a single night. After five months only forty-six of the hundred and twenty were still alive.

Since the company had ordered the colonists to explore, John Smith and others sailed up the James River as far as the present capital of Virginia, still looking for a passage to the South Sea and the Spice Islands. They found the Indians friendly; but they did not reach the South Sea, which they thought must be about five or six days' journey to the west.

In the fall things seemed better. Many wild fowl flew by, and it was easier to get food. John Smith as cape merchant was put in charge of the food supplies and had to get corn for the colony. Only a few acres had been planted; so it was necessary to buy from the Indians.

Smith set out on a trading voyage up the James River. After getting thirty bushels of corn he left the boat and went inland with two of his men and their Indian guides. They had hardly started when they were attacked and the two men killed. Smith kept the Indians off for a long time, but while fighting he fell into the mud and was taken prisoner. He was carried before the chief. In order to gain time he showed him a compass which he had in his pocket. The whole tribe was much interested in the needle, which they could see through the glass cover, but could not touch because the glass stopped their fingers. They had never seen a piece of glass. The chief sent Smith from one village to another so that all might have a chance to look at him. In one place he found a bag of gunpowder which the Indians had stolen. They were keeping it till spring to plant it. They thought it would grow and give them more gunpowder.

At last Smith was brought to the great chief of all the tribes in that part of the country. This chief was called the Powhatan. The Powhatan and his council,

John Smith trading with the Indians

How do you think the Englishmen are able to make the Indians understand them?

"fifty armed savages of the tallest in his kingdom," decided that John Smith should die because he had killed several Indians in the fight.

Later the Powhatan decided to let Smith go, and made him a member of the tribe; then he sent him back to Jamestown to get the tribe some cannon and other gifts (find Jamestown on the map on page 190). Smith brought the other gifts, but said that the cannon were too heavy.

After this the Indians were friendly for a time, and once or twice a week carried food to the settlement — corn, deer, and wild turkeys.

Soon one of the ships from England came again with supplies and almost a hundred new settlers. Before it returned a great fire broke out and burned half of Jamestown, but instead of building their houses again the settlers had to get a load of lumber ready to send back. John Smith sent a letter to the company asking them not to send any more "gentlemen," but to send carpenters, farmers, gardeners, fishermen, and "diggers up of trees' roots." He also sent maps of the explorations he had made along the coast and up the rivers.

The Second Year

The colony was now a year old. John Smith had become president of the council; all the other members had died, or had gone back to England, or had become so discouraged that they would not even try to help themselves.

The colonists had seen some shining yellow sand along the banks of the river, and for a time took no interest in anything but digging this up with shells and loading it on the ship to send to England. They thought it was gold. They wasted much precious time; for when the ship arrived in England the sand was found to have no gold in it and to be worth nothing.

Spring and summer went by. Only four acres of corn had been planted, for the colonists had been busy digging sand and attending to other less important matters. Smith decided that if the colony was to live he would have to take things into his own hands. He called the men together and told them that no success could be expected except by hard work. Then he made some strict laws. This was one of them: "Every man that gathers not every day as much as I do, the next day shall be set beyond the river and forever be kept away from the fort, and live there or starve." Smith said further, "He that will not work shall not eat."

At first those who had not been used to hard work found that cutting down trees made them tired, and often they would swear. Smith ordered that every time a man was heard to swear, a can of cold water should be poured down his sleeve. The swearing soon stopped.

But in spite of all Smith's efforts the colony would have died out if it had not been for the food brought by the friendly Indians.

The months dragged on, and the second supply ships came from England. This time they brought workmen and some women who would help to make homes. But they also brought orders to find a gold mine, to discover the South Sea, to crown the Powhatan with a gold crown, and to find Raleigh's lost colony or not to come back. Smith must have been discouraged to find that the company did not understand even yet what was necessary to found a colony. He could crown the Powhatan, but it was impossible to carry out the other orders. Wishing to please the company, he did what he could; he and the captain of the vessel crowned the Indian chief and gave him a coat of many colors. In return the Powhatan gave them the old fur cape that he had been wearing, which may even yet be seen in England. But better than his crown he liked the blue-glass beads which Smith used in trading.

When the ship went back to England it took a load of pitch, tar, and iron, and a sharp letter from John Smith to the company.   He told them that he needed supplies for another year and more "honest workmen, such as carpenters, smiths, fishermen, brickmen, and such like."   He showed them that this new struggling colony needed to spend its time in raising food, and that if they wanted lumber they should buy it in Europe. He also told them that for many years they need not look for any profit from the money they had spent on the colony.   The first thing for the colony to do would be to learn to support itself.

The newcomers in the supply ships knew nothing about the hard life in the wilderness; they were only so many more mouths to feed. The workmen did not prove any better workers than the gentlemen. To make matters worse, rats got into the colony's corn and ate it all.

But Smith kept the colonists at work.   He made them dig a well so that they should not have to drink river water.   Under his direction they built twenty log houses and planted forty acres of corn.

The Indians were angry when they saw so many white people coming, and they refused to sell any more food. They even attacked Jamestown, but Pocahontas, daughter of the Powhatan, gave the colonists warning, and the attack failed.

The end of the second year came.   Although there was still suffering and although everyone had to work very hard, the colony seemed at last to be growing.

Then a terrible thing happened.   One day John Smith was returning from an attempt to find a better place for settlement. As he lay asleep in his boat his gunpowder in some way caught fire and exploded. He was burned so badly that he had to go home to be treated by the doctors in England. He was never in Virginia again, though later he came back to the northern coast and made a map of New England.

The "Starving Time"

While Virginia was having all this trouble the London Company had decided to stop the constant quarrels in the colony by sending over a governor. This governor set out with nine ships and five hundred colonists. But the ill fortune of the colony seemed to follow him; some of his ships were wrecked, and for months his men had to keep themselves alive on a lonely island.

When at last they built new ships and reached Virginia they found the colony in a terrible condition. After Smith had left, everything had gone to pieces. The fields were not plowed, the cattle were killed for food, all the corn in the storehouse was used up, and the colonists had eaten the dogs and horses and finally the roots of plants. The Indians would no longer sell them corn. The empty houses were broken up and burned to keep the starving people warm; then fences and gates followed. There had been more than four hundred colonists in the fall, but by spring only sixty were living.

What should the governor do? He had food enough to last the people only a few weeks. They would all be dead before any harvest could be hoped for. It was at last decided to leave Jamestown and go back to

England. The colony had managed to keep itself alive for three years, but it seemed as if the end had been reached. Was England to fail again? Sadly the men stripped the houses of everything which could be moved, went on board ship, and rowed down the river, leaving Jamestown behind. The next day they were surprised to see boats coming toward them. Who could the strangers be? With great joy they learned that a new governor and more settlers were coming, with plenty of supplies. The colony was saved. The new governor fell on his knees and thanked God that he had come in time.

Never again did the colony think of giving up. Jamestown was the first *permanent English colony* in the New World. One of the settlers had written three years earlier

> We hope to plant a nation
> Where none before has stood.

That nation had at last been planted.

Getting Ready

A good way to get ready for the matching game below is to ask yourself these questions:

1. Why were companies formed to carry on trade?

2. What four kinds of people agreed to go to America?

3. What did the London Company do for the colonists?

4. What did the men have to do to get their food? Was this a good plan?

5. What happened after John Smith left Virginia?

6. What saved the colony?

Saving the Jamestown Colony

From a painting by Fred C. Yohn

A Matching Game

In the column at the right you will find words which describe the words in the column at the left. Copy the words in the *right-hand column* and put the figure 1 before those which describe John Smith (No. 1 in the left-hand column); put the figure 2 before those which describe Pocahontas; and so on.

1. John Smith	the first English settlement which lasted
2. Pocahontas	the Indian girl who helped the settlers
3. Powhatan	making settlements in a new country
4. James River	the year in which Jamestown was settled
5. Jamestown	the leader of the settlers in Jamestown
6. 1607	any settlement which lasts
7. permanent colony	the water near which Jamestown was built
8. colonization	the chief of the Virginia Indians

Virginia was the first permanent English colony in the New World.

At first the colony had a very hard time.

What nation succeeded at last? In what task was it successful? Do you think a plant could help a colony to succeed? Let us read and find out.

SUCCESS AT LAST

The new governor at once set to work. He had brought with him a hundred and fifty settlers, chiefly soldiers and laborers; also supplies enough for a year. Every man was given something to do. Some cleaned the streets and the well, some planted vines, some repaired the houses, and some put a new roof on the church. The church bell gave the signals every day for beginning and ending work. Two forts were built. In these all the people who had just come from England stayed until their work was laid out for them.

But sickness could not be prevented. It broke out again, and the governor became so ill that he had to go home to England.

Free Land

The new ruler who was sent out was an old soldier. He had a strong will, and he decided to bring order to the colony by making the settlers work harder. His three ships had brought over three hundred people, twelve cows, twenty goats, and other things that were necessary for the colony. He sent out stern orders. Everyone had to go to church twice on Sunday. No cattle could be killed without his permission. If men tried to run away from their work he had the Indians catch them and bring them back. The laws were written down, so that there might be no mistake.

Though the colonists hated their ruler they had to obey him. The rest of the ruined houses were repaired; a barn, a powder house, a new well, a salt factory, and a bridge were built. Farther north another fort was set up to keep the Indians from killing the cattle. Hay was cut, gardens were laid out, and barrels were made to hold the salted fish.

When the Indians saw how strong the colony was growing they no longer wanted war. In order to make peace between the two nations, Pocahontas married an Englishman, and as long as she lived peace lasted.

There were still too many lazy men in the colony. The old soldier's plan was to make men want to work rather than to punish them for not working, so he did away with the common storehouse. Each man then had to work for himself. Each was given three acres of land, two acres of which had to be put into corn. Later each received fifty acres. All the colonists still had to give one month of every year to the London Company, but the rest of the time they could work for themselves. This plan succeeded well, and much more work was done.

Yet the colonists were glad at last to get rid of their stern old soldier-ruler. When he went back to England he told the company that he believed strongly in Virginia, and warned them not to give it up. Pocahontas and her husband went to England with him. The king and the queen received the "Indian princess" with great honor, and everyone was eager to see her.

What made the Success of the Colony Certain

The real success of the colony came from raising "the weed," as the king called it. He meant tobacco. Some of the countries of Europe had used tobacco for years, but it had not been used much in England. The king hated it.

The husband of Pocahontas had been the first to plant tobacco in his Virginia garden, and he had found a new way of drying it. Soon all the colonists wanted to raise it, for the leaves sometimes sold for what would amount to twelve dollars a pound in our money today. As long as the stern old soldier ruled the colony he would let no man grow tobacco until two of his three acres had been planted to corn.

But when he went back to England all the colonists began to raise tobacco. They raised nothing else. Soon tobacco was growing in all the fields, along the sides of the roads, in the market place, and wherever there was any vacant ground. The colonists no longer sent corn to England; they did not raise enough even for themselves. They traded their guns to the Indians for corn, so that they might go on raising tobacco. Tobacco was used for money; if one man worked for another he was paid in it. By the time Jamestown was fifteen years old it was sending out sixty thousand pounds of tobacco a year to England.

The people in England were interested when they saw how much money the planters in America were making. Hundreds of new settlers began to arrive; they were good, hard-working men of a better sort than the first colonists. The company no longer found it

Raising tobacco

For what are the barrels to be used?

hard to get men to go to Virginia, but it was of no use to tell them to plant cotton and grapes when they reached the New World. They could earn more in tobacco. So they planted it.

But tobacco wears out the soil very quickly, and the colonists did not know how to use fertilizers on it. After a field had been planted with tobacco three years it would not raise any more that was good enough to sell, and new land had to be found. So the planters had always to get more and more land. One man might own perhaps five thousand acres. The plantations had to be very large and the houses far apart.

How the Planters handled Problems Common to All of Them

By the year 1619 there were more than a thousand people in Virginia. Some lived in villages and some on plantations along the river banks. Most of the houses were scattered through the country, but here and there a few were built together in a village of one street. Nearly all the men were planters of tobacco.

Soon many questions began to trouble them. How could they protect themselves against the Indians? How could they be sure that every planter would hold his tobacco until the price was high enough to make a good profit? Who would pay for making roads from one plantation to another?

It soon became clear that they needed to come together in one place to talk over such matters and to make laws about them. But what house would hold a thousand people? And if everyone went to make laws, who would take care of the cattle and who would guard the houses against the Indians? Many of the settlers lived a long way off and could not come so far.

So it was agreed that all the people living near one another should come together and choose two of their number to go to Jamestown and vote for what their people wanted. These two were called *representatives*.

These representatives first met in Jamestown in 1619, and almost every year after that. Some came in boats on the river and some came on foot. They met in the old wooden church an hour after sunrise. The governor and his council, all in velvet and gold lace, sat together on the platform; the representatives sat in the lower part of the church. After prayer they began to consider what laws they should make. They met every day for six days. Some of their laws seem strange to us. If a man was drunk the minister was to tell about it in church. No man or woman should dress too finely. No one could go on a voyage on Sunday unless it was very necessary. Every family must always have a spare barrel of corn in the house for use in case of trouble. The price at which tobacco was to be sold was fixed. No one was allowed to sell guns to the Indians; all were to try to make them Christians. No man should be idle, and no man should swear. The king was asked to found a college in Virginia as soon as possible.

After the colonists had the right to vote and to choose representatives they were better satisfied.

New Kinds of Settlers

All this time there had been very few women in the colony. But the London Company soon learned that if the colony was to be a success the settlers must feel *at home* in the New World. So the company sent out a ship with ninety young women to be wives for the men in Virginia. When the ship arrived the men came down and chose their wives, but before they could be married each man had to pay the cost of the passage of the one whom he wished to marry. This would amount to about five hundred dollars in our money.

After a while more ships came with the same kind of load. Then homes were set up in the colony.

There was another kind of settler in Virginia. In 1619 a Dutch ship came from the West Indies with negro slaves and sold twenty of them to the planters. The planters were glad to get help, for the tobacco crops needed much labor. So in the same year that the colonists began to send representatives to make laws, they also began to use slaves.

For a long time the number of negroes was small. Most of the planters' work was done by white servants. Few servants could be secured from the New World, for every settler had land of his own to work. But in England there were many poor people who had not money enough to pay for their passage to America, many boys and girls without homes, and many prisoners who if they were let out of prison would be glad to come to the New World. Ships would bring such people over and have them work for the colonists for two or three years or for six or seven years. During that time they had to work just as if they were slaves, but at the end of it they were made free and were given land for themselves. In a few years they might have small plantations of their own and might get other white servants to work for them, or they might stay with their former masters and work for wages.

The Indians were not made slaves. They would not work for the white men.

Thinking about the Story

How much of the story do you remember? Can you answer the following questions? If not, turn back in the story and find the answers.

1. Why was land given to each settler?

2. In what way did tobacco help the growth of the colony?

3. What were some of the planters' problems?

4. Why did they choose representatives instead of all going to the meeting?

5. In what way were the white servants different from slaves?

Filling in Blanks

I. Tell the right words for the following blanks:

1. The oldest of the English colonies in America was named _ _ _ _ _ _ _.

2. Slaves were brought into Virginia in the year _ _ _ _ _ _ _.

3. The representatives of the Virginians met first in the year _ _ _ _ _ _ _.

II. Which of these words belong in each blank below?

representatives   voted   plantations   making laws   colonists

1. People who live in new settlements are _ _ _ _ _ _ _.

2. The Virginians liked to live on large _ _ _ _ _ _ _.

3. They had _ _ _ _ _ _ _ to make their laws for them.

4. They wanted the right of _ _ _ _ _ _ _ _ _ _ _ _ _.

5. The representatives _ _ _ _ _ _ _ for the laws the colonists wanted.

When each man was given a farm of his own the colony grew.

In 1619 slaves were brought into Virginia.

In 1619 the colonists had the first representatives in America.

Should you like to have been a child living in Jamestown?
Make a list of the things you would have liked. Make
another list of things you would not have liked. After
you have read the story, correct your list or add to it.

LIFE IN EARLY VIRGINIA

Plantation Homes

The settlers coming from England to Virginia found
many interesting sights.

The first thing they noticed was that the new country
had few towns. The largest town had only about two
hundred houses, and its streets were thick with mud
or dust.

The planters lived on their great farms, or plantations,
on the banks of the rivers. New settlers who came in
moved farther up the rivers and took wild land instead
of staying near the others. Because the farms were
very large the houses were generally two or three miles
from the nearest neighbor and sometimes even farther.

Newcomers sailing up the rivers had a good chance
to see the plantations. They found that the greater
part of the land was not yet cleared; it was used only
as a feeding ground for the half-wild cattle. Some of it,
however, was planted with tobacco and surrounded by
wooden fences.

At the top of a little hill could be seen the "great
house" of the plantation, with a smooth yard in front
reaching down to the river. Roses were growing in the

An early view of Mount Vernon

Can you tell the uses of the small buildings? (From an old engraving)

yard. The plantation looked like a little village in itself. Back of the great house and at either side were many smaller buildings: kitchens, carriage houses, barns, washhouses, chicken houses, smokehouses, spinning-rooms, and sometimes separate rooms for guests. The *slave quarters* were rows of little log houses behind the great house. These contained only a rude bed, a few chairs, and some pots and pans. The fruit trees and the garden were near and were surrounded by a wooden fence to keep out the cattle.

The master's house was a story and a half or two stories high. In the earliest times it was built of logs, but later it was built of boards and still later of brick. At each end rose great brick chimneys. A broad road ran up to the front door, which opened on a large porch.

The windows were protected by heavy shutters. Washington's home, Mount Vernon, was built in this way.

Inside, in the middle of the house, was a great hall with smaller rooms on each side, and many bedrooms upstairs. The rooms were large but low. All were finished in beautiful woods, and in each was a fireplace. One such house had twenty-eight fireplaces, which required four loads of wood a day.

At the river side, in front of the house, was the "landing," or *wharf*, with its storehouse for tobacco. Since the ships came direct from England to each man's private wharf, shops and merchants were not needed, and towns did not grow.

Some of the richer colonists owned brick town houses besides their plantation homes, and once a year, when the House of Representatives met, they went in to town for a few weeks. But they did not care to stay long. City life did not please the people of Virginia.

Household Furnishings

At one end of the great hall in some of the finest plantation houses was a fireplace big enough to burn many whole logs at once. In the center of the room was a long table, large enough to seat twenty persons at a time, with benches to sit on or (if the family were rich) with chairs. All the silver and china could be seen in cupboards along the wall. The walls were covered with paper and hung with paintings from England or with family pictures. The fine carpets came from Europe; the beautiful "grandfather's clock," from

The kitchen at Mount Vernon

How many of the articles in the picture can you name?

England. For lighting, the colonists used candles or pieces of pine wood. Each family made its own candles for winter; a good worker could make two hundred in a day.

In the bedrooms stood the huge beds, high up from the floor, so that the servants might sweep under them easily. Over each was a mosquito net, for the new country was full of mosquitoes. In some rooms there was a chest of drawers, but most of the clothes not in use were kept in great boxes or chests. On a stand in one corner of each bedroom was a washbowl. The water must have been cold on winter mornings, even in a land as far south as Virginia. There were no bathrooms.

After the great hall, the kitchen was the most interesting room in the house. Its huge fireplace took up almost an entire wall. At the back of it was a rod from which hung the pots and the long-handled pans. Brass kettles were much used; there was very little tin. At one side of the fireplace stood the great brick oven, which was used only once a week. If the fire went out at night, coals had to be brought from the neighbors, or a light had to be struck from a flint and steel. The mistress of the house spent much of her time in the kitchen, directing the work of the slaves.

Food

The boys and girls of Virginia had plenty of good things to eat. Their chief food was corn, which was planted among the dead forest trees without plowing the soil. It was called "turkey wheat." Many times it saved the lives of the colonists. They ground it into meal between two stones and made "johnnycake" of it, and sometimes they boiled it. They learned to use pop corn too, and one of the colonists wrote that they liked to see the corn "turn inside out, all white and floury within."

Fish and game were the next important foods. The rivers of Virginia were full of all kinds of fish, and in the bay were huge oysters. Most of the fish were salted or smoked. Deer meat was sometimes cooked over the open fire, but it was usually cut in small pieces and boiled. The pigs which the colonists raised were very good, but their cattle were small and lean. The woods were full of wild turkeys, which were very large, weighing as much as thirty pounds. It was easy to get fresh meat, but because the colonists had no ice they could not keep meat long in summer. Often they had to eat smoked and salted meat.

Some wheat was grown in the hill country, but it was not very good. Peas, beans, and potatoes grew to a great size in the rich soil. There was much fruit of all kinds. Wild honey was used for sweetening, but spices had to be brought from the Far East.

For breakfast the planter might have tea, coffee, or chocolate, bread and butter, and cold meat. His dinner, which he had at noon, was of meat, vegetables, sweets, and wine. At night he had a very light supper or none at all.

His table linen for every day was plain, but for best he had fine linen and napkins. He needed the napkins, for he had no forks to eat with. The spoons were of silver or iron or, among the poorer planters, of wood or horn. The dishes were of china or wood; there was very little glass. All the family drank from one vessel, passing it round from mouth to mouth. The salt was always placed in the middle of the table; the planter and his wife and the honored guests sat at one end, "above the salt," and the children and the servants at the other end, "below the salt." Many of the chairs were only benches without backs, and sometimes the children had to stand while they ate.

Though so many people lived on each plantation, they did not raise much of their own food. They spent so much time raising tobacco that they had to buy flour, cheese, and other things from the colonies farther north.

Clothing

If we could have seen one of the splendid parties in the great house, we should have been surprised at the fine clothes. Men did not wear plain suits of dark colors as they do now. They wore blue-velvet coats lined with red satin, waistcoats, or vests, of embroidered white satin, breeches of blue velvet or black satin coming only to the knee, long silk stockings, shoes with huge silver buckles covering half the foot, lace around the neck and the wrists, and colored gloves. The large buttons on their coats were of brass or pearl. They surely made a fine show.

Men wore their hair long in the earliest times, but later they began to wear wigs of hair or silk, powdered white. These wigs must have been heavy and hot, but even little boys wore them. For riding, heavier and darker clothes were worn; for every day, suits of home-spun. When it was raining, heavy capes were put on.

The women's clothing was almost as grand. They had flowered silk dresses, with long full skirts and large sleeves. Like the men, they wore silk stockings, colored gloves, and silver lace. Even their little high-heeled shoes were of silk. Sometimes they wore fine straw hats, but oftener hoods of velvet. They had beautiful fans and buckles and bright-colored ribbons.

Neither men nor women had many precious stones, though they wore plain rings and chains. Few watches were to be found in all Virginia.

Little boys were dressed just like their fathers, and little girls were dressed like their mothers. One little girl about whom we read had twelve silk dresses. Perhaps you think that it would be nice to have lived at that time; but when you learn that the girls had to wear linen masks to keep the sun from their faces and long gloves to keep their arms white, and had to sit quietly in chairs instead of running about and playing, you will be glad that you live today instead.

All these fine clothes had to be ordered from England, and the ship's captain had to choose them. Should you like to have him choose your best dress or your best suit? The planters sent their measures to a London tailor, and, of course, could not try on their clothes while they were being made. Often they did not fit very well, but at least they were sewed by hand and lasted a long time. The planters had news of the styles from friends in the Old World and tried to follow the London fashions.

The slaves wore a single cotton dress of the cheapest kind of cloth, made in the workroom of the plantation.

It seems strange to us that the representatives should make laws about the kind of clothing people should wear, but they did. Only the most important men were allowed to wear gold lace. If a common man wore clothing too fine for him he had to pay a heavy tax.

The Work of the Planters

Tobacco, as we have seen, was the chief product of the colony. Every plantation raised this one crop. First the forests were cut down, the trees dragged away, and then the tobacco was planted. In the rich soil, which had never been farmed before, it grew to a great size. Slaves and white servants did all the labor.

When the leaves were gathered they were dried and put into great barrels, which were rolled down to the wharf and loaded on boats, to be sold in England. Every ten or twelve miles there was a storehouse where these barrels were stored until the ships came. Before the tobacco could be offered for sale an officer appointed by the representatives came and looked it over to see if it was good.

Usually the planter himself attended to the sale of his tobacco, but not to the work of raising it. This was done by *overseers*, poor white men who directed the slaves. The planter also had to see that his negroes learned all the trades necessary for the work on the plantation.

The planter's wife had heavier duties. She had charge of the great house and of the guests. She directed the spinning, weaving, and making of all the clothes for the slaves and the everyday clothes for the family. She taught the negroes how to spin, weave, sew, cook, and make soft soap. She was nurse when anyone on the plantation was ill. Once a month she directed the washing of clothes. Once a year she saw that the negroes picked geese for feathers for the warm beds. She always carried a great basket of keys — keys to all the storehouses and smokehouses.

Other kinds of work done on the plantation were cutting lumber in the winter, making barrels to hold the tobacco, and preparing hides for leather. Cattle and pigs were raised, but they were not fed nor kept in warm barns. They had to find their own food in the woods. For this reason the planters often had to buy meat from the Northern colonies.

In general, farming was poorly managed. Oxen were used to draw the plows. Sometimes there would be only one plow in a whole town. It was usually made all of wood and was so heavy that it took four oxen and three men to run it.

The king had been eager to have the colonists begin manufacturing, and had begged them "not to build the plantations wholly on smoke." (What did he mean?) Ironworks had just been started when the Indian trouble came; they were not built up again. John Smith had hoped to establish glass and soap works, but he had not succeeded. Silk-growing was tried and given up. Back in the hill country, however, men gathered a little pitch, tar, and salt.

Only the most common goods needed on the plantations were made there; even chairs, tables, bowls, boxes, and cart wheels had to be brought from other places. Saws, knives, and other tools were brought from England. The planters were proud and did not think much of tradesmen, so manufacturing and trade were of little importance.

Churches

Most of the colonists in the South belonged to the Church of England. Today we call it the Episcopal Church. England sent out ministers to the colony; and the people had to keep them, whether they liked

Going to church in Virginia
Courtesy of the Metropolitan Museum of Art

them or not, so we are not surprised to find that little interest was taken in the services in the South.

The first church buildings were of wood. Later many of them were of brick. The churchyard was surrounded by a brick wall, and in it the dead were buried. Inside of the church, at one end, was the high place where the minister stood. The seats looked much like great empty boxes; one could hardly see over the top into another seat. Each family owned its own box. The poorer people had to sit at the back. The children all sat together in one part of the church.

There were no lights nor fires, but the sermons were not long. Some churches had music and were gay with flowers. Some had brass plates on the walls in memory of members who were dead.

The people who lived far away came to town on Sundays to spend the day. They left their horses in sheds on the church grounds and visited with the other planters. Half an hour before church time the bell rang, and the captain of the watch sent men to search the houses round about to see that everybody came to the services. After church the crowds would again gather in small groups to talk and laugh and do business before returning home.

The ministers were not so learned as those of England; some of them were not very good men. Many were planters during week days and were more interested in tobacco-raising, fox-hunting, and card-playing than they were in their churches. So the people of Virginia did not think about religion as much as those in the Northern colonies did.

Schools

The schools of Virginia were very poor. It was hard to have good schools, because the houses were so far apart and most of the colonists did not care enough about education to send their children so far. They were more interested in cutting down trees and in planting tobacco than they were in books.

At first each family taught their own children. Then some of the planters asked to have teachers sent from

England, and these teachers taught the children of several families at once. Often the teachers were white servants who were sold to the planters for a certain number of years, and they were not greatly respected. The boys spent more time in hunting and fishing and playing with the negro children than they did in study. When the sons of the very richest men were old enough, they were sent to the great colleges in England. But not many were able to do this.

After some time a college was begun in Virginia, the second one in our country. It was named the College of William and Mary after the king and queen of England, who were much interested in it and gave it rich gifts. Only the sons of the rich could attend. The colonists had thought that Indians would come to some of the classes, but they did not. Three presidents of the United States were trained there.

Today we think that schools for children are even more necessary than colleges, but there were very few free schools in Virginia. One had been started, but Indian troubles had put an end to it. There were some private schools kept by ministers, but parents had to pay for their children to attend. For girls there were not even private schools. At one time the governor of Virginia said that he thanked God that there were no free schools, and hoped that there would be none for a hundred years to come. For a long time printing was not allowed. The colony was a hundred years old before it had a newspaper.

Many people had only one book in their houses. That was the Bible. Others had a church songbook and perhaps an almanac. A few of the planters had libraries, but most of the people learned only from talking with their neighbors or from hearing speeches.

Good Times

If the planters did not work hard, they played hard. They were very fond of horse-racing. The races were held at the fairs. The horses were fast and beautiful and well cared for. A traveler in Virginia wrote: "Almost every person keeps a horse. I have known one to spend the whole morning catching his horse, which was running free in the woods, in order to ride three miles to the courthouse or church."

Fishing and hunting were thought very good sport. The hunting dogs had fancy names and were much loved. Nothing would draw a larger crowd than a cock-fight. It was talked of long before, and when the time for it arrived all the men for miles around would come to see it.

At harvest time or whenever a new house or barn was to be put up, all the neighbors came and helped, and then they had a party. There were many outdoor picnics in the woods, at which whole oxen were roasted. Christmas lasted a whole week.

Most of the good times were among the families themselves. The people married early, and the families were large. There were often fourteen children or more in a family. They visited their friends frequently. Whole families with all their children and several servants might drop in for a visit at any time; they might stay a day, or perhaps a week, or a month. They were always welcome. If no guests came to a plantation for a long time the planters would send their slaves down to the nearest road to wait until a traveler came along, and they would invite him to come and stay as long as he wished. They liked to talk with strangers and to hear what was going on in the world.

Once a year, when the House of Representatives met, the whole family would come into town — to their town house if they had one. The women rode in their coaches and the men on horseback. Then what dances and dinners and balls there would be!

Punishment

In such a society we are not surprised to learn that many laws were broken — more than in the colonies farther north. Every courthouse was fitted out to punish men who did evil deeds. Some were put in prison, into little dark rooms without any sunshine and with little air. Others were punished in ways that we never see today. Some had to stand up on a high box with their heads and hands caught in a piece of wood. This was called the *pillory*. Everyone who passed would throw mud or stones at them. Others had to sit on a high box, with their hands and legs caught in a board, and passers-by would throw things at them also. This was called the *stocks*. Then there was the *whipping post*, to which a lawbreaker was tied. An officer gave him a certain number of blows on his bare back with a heavy whip.

How criminals were punished

Which are the stocks? Where is the pillory? What do you think the passers-by are saying?

One very strange way of punishing was by the *ducking stool*. This was a sort of wooden chair at the end of a long pole. The man or woman to be punished was tied into the chair and then ducked into the water a number of times. If the man who handled it was not careful the prisoner might be drowned. At any rate, he suffered a great deal of discomfort.

Other terrible punishments were burning the face, the hand, or the arm with a hot iron, cutting off an ear or part of an ear, or boring a hole through the ear or tongue. These were not so bad as cutting off a hand, for the man could still work.

Today we do not think such terrible punishments should be allowed, but in those days they thought it was the only way to make people obey the laws.

"*Prove It*"

Prove to yourself that you understand the story by answering these questions:

1. Why were the houses far apart?

2. Why were there few shops and few merchants?

3. Why did the planters have to buy some food from the other colonies?

4. Could a planter sell any quality of tobacco that he pleased?

5. What were five ways of educating children?

Something to Do

This time you may make sentences of your own, using these new words.   The class will decide whether or not your sentences are right.

Mount Vernon	Church of England
coach	wharf
slave quarters	

Each large plantation was a little world in itself.
The chief crop was tobacco.

The plantation owners owned much land.

What Spanish colony was nearest to the English colonies? Do you think that colonists of different nations liked to be neighbors?

ENGLAND REACHES AS FAR AS SPANISH AMERICA

We are now going to pass over a great many years, during which colonies were being made in the North. These were very different from Virginia; so we shall not try to learn about them at this time, but shall go on for half a century until we find other colonies more like Virginia being settled in the South. After we have read about those that are alike, we shall go back and read about those in the North.

The Beginnings of North Carolina

The region which Sir Walter Raleigh had tried to settle was south of Virginia. Since he had failed, no one had thought much about that land.

As Virginia became more settled some of her people grew tired of the quiet life of the plantations and moved on into the unknown South, looking for further adventures. Some left Virginia because they did not like the Church of England. They set out with their guns on their shoulders, for the country was very wild. At one place they found a paper nailed to a post. It had been left by some earlier settlers, and said that "all such as should hereafter come into these parts to settle" might as well go back, for the land was very poor.

Pioneers in North Carolina
Does the picture show how the white settlers earn their living?

But the men from Virginia found many animals for food; the weather was warm, and they liked it so well that they decided to stay. Their homes were far apart, and they had to work hard. They got lumber, pitch, tar, and other supplies from the forests and sold them to ships from the Northern colonies. In return they secured sugar, rum, and molasses that these ships had brought from the West Indies.

All the land south of Virginia soon came to be called Carolina from the name of the English king Charles, (in Latin "Carolus.") This part that we have been reading about was North Carolina. (Find North Carolina on the map on page 190.)

The Beginnings of South Carolina

During the time that the northern part of Carolina was being settled by people from Virginia, England was at war. When the war was over, the king wanted to do something for the people who had helped him. The best gift that he could think of was a gift of land, so he gave all Carolina to eight of his great lords. He probably did not know that some of the Virginia colonists were already living in the northern part of this region. But when he gave Carolina to his great lords he had three things in mind. He not only wanted to pay these lords for their services, but he wanted to get the country settled before France and Spain could start colonies there (for they both claimed the land), and he wanted to build up a good trade for England in Carolina.

The great lords were given as many rights as if they had been princes; they could make all the laws themselves. In return they were to raise silk and "raisins of the sun" in their land, which, the king said, stretched "from sea to sea." (From what sea to what sea?) Only one of these lords went to America to live, however, and he was governor of Virginia as well as lord of Carolina.

The settlements in the South, later known as South Carolina, grew rapidly. Many colonists came from the West Indies and many from Europe. They had a House of Representatives, or assembly, like that of Virginia. People of any religion except the Catholic were allowed to come to the colony. It grew steadily. (Find South Carolina on the map on page 190.)

Life in North Carolina

Since the northern part of Carolina was so near to Virginia, it offered a home for servants who wanted to run away and for others who did not like the Virginia laws. We are not surprised, then, to learn that the settlers were at first rather hard to manage.

They could not carry on much trade, for there were no good ports along the coast. So they turned to farming. Every man owned his little piece of land and did his own work. There were not many slaves. It was very different from Virginia.

Along the northern border some tobacco was raised and was sent to Virginia. In the hill country some wheat was grown. Many men owned great herds of cattle, sometimes as many as a thousand, which ranged the woods all day and came up at night at the sound of a horn. Meat was sent to the West Indies and hides to the New England colonies. The chief products, however, were those of the forest: pitch, lumber, and tar.

The settlers had no money, but traded pigs for corn, tar for salt, and hides for ammunition. All manufactured goods were bought from England or from the Northern colonies. The people lived back from the coast, and no towns grew up.

For almost a hundred years there was no printing press in the colony and very few schools and churches — fewer even than in the neighboring colonies.

The coast line of North Carolina was broken by many small islands, to which the pirates loved to come.

Blackbeard and other pirates had been coming here
for years, but at last Virginia and South Carolina sent
men to catch them.

Though there were more people in North Carolina
than in South Carolina, the governor usually lived in
the south and left the north to take care of itself. One
of the people in North Carolina wrote, "We still continue much behind the rest of the British settlements
in making a proper use of a good soil and an excellent
climate." It was true. This colony did not become
great until the time of the Revolution.

Life in South Carolina

South Carolina was different. Next to Virginia, it
was the most important of all the Southern colonies.

At first its people, like all settlers in the new lands,
had to spend their time in cutting down trees and fighting Indians. But soon they built up a good trade with
the West Indies.

They also traded with the pirates and let them hide
in the many small islands along the coast. The pirates'
pockets were full of good Spanish gold, and they were
willing to pay a high price for food. Indeed, South
Carolina became known as "the delight of pirates."
But at last, when the pirates began to seize the goods
of the Englishmen, South Carolina and Virginia united
against them, and put an end to their robbing.

Once a ship passing the harbor of Charleston, the
largest city of South Carolina, left a bag of rice from
Africa. The planters found that this rice grew very

well in their low lands, for rice, you know, grows in the water.   So it happened that before long the rice crop became as important to South Carolina as the tobacco crop was to Virginia.   Of all the products of this colony, one half was rice.

The plantations were much the same as in Virginia. Every planter was given a hundred acres of land for himself, a hundred for his wife and for each child, a hundred for each man servant, and fifty for each woman servant.   The plantations were not so large as some of those in Virginia (including perhaps two thousand acres instead of five thousand), but there were no small farms such as were to be found in parts of Virginia and in North Carolina.

Workers on rice plantations have to stand knee-deep in the mud, bending their backs hour after hour in the hot sun.   White men could not and would not do such work, so great numbers of slaves were brought from Africa and from the West Indies.   The worst punishment that could be given to a Virginia slave who would not obey his master was to sell him to the rice-planters of Carolina.   Even the negroes grew sick and died in the rice fields, and the planters had always to buy more. They bought slaves in the market place, like cattle. Soon there were three black men to every white man in the colony, and the whites were always afraid that the slaves would rebel.   Slaves were not allowed to hold meetings nor to learn to write; they could neither buy nor sell, and could not travel from place to place without permission from their masters.

Hoeing rice in South Carolina
How can water be let in upon the rice fields? Who is the man
on horseback?

A woman in South Carolina had tried many times to raise indigo plants, from which blue dye is obtained; up to that time they had been grown only in the Indies. At first she had no success. Either the plants died or the dye was not the right color, but at last she learned the secret. Then indigo became an important product of South Carolina, second only to rice.

Many of the planters when they became rich did not like to live out on their plantations, so far away from their friends. Then, too, there was much sickness because of the rice swamps. So they left their slaves in charge of overseers, who were far more cruel than the masters would have been. The masters themselves went to live during most of the year in Charleston, which was then the only large city in all the South. At the time of the Revolution it had fifteen thousand people. (Find Charleston on the map on page 190.)

There they lived in great ease and comfort. No family of importance in Charleston had less than twenty house slaves. There was much company, many parties and horse races (some of the richest men even kept up their own race tracks), and in general the planters had very good times. The houses were handsome, each with its own yard and garden at the back, where there were beautiful flowers and orange trees. The living and dining rooms were on the second floor.

Besides the English, there were a number of French people of good education and good training, who added to the strength of the colony.

The churches were better than those of Virginia, and the ministers were also better.

There were few schools, and even those few were private. The sons of the richest planters were sent to England for their education. For the first time in the New World we find in Charleston a public library. There was also a theater. How different this town life was from the plantation life of Virginia!

But there was no manufacturing. South Carolina received its money from rice and indigo, and with that money bought everything it needed from other colonies, even its flour and meat.

A Long Time Passes

We are now going to pass over almost three quarters of a century in order to hear about the last of the English colonies. The reason for learning about it now is that life there was so much like life in Virginia and the Carolinas.

The Last English Colony

The land between the Carolinas and St. Augustine was claimed by both Spain and England. These two nations wanted it more for the trade with the Indians of that region than for the land itself. It was low and sandy, with a warm climate, and "a fair coast stretching a great length, covered with a great number of high and fair trees and the fairest vines in the world." England had tried to build forts there, but had failed, though the Indians had been friendly to the English.

There was in England at this time a good man who was much interested in having prisoners treated less cruelly while they were in prison. He had visited many prisons in England to see how they were managed, and he had found that a great many of the prisoners had been put into prison because they could not pay their debts. At that time a man could be put into prison by those to whom he owed money, if he was not able to pay.

This good Englishman believed that many of the debtors were honest and would pay their debts if they only had a chance to work and earn the money. So he went to the king and said: "Will you let me make a colony in the New World? I should like to take with me some of these debtors from the English prisons, who I believe are honest, and also some of the people of Europe who are being cruelly treated because of their religion. My colony could settle south of the Carolinas and could protect Charleston against the Spaniards of Florida. I have fought against the Turks, and I could lead an army again, if necessary."

The king was not much interested in the debtors, but he liked the idea of having someone protect Carolina from the Spaniards, so he agreed to the plan. He named the new colony Georgia in honor of himself. (What do you think his name must have been?) He gave to the new colony the land south of Carolina, from sea to sea. (On the map on page 190 find Georgia.)

Many good people in England took a great interest in this last of the colonies. Many gifts were made to it. The great assembly, or Parliament, of England gave a large amount of money. Only such settlers as could work were allowed to go. There were carpenters, bricklayers, and farmers. They had plenty of money to keep them until they could take care of themselves. The motto of the colony was "Not for ourselves, but for others."

They set out from England with great hopes. The people of South Carolina were glad to greet them (why?) and helped them all they could. The kind man who had been made governor of the new colony went out from the ship in a small boat to choose a place for the settlement. He found one on a high bank where ships could come close to shore.

A trader from South Carolina and his Indian wife were already living there; they persuaded the rest of the Indians to be friendly. The governor bought the land from them and treated them justly. Food was to be had in plenty; a deer cost six pennies, and wild turkeys four pennies.

Each of the settlers was given a town lot, a garden, and a farm. While their houses were being built they lived in huts made of branches and leaves. They had been ordered to make silk, and silk-makers had been sent from England to teach them, but the worms which make silk could not be raised successfully in Georgia; so this industry died.

Then there was fighting between the Spaniards of Florida and the English colonists. But the Spaniards could not drive the English out of Georgia, nor could the English drive the Spaniards away from St. Augustine. So each settled down in its own part of the country. The governor's plan had succeeded: he had saved two English colonies for the king. (Which two?)

Slow Growth of Georgia

At first matters went smoothly in the little colony. Many hard-working settlers came from Europe. Each was given his tools, food, seeds, and his way was paid.

But trouble soon began. One of the rules under which the colony had been formed was that no slaves should be brought to Georgia. This rule was passed partly through fear of a great negro rising and partly because slavery was beginning to be considered wrong.

What crops could be raised without slave labor? The growing of silk and the making of wine had been tried, and both had failed. Then the colonists wanted to raise rice and indigo, like their neighbors in South Carolina. But for such work they needed negroes; for there were few white servants, and the white men could not stand the heat of the rice fields. The debtors had not succeeded much better in the New World than they had in England; they had disappointed the governor. So if any work were to be done, it seemed as if negroes were necessary.

At last the rule against slavery had to be given up. Slaves were brought in, and rice and indigo were raised; but the plantations of Georgia were not so rich as those farther north.

Another rule under which the colony had been founded was that there should be no trade in rum. Again the settlers objected. They pointed to the large trade which South Carolina had built up. They believed that they could do as well if they were allowed to trade in rum with the West Indies. Some brought it in secretly, although it was against the law. At last this rule also was changed.

But the colony did not grow fast. There were fewer schools and churches than in the other colonies. There was much crime. There were no manufactures and no town life. After a time the governor went back to England; then matters became worse. The king at last took over the government of the colony himself, and it was called a royal colony. Virginia and North and South Carolina were treated in the same way.

Partners

After you have proved that you can answer these questions, perhaps your teacher will let you choose a partner and ask the questions of him.

1. Why did the eight lords have trouble with their colony?

2. What were three industries of the North Carolina colonists?

3. What was the chief industry of South Carolina?

4. Why did the planters of South Carolina live in the city?

5. Which was the last of the thirteen colonies?

6. What were the two purposes for which the colony of Georgia was founded?

Serving as Judge

Write sentences containing the following words that were used in the story. Exchange papers and correct the sentences.

the South   the Carolinas   Georgia   debtors

Carolina grew because it could trade with the Spaniards and because of its rich crops.

Georgia was founded as a home for debtors who had been in prison.

LIFE IN NEW NETHERLAND

Now we shall go back to the time when negroes were first being brought to Virginia, before the Carolinas or Georgia had been thought of. While the people of Virginia were learning how to carry on business in their House of Representatives, what were the Dutch in the colony of New Netherland doing? (Find New Netherland on the map on page 242.)

The Dutch West India Company had built forts and had brought a few settlers to New Amsterdam, but had been so interested in the fur trade that it had paid little attention to making colonies.

For a long time the Dutch people did not care to go to America to live, and the few who came turned to the fur trade instead of to farming. Few permanent settlements were made, and the colony was not growing.

The Patroons

What should be done? The company decided to let any of its members come to New Netherland and buy land from the "wild men," as they called the Indians. For a few trinkets one might buy all the land

240

for sixteen miles along one side of the Hudson River or for eight miles along both sides, and as far back as he wanted to go. These landowners were known as *patroons*. The patroons had to make settlements on their land and pay the expenses of fifty grown-up people who would come there to live. Patroons had to clear the land, build farmhouses and barns for their settlers, give them tools and cattle, and bring a minister and a school-teacher from Holland to preach and to teach. They could hold their own courts to try anyone who broke the laws, and they alone had the right to hunt and to fish on their lands, or *estates*.

The colonists whom the patroon brought over had to work part of the time for him. They were not allowed to leave his land without permission, they had to help keep up the roads on his estate, they had to take their grain to his mill and give him some of it for the grinding, and if they raised cattle or made butter to sell they had to give him the first chance to buy. They were not allowed to trade in furs. They could not manufacture cloth; for the Dutch people in Europe wanted to sell their products in the New World.

Many rich men in Holland were eager to get these great estates — of sometimes a million acres — along the river. It was easy to find patroons, but it was not so easy to find colonists. Yet enough were found to give the patroons a chance to take up the best land. The houses of their people were widely scattered over their estates. (Find the Hudson River on the map on page 242.) Some great names in our history are those of Dutch settlers, for example, *Roosevelt*.

LAKE CHAMPLAIN

LAKE ONTARIO

Connecticut River

Fort Orange

Hudson River

NEW NETHERLAND

New Amsterdam

ATLANTIC OCEAN

Dutch Possessions

The Dutch in North America

Slow Growth of the Colony

At last it was decided that more settlements would
be made if the patroons were given less land; so the
later patroons were allowed to buy only one mile of land.
But even then settlers would rather go to other colonies

where they could own their own farms instead of working for patroons. Many foreigners came, however, and in a few years eighteen different languages were spoken in New Amsterdam. (Find New Amsterdam on the map on page 242.)

The Dutch colony grew very slowly, but the English colonies were growing fast. What could be done to make the Dutch colony grow too? At last it was decided to give every settler a little farm for himself and to let him trade in furs if he wished.

After that the number of settlers grew larger. The company gave each colonist free passage to America, a farm, a house, a barn, four horses, four cows, some sheep and pigs, and tools. He had to pay rent for six years, but after that the land was to be his.

When the fur trade was made free for all, the traders began to trade guns with the Indians for furs. The Indians would give twenty beaver skins for a gun. But it was not safe to let the Indians have guns, for they soon began to use them on the settlers. An Indian war broke out, and many of the Dutch were killed. For these reasons the colony grew slowly.

The City of New Amsterdam

Let us try to think how the Dutch city on Manhattan Island, at the mouth of the Hudson River, must have looked. The first things that we should have seen would be a tall flagpole with the flag of the Netherlands flying from it, a small fort at the edge of the water, and the "government house," built of stone.

Along the main street were the governor's square stone house, a storehouse, a large barnlike place where liquor was made, and the minister's house with its bright flower beds. On other streets were the great stone church, the town pump, the prison and stocks, and, at the water's edge, a great heap of oyster shells.

The broadest street had a canal running through it; today we call the street "Broadway." Farther back was a brook where the women of the colony did the family washing; the street where the brook used to run is known even yet as "Maiden Lane." Close by were the blacksmith shop and a great open place where the people came to play games. The game that they played most was ninepins.

If one wished to row over to Long Island he would find a boat tied to a tree, and a horn ready for use. When he blew the horn a man would come out of a house near at hand and row him over for perhaps six cents.

Sights which would seem very strange to us were the tall windmills with their arms covered with cloth; the lamp which was hung on a pole at night from every seventh house; and the night watch with his lamp, walking about from dark to dawn, calling out at each hour, "Midnight and all is well" or "Five o'clock and a cloudy morning."

We have thought of New York as the largest city in the United States for so long that we sometimes think also of New Amsterdam as the largest city in the colonies. But it was not. Boston was larger; and Philadelphia, founded almost three quarters of a century later than New Amsterdam, was also larger.

The Homes of the Dutch in the New World

On their great estates the patroons lived like princes. Most of their land was rented to farmers, who came up to the great house twice a year to pay the rent. At that time the patroon gave a great feast.

The houses of the richer colonists were built of wood or of wood and yellow brick from Holland. The front wall had figures in color worked in the bricks, and sometimes the date when the house was built. The windows were small and had shutters of wood. At each corner of the house were great barrels to catch the rain water from the roof. At both ends were large chimneys. The second story hung out over the first, and the roof came down to make a cover for the porch. All round the porch were seats, and it was covered by climbing vines. There the family sat in summer.

The front door was divided into two parts, an upper and a lower, so that the lower could be kept shut while the upper was open like a window. On the lower part was a great iron knocker.

The house was very pleasant inside. A wide hallway ran through the middle, where the family sat in winter. Heavy beams of wood showed in the ceiling. The fireplace was covered with squares of blue or pink china and sometimes with pictures of Bible stories. Burning wood gave the only light except for a few candles.

Rows of wooden dishes, blue-china plates, and pipes ran round the walls. In one corner stood a tall "grandfather's clock," and in the place of honor lay the great Dutch Bible.

The floor was the pride of the housekeeper's heart. There was no carpet to catch the dust; the bare floor was washed every day and covered with clean white sand. The mistress sometimes drew figures in the sand.

The bedrooms were kept shut in summer because of the flies; in winter they were so cold that the water froze in the bowls. They were furnished with large boxes or chests of oak, in which were stored the linens and laces that the good wife and her daughters were always making. Tall cases of drawers held what the boxes could not.

But the most interesting sight was the great bedstead, with its four tall posts and its mattress of straw covered by a huge feather bed. It had curtains all around, and it was so high above the floor that the children's beds were kept under it during the day and were "trundled" out only at night. So the children's beds were called trundle-beds.

The storehouse was deep under the house and was dark and damp, but in it were stored all the good things to eat: pounds and pounds of butter, barrels of salt meat and of fat, and piles of apples, potatoes, and other vegetables. There were big cans of fruit, barrels and barrels of cider, and generally some rum. For in Europe the water had not been pure enough to drink, and the settlers had not yet learned to like water.

Outside the house a row of trees with a fence of white boards nailed from tree to tree ran down to the river. The gardens were full of bright flowers; and here the women, even those of rich families, spent a great deal of time working.

Peter Stuyvesant at Fort Amsterdam

The picture shows you how the Dutch colonists dressed. (From a painting by Stanley M. Arthurs)

There is not time to tell about the great barns full of cattle, horses, and corn, with a floor in the center, on which the Dutch settlers pounded out their grain; but we may be sure that they took as good care of their animals as they did of their other property.

Food and Clothing

From our glance at the storehouse we have some idea of what the Dutch colonists liked to eat. They were very fond of all kinds of food made from corn. They had corn meal and milk three times a day. Peas and beans were also eaten.

For meat they had deer, which cost about half a cent a pound, and wild turkey and wild geese. Every farmer also kept pigs. The colonists who lived near the sea had all kinds of fish and oysters. Apples were the chief fruit.

The tables were covered with fine linen and, on feast days, with china, but only a few of the richest families used forks.

On great occasions the clothing of the richer families must have been very gay. The men wore long coats of velvet lined with silk and trimmed with silver lace. Their knee breeches were of black satin; their waist-coats, of red satin. Their white shirts had ruffles all down the front. Their stockings were of gray silk, and their shoes had great silver buckles.

On their perfumed wigs they wore wide hats of black felt with bands of gold lace; and some of the gentlemen wore at their left side a long sword with diamonds in the handle.

At such times the women also wore beautiful clothes, some of which came from the Far East: blue and gold dresses, lace ruffles, very full black-velvet skirts trimmed with silver, red-silk stockings, and fine red-leather shoes. Caps of white linen covered the whole head and came far down over the shoulders. They wore so many clothes that they looked very fat.

Work in New Netherland

The most important business in the colony was the fur trade. Dutchmen went far up the Hudson to the country of the Iroquois, where they exchanged guns, rum, and trinkets for beaver skins. We read of one ship which carried five thousand beaver skins to Holland.

The cattle fair at New Amsterdam

How many different things for sale can you see in the picture?

There was some trade in other goods also, especially in lumber, which was sent to the seashore to build ships. In return for these things, wine, sugar, and manufactured goods were brought from the Netherlands.

Goods were sold at the "cattle fair," at which not only cattle but cheese, butter, laces, and linen were shown. The Indian women brought furs, baskets, and things made of bark. They exchanged what they had made for whatever they wanted. After selling their goods the people would dance on the grass before going home.

Farming was also important, for the soil was very rich. The settlers raised wheat and sent this and flour to Europe. For themselves they raised potatoes, corn, and other grains. At first they tried to grow tobacco, but they found that it did not pay, so they used tobacco from Virginia.

The Dutch did not use the plantation system of raising only one crop; instead they raised many different products. Except for the estates of the patroons, the settlers' farms were small.

There was not much manufacturing. Flour, leather goods, plain furniture, bricks, salt, and beaver hats were made. Almost everything else was brought from Europe.

The colonists had cowherds to take care of their cattle. Every morning the cowherd and a good strong boy went through the town sounding a horn. All the cattle followed, out to the meadows. At sundown the two brought them back to town and called the owners by again blowing the horn. Each man then came and took his own cows home to milk.

There were few doctors, but the ministers were men of wide learning and were held in deep respect.

Good Times

The Dutch people seem to have had more good times than any of the other colonists; they had many holidays, and feasted at each one.

In summer the patroons lived out on their estates with their large companies of servants; in winter they came into New Amsterdam to their town houses. There they lived in great style, dancing, drinking, and playing cards. They had sleighing parties, horse-racing, turkey-shooting, and cock-fighting. They had the first theater in America, a great barnlike building, but in it many good plays were acted. There were many clubs, which usually met in the inn or at the coffeehouse.

The plain people rose at dawn, had their dinner at noon, and spent the evening in having a good time. They were a gay people; they lived happily and were kind to the strangers who came among them.

Testing your Memory

Test your memory by asking yourself these questions:

1. Why was settlement slow under the Dutch West India Company?

2. What did the patroon have to do for his people?

3. What did his people have to do for him?

4. What are two streets in New York whose names today make us think of the Dutch?

5. What was the most important industry in the Dutch colony? the next most important?

Choices to Make

Choose the right words to complete the following sentences:

1. The Dutch colony in the New World was

Carolina   Virginia   New Netherland

2. Their city at the mouth of the Hudson was

New Amsterdam   Albany   New York

3. Any man who could bring over fifty people was called a

nobleman   patroon   rich man

4. Such men lived on large stretches of land called

townships   plantations   estates

The Dutch people had large estates.

The land belonged to only a few men.

For a long time a common man might not own a farm.

The name "New Netherland" was later changed to "New York." The English king's brother was the Duke of York. Do these facts tell you what nation took the colony away from the Dutch?

THE END OF DUTCH RULE IN NORTH AMERICA

However happy the Dutch people may have been in their family life, they were not so fortunate in their government. There were always quarrels between the people and their governors, between the governors and the patroons, and between the Dutch and their English neighbors to the north and south. These quarrels partly explain why the colony never grew so fast as its English neighbors.

This story will show you how the governors got along with their people. Once a governor was very angry at the minister of the Dutch church, but he did not dare to have him arrested because the minister was greatly respected by all the people. The minister was angry too and preached against the governor in the church. At this the governor had his soldiers stand outside the church and beat drums so that the people might not hear the minister. The louder the minister talked, the louder the soldiers beat their drums. At last they even fired off their cannon to drown his voice.

People from another country in Europe had settled a little south of the Dutch colony. They were few in

New Amsterdam

Can you see the church? the fort? Wall Street? (From an old engraving)

number and went quietly about their business. But the Dutch claimed that land, so they sent out soldiers who drove the strangers away.

Peter Stuyvesant as Governor

The governor in whom we are most interested was the last of the Dutch governors. His name was Peter Stuyvesant. He was an honest, well-educated man, who worked long and hard, but he had a strong will and believed that the people should do exactly as he told them and that they should not be allowed to help in making the laws.

In a war with Portugal many years before, he had lost one of his legs. In its place he had a wooden leg. The story is told that it was bound about with silver bands and silver nails, so the people called him "Old Silver Nails" or "Old Silver Leg." At meetings of the council, if any man did not agree with him he pounded on the floor with his wooden leg and sometimes even struck the man.

But with all his faults he did more for New Netherland than any of the other governors had done. He made peace with the Indians, who had been carrying on a terrible war with the colonists before he came; and he captured the colony of the other nation from Europe which had settled too near him on the south.

Trouble with the English

The enemy that Stuyvesant feared most was the English. England claimed that the land on which the Dutch had settled belonged to her because of John Cabot's discovery. The Dutch replied that Cabot had not found the Hudson River; and that if the man who first discovered land in the New World could claim all of it for his nation, then all of America belonged to Spain, and England had no better right to it than the Dutch had. It was plain that war between England and the Dutch would come some day.

Meanwhile matters in New Netherland were growing worse. These were some of the reasons: (1) The Dutch people saw their English neighbors holding assemblies and helping to make the laws, while they themselves were allowed no such rights; (2) the Dutch West India Company had not been willing to spend money enough to protect the colony against the Indians, and many of the colonists had been killed; (3) for years only the patroons and the rich colonists had been able to own land or to engage in the fur trade; (4) Stuyvesant had ruled so harshly that the colonists hated him. He whipped or put in prison those who would not obey him. They said, "He is like a wolf: the older he gets, the worse he bites."

England takes New Netherland

Just at that time a new king came to the throne in England. He was interested in the Dutch colony for several reasons: (1) The Dutch colony was in the midst of the English colonies in America and divided them; some were to the south and some to the north of it (see the map, p. 242). (2) The Dutch had the best harbor on the whole Atlantic coast (New Amsterdam). (3) The Dutch had traded with the English colonies, and the law was that only England should trade with them. (4) The English claimed all the country that the Dutch were settling and all the coast of North America because John Cabot had discovered it and sailed along the coast.

For these four reasons the king decided to make war against the Dutch. The best plan, he thought, was to strike at once, while the two countries were at peace, so that the Dutch should not have time to get ready. So he gave all the land along the Hudson River to

The Dutch surrendering New Netherland to the English
Which are the English soldiers and which the Dutch?

his brother, the Duke of York, and told him to go and take it away from the Dutch settlers.

One day when Peter Stuyvesant was at Fort Orange (now called Albany) a messenger came riding to tell him that four English ships had appeared in the bay near New Amsterdam and had already seized the fort on the island. (On the map on page 242 find Fort Orange.)

What should he do? He had built a wall of posts twelve feet high to protect the city (from this wall, the Wall Street of today takes its name), but the stone fort was old, and he had no money to buy powder and shot. He had only twenty cannon, and these could do very little against the hundred and twenty cannon of the English.

He hurried back to New Amsterdam and called a meeting of the people, asking them what to do. They were not much interested. For a long time they had wanted assemblies of their own, as their English neighbors had. They hated Governor Stuyvesant because he had been so stern with them. Many were themselves English and would rather be under the rule of their countrymen. Some of the Dutch were afraid of the English and thought it was of no use to fight against such great numbers. The English colonies on both sides of them would surely help the Duke of York, and there were ten Englishmen in America to every Dutchman. The council was about ready to surrender.

At this point the leader of the English sent the governor a letter. It was a kind letter promising the Dutch that he would not harm them, that he would not take away any of their property, that they might trade freely, and that they might keep their own religion if they would not fight. He also promised that they might have an assembly and the right to make their own laws.

Peter Stuyvesant, in great anger, tore the letter into bits. But the colonists gathered up the pieces, put them together, and read the message. They looked at the English ships coming on under full sail, with all their guns loaded, and told the governor to surrender. "I would rather be carried to my grave," he shouted.

But the people refused to fight; and no man, however brave, can meet an army alone. When Stuyvesant's own son begged him to give in, he at last consented.

The Dutch flag came down, and the English flag rose in its place.   Dutch rule in North America was over. No longer were the English colonies cut in two by a section which foreigners held.   The Dutch people were allowed to stay, but they were under the rule of England. England now owned all the eastern coast from New France as far as Florida.

New Netherland becomes New York

The Duke of York, to whom the king had given the land, changed the name of New Netherland.   He called it New York.   The city of New Amsterdam he also called New York.

But, except for the name, he made few changes. The Dutch customs remained; people still spoke the Dutch language and went to whatever church they wished, just as they had done before.   Some of the officers were Englishmen and some were Dutch.   The settlers were given the same rights as their neighbors in the other English colonies; they were allowed to vote and to have an assembly.

Years afterwards the king took the government of New York into his own hands, and it became another royal colony.

Finding Sentences

After you have found the sentences which answer the following questions, call on someone else in the class to find them.   The rest of the class will decide whether he finds the right sentences.

1. What two things did Governor Stuyvesant do for the colony?

2. What were the four reasons why matters grew worse in New Netherland?

3. What were the four reasons why the king of England was interested in the Dutch colony?

4. For what four reasons did the members of the council not want to fight?

5. What did the English leader promise?

Reminders

These new words should remind you of something you read in the story.   Give a sentence, using each word or group of words and telling a fact you learned about each.

1. Peter Stuyvesant   2. New York   3. surrender

The English claimed the land on which the Dutch had settled.

The English conquered the Dutch.

The name of the colony was changed from New Netherland to New York.

Why does our country hold a day of Thanksgiving every year? Who held the first Thanksgiving Day in America? Should you like to learn why the Pilgrims had left their comfortable homes in the Old World and had come to live in a new, wild land?

THE PILGRIM FATHERS

Now we must again go back to a few years after Jamestown was founded, to the time when Virginia was the only English colony in the New World and had been settled only thirteen years. Patroons were just beginning to come to New Netherland, and no one had yet dreamed of the Carolinas or Georgia. The year was 1620.

Trouble in England

While Elizabeth was queen of England she made all her subjects live in peace together. But the king who came to the throne after her was very different. He thought that everyone ought to do just as he said, and that he himself was so wise that he could do no wrong.

In those days it was very common for the king to decide what church all his people should attend. Elizabeth and the rulers who came after her decided that all their people should belong to the Church of England.

But some of the people said: "We belong to the Church of England, and wish to remain in it, but we think some changes should be made. We do not want to have our prayers read from a book. We want the church buildings to be plainer and more simple. People now have so many things to look at in church that it takes their attention away from the services." Because these people wanted to make the services more simple and pure, they were called Puritans.

There were other people who said: "We will not attend the Church of England at all. We believe that people should be allowed to form such a church as they wish. They should do what they think is right, and not have anyone over them to make rules for them. The Bible should be their only guide." These people wanted to separate entirely from the Church of England. So they were called Separatists.

The king did not intend that either of these groups should be allowed to carry out their ideas. He ordered that all ministers should use the service of the Church of England just as it was, without any change. "And if they do not do as I say," he added, "I will drive them out of the kingdom, or else worse."

What could the people who wanted to separate from the English Church do? They must have church services, but where should they meet? They met in private houses, in halls, and even in the fields. Since most of them were poor, — farmers, traders, and working-people, — the king at first did not pay much attention to them. But their neighbors made fun of them, and sometimes rough crowds would attack and beat the ministers. Sometimes the meetings were broken up. Later the houses of some of the members were watched day and night, and soldiers came and put the leaders in prison; sometimes they even hanged them.

Once in a while a few would escape over the sea, and at last a number of them planned to leave England. But where could they go? The Netherlands was the only country which allowed all Christians to live within its borders and attend whatever church they wished; so the English Separatists decided to go there. It took brave men to make such plans, to leave the only homes they had ever known and the country they loved, and to live in a strange land whose very language they did not understand. But they would rather do that than stay where the king would not allow them to have their own religion.

The Escape to Holland

It was against the law of England for people to leave the country unless the king had given his consent, so whatever was done had to be done quietly. Once the people who wished to separate from the English Church secured a ship and prepared to go to Holland, but the captain of the ship told the soldiers, and the soldiers seized the Separatists, put them in prison for a month, and took all their money and goods.

After a while they secured another ship. The men were already on board and the women and children were coming out in small boats, when the captain was seized with sudden fear and put up his sail and hurried off. Thus many families were separated.

A few months afterwards the rest managed to escape also, and reached Holland in the same year that James-town was settled. (What year was it?)

In Holland these simple country folk saw for the

first time great cities strongly walled and guarded. They were surprised at the strange manners and customs, and they found the prices of everything so high that they had a hard time to earn a living. Some of them worked at weaving wool and others at printing and teaching. One, of whom we shall hear later, became a silk-weaver. His name was William Bradford. He had lived three miles away from the meetinghouse in England, but had walked back and forth every Sunday to hear the services. He was only eighteen years old when he left his home, but he became one of the leaders of the little colony.

Although the English people had to work very hard, they learned many things from the Dutch. The Dutch people liked them and never had any cause to quarrel with them.

Slowly their numbers increased. Miles Standish joined them during these years. He had been a soldier in the Netherlands. He did not belong to the same church as the others, but he was a splendid fighting man and proved to be a faithful friend.

Thirteen years went by. The English people felt very kindly toward the Dutch for having given them a home, but they were not happy. There were several reasons: (1) The health of some of them was breaking under the hard work. (2) Their children were learning the Dutch speech and customs, were forgetting their English, and were not so strict in their religion as the parents would have liked. (3) War between Holland and Spain was likely to break out again. (4) They did not want always to live as strangers in a strange land.

Where could they find a country in which they might remain a part of the English nation and still keep their own religion? They thought of going to South America, but decided that it was too hot and that there was danger from Spain. The land in Europe had been settled many years. They thought of Virginia, but the Church of England was established there. They thought of New Netherland, but that would be too much like the old Netherlands.

At last they decided to go somewhere north of Virginia. John Smith had sailed along the coast and had made a map of it. They thought that they could find a place there. The old and the weak could not go; only the strongest would be able to found the new colony.

Getting Ready to make a New Colony

There was much to be done. First men were sent to England to see about getting land in the New World, so that when the colonists arrived they might call the place their own. After much trouble land was secured from the London Company, but it was good only for the territory south of the Hudson River.

Then they asked the king to give them a paper telling what kind of government they were to have in the New World, but he refused. They were lucky to be allowed to go at all.

The next question was how they were to raise money to pay for the voyage. They themselves had very little. But at last some rich merchants agreed to lend them the money if they would give in return half of all they should earn for seven years. This was hard for them, but it was the best that they could do.

It took three years to settle these questions, but at last all was ready.

The *Mayflower* crosses the Ocean

Sadly the little company in Holland prepared to leave their friends and the land which had been home to them for thirteen years. As they were going on a long journey they called themselves Pilgrims. William Bradford and Miles Standish were among them. The colony was to be established not to find riches nor to earn a better living, but to have *freedom of religion*.

All the friends of the Pilgrims came down to the shore and wept as they saw them go. The minister knelt down and asked God to keep all the company safe until they should meet again.

The ship went first to England, where some more of the Separatists and another ship, called the *Mayflower*, were waiting. The two vessels set sail; but it was soon found that the one that had come from Holland was leaking, so the Pilgrims had to turn back and have it repaired. They started a second time, and a second time they had to return. The leaky ship was too bad to mend. It would have to be left behind.

They decided to go on in the *Mayflower*, taking as many as the ship would hold. Twenty had to stay in England; the others, one hundred and two of them, crowded into the *Mayflower*. Twenty-one were women, twenty-eight were children, and the rest were men.

The first boat ashore from the *Mayflower*

Who is standing in armor at the back of the boat? (From a painting by H. A. Ogden)

They had to pack themselves in closely; for besides the people, room had to be made for food and supplies and for the many boxes, bags, chests of drawers, and heavy furniture which the families had brought. There was little space in which to cook and there was less in which to bathe.

For more than two months the *Mayflower* labored through the heavy seas. Once, in a great storm, the ship cracked; and if it had not been for a huge iron screw that one of the men had with him, the Pilgrims probably would all have gone to the bottom of the sea.

When they sighted land they did not know what coast it was, but they soon found out that it was far north of the land that had been given to them by the London Company.

What should they do? Should they try to go farther south through the roaring seas? They decided first to find out what kind of country it was. Miles Standish and a few others went on shore to bring back wood and to explore. They put on their heavy armor and marched up and down, but saw only a dog and five Indians, who ran away in fear.

Later a second exploring party found some Indian houses with grass mats in them and many pots for cooking, but the natives kept carefully out of sight. On returning to the ship the party found that a baby had been born while they were away, the first child born in the Pilgrim colony.

A third party that went out was attacked by the Indians. The natives hated white men because one of

John Smith's captains had seized some Indians many years before and had carried them to Spain as slaves.

Five weeks went by before the Pilgrims decided where to make their settlement. Before landing they had a meeting on board the *Mayflower* to talk over their plans. There were two hard problems: (1) they had no right to this land, because it was not the land that had been given to them; (2) they had no form of government to follow.

They decided to settle where they were and to try to have the land given to them afterwards. As to government, they agreed that they would make their own laws "for the good of the colony" and would see that everyone obeyed them. These things were written down in a paper which forty-one of the grown men of the colony signed.

Making a Settlement in Winter

At last the exploring parties had found a place "fit for shipping," with a clear brook running into it. By this time it was the middle of winter.

Back and forth went the small boats from the *Mayflower* to the shore, moving goods and people. A great rock can still be seen on the shore near where the boats landed. It is called Plymouth Rock. (Find the village of Plymouth on the map on page 271.)

A busy time followed. Some of the men were set to cutting down trees, others to making boards. The women began to wash clothes in the clear cold water of the brook. On Christmas Day of the year 1620 they began to build the storehouse which was to hold the supplies for all the people.

The new town was called Plymouth, after the English city from which the Pilgrims had sailed.

As the winter wore on they suffered severely. None of them understood how to live in a forest. Most of them did not know much about fishing or how to handle guns, so they lived chiefly on oysters and other shellfish which they found on the shore.

Before the winter was over, almost all were ill. At one time only Miles Standish and six others were well enough to go about. They had to cut and bring in wood, keep the fires, cook, make beds, wash clothes, and nurse the sick. There were hardly enough of the living to bury the dead. When spring came more than half the company had died and had been buried under the snow.

Cannon had been placed on a high platform to protect the colony against the Indians, but no Indians had been seen.

Work of the First Spring and Summer

Much work was yet to be done, but the colonists were glad to be able to do it. A fort was built, and six guns were placed on its flat roof; the lower part was used for a church.

Two streets were laid out, with wooden gates at each end. There were now nineteen families. Every man had begun to build his own house; seven houses were finished, each with its garden around it, arranged in

Early New England

very good order. The governor's house stood in the middle. A stockade was put up around all the buildings.

Twenty-six acres of land were cleared, and corn was planted in the fields which the Indians had left. The soil was not so good as in England. It was full of stones; but corn and other grains grew in it. Never again was the colony in danger of starving.

In the spring the *Mayflower* returned to England with a load of beaver skins and some lumber.   Instead of taking this chance to give up their attempt and go back to England, the Pilgrims stood on shore and watched the ship out of sight.

The Colonists and the Indians

During all these months no Indians had been seen. One reason was that there had been a terrible disease in the country some time before the Pilgrims had arrived, and half of the tribe had died.   Few were left around Plymouth, and these few were afraid of the white men.   They had had a meeting in a swamp close by, and their medicine man had tried to drive out the Pilgrims by casting a spell over them, but had failed. So they did not even visit Plymouth until the end of the winter.

Then one day in spring a tall Indian entered the village and said "Welcome, Englishmen."   The colonists welcomed him and gave him a knife, a ring, and a coat. In return he told them about the Indian tribes that lived in the country round about.

Later he came back with another Indian who could speak English very well, for he had once been captured by some sailors and taken to England for a time.   This Indian liked the Pilgrims so well that he stayed among them, living sometimes with one family, sometimes with another.   He taught them how to grow corn by putting three or four fish in each hill for fertilizer.   He also showed them how to use wampum as money.   Wampum was beads made of pieces of shells; there were both black and white beads, but the black were worth more than the white.

When Massasoit, the chief of the tribes near them, heard that the Pilgrims were friendly, he decided to visit them himself. With many painted and feathered warriors he came to the governor's house. Some of the Indians were painted black; others, yellow or white. Their heads and faces were covered with oil. They had strings of white wampum around their necks, with bags of tobacco hanging down behind.

They sat very quietly on the green carpet in the governor's house and smoked the pipe of peace. Then they made a treaty promising to be friends. As long as Massasoit lived this promise was faithfully kept.

The Indians then began trading in furs, and from them the *Mayflower* secured the beaver skins which it carried back to England.

Massasoit was not chief of all the tribes. Another tribe, of two thousand warriors, wanted to drive the white people away, and sent them some arrows tied up in a snake's skin. That was the signal for war. The messenger threw the skin in at the governor's door and ran quickly away.

The governor was William Bradford. He had only fifty men, but he had guns and powder and bullets and a good captain, Miles Standish. So he filled the snake's skin with powder and bullets and sent it back. The chief knew what that meant; he would not keep the skin, but sent it away, out of his sight. There was no war.

The First Thanksgiving

When fall came and it was time to harvest the crops, the hearts of all the Pilgrims were full of joy to see how much corn they had raised. And there were plenty of deer and wild turkeys and fish, besides the oysters and shellfish. Much wood had been piled up. The coming winter would be very different from the last one.

Governor Bradford set aside a week in which the people should thank God for his care of them. Four men were sent into the woods to hunt deer and turkeys for the feast. The Indians were invited; and because they often had feasts for giving thanks to their own gods, they understood what was meant.

They came with loads of deer, corn, and wild turkeys. They attended all the church services, sang their songs, and played their games for the white men. The first Thanksgiving was a season of great happiness.

Finding your Score

If you can answer all these questions correctly without looking back in the story, your score is 7. If you had to look back once, your score is 6; if you had to look back for two answers, your score is 5; and so on. Write your answers on a piece of paper. Then prove your answers by turning back in the story. What score did you make? Wrong answers subtract from the score.

1. What things about the Church of England did the Puritans want to change?

2. Why did some other people want to separate from the church?

3. Why did they go to Holland?

4. For what four reasons did they decide to leave Holland?

5. What three matters of business had to be attended to in England before beginning a new colony?

6. Why did the settlers think they should sail farther south in the New World?

7. What did they do about a government for the colony?

Sentences to Complete

Supply the missing words in these sentences. Make them into a list and show your list to your teacher.

1. The man who sent the snake's skin back to the Indians was Governor _____ _____.

2. The great captain of Plymouth was _____ _____.

3. The Indian who was a friend of the settlers was _____.

4. The settlers were called _____ because they had wandered so long.

5. They founded a settlement which they named _____.

6. The Pilgrims reached America in the year _____.

7. The ship in which they crossed the ocean was the _____.

8. They were seeking _____ _____ _____ for themselves.

The Pilgrims came to America to secure freedom of religion.

The king "shut his eyes" but refused to grant a charter.

What do you think the title of this story means? What
kind of spirit did the Pilgrims have? From what country did these other people come? The story will tell you
about them.

THE SPIRIT OF THE PILGRIMS IS CAUGHT
BY OTHERS

Many Englishmen had watched the settlement of
the Pilgrims with interest. For at home the king continued his strict laws, and his soldiers continued to throw
ministers into prison and to break up church services
that were not carried on according to the rules of the
Church of England.

You will remember that many people had hoped to
stay in the Church of England, but they did not believe in using colored-glass windows, beautiful robes
and images, or in reading prayers from a book. And
because they said that they wanted a plain, *pure*
church they were called Puritans.

But the king would not allow any changes to be
made; and as time went on the Puritans began to see
that they too should have to leave England, as the Pilgrims had done. A writer of that time said, "Then God's
people turned eyes of longing to the free and open
spaces of the New World, where they might be at peace."

Naturally their thoughts turned to New England.
At first only a few at a time left their homes, but later
they left by thousands.

The Settlement of Massachusetts Bay

The first settlers on the shores of Massachusetts Bay were either traders or adventurers, who built little villages for the purpose of carrying on fishing, cattle-raising, or fur-trading.

The fishermen and sailors in these villages soon found that fishing and farming could not be carried on together very well, so they gave up the sea and settled down to farming.

At the same time a company of Puritans in England, called the Massachusetts Bay Company, was being formed for the purpose, they said, of trading in the New World. They secured from the king a paper giving them the land north of the Plymouth colony from sea to sea. They were allowed to choose their own governor.

They sent a few of their number ahead. These founded a town called Salem, which means "Peace." There they started a Puritan church which was to have as much power in the colony as the Church of England had in England.

The Puritans were much more stern and strict than the Pilgrims. One of the first things that they did was to send men to one of the little trading villages on the shore of the bay to cut down their Maypole and to warn the people there that they should live a more sober life.

When the Puritans who still remained in England heard that the settlers in the new lands were getting along well, a second group came out to join them. In this group were four hundred people, with one hundred and forty cattle, forty goats, and many guns and tools.

Beginning life in the wilderness
How many different kinds of tools do you see?

How strict the New England settlements were! The colonists had given up everything that they loved at home in order to worship God in their own way. They meant to set up their own church and to allow no other. They had freedom of religion, but it was freedom for themselves alone. Anyone who did not belong to the Puritan church was not allowed to come into the settlement. One might think that such a colony could not grow, but there were so many Puritans who wanted to get away from the power of the king that within a year their town had grown to be larger than Plymouth.

The Great Moving out of England

In the meantime matters in England had been growing worse. The king punished more and more severely all who would not obey him; he himself decided how much tax the people should pay. For years he ruled quite by himself.

At last all the Massachusetts Bay Company decided to move to New England and to set up a government. The first thing that they did was to elect one of their number, John Winthrop, governor. Then the trading company itself prepared to move to the New World; for the first time a *company* prepared to found a *colony* itself.

In 1630 the Massachusetts Bay Company was ready to leave. Never before had so many set out in one year for the New World. A thousand people set sail in seventeen ships. Many of them were rich and respected at home, but they would not stay where the king could make them do just what he wished. Each gentleman needed the following things for the journey: three servants with all their supplies, a feather bed, pillows, sheets, carpets, curtains, guns, and food enough for a year.

After a stormy voyage of nine weeks they arrived safely in New England. The "Peace" colony, Salem, which they had sent out earlier, was in a bad way. Its settlers were hungry, sick, and discouraged. Two hundred of the newcomers, seeing this, decided that making settlements in the New World was too hard work, and they returned to England in the same ships in which they had left home.

The rest set to work to see what could be done. They set many of their white servants free and told them to find food for themselves. They put up tents to live in and began to build log houses, but many were not strong enough for that sort of life, and a large number of them died. At last they decided that the sickness was caused by bad water, and that the settlement would have to be moved.

The Founding of Boston, 1630

Exploring farther south along the coast, they found, near the Charles River, some springs of clear water. There they chose a place for their town, and called it Boston, after the town of the same name in England. (Find Boston on the map on page 271.)

Each settler was given twenty acres of land, a house lot in the village, and the right to feed his cattle and cut hay in the meadows which belonged to the town. After a while each was allowed fifty acres instead of twenty.

Their food supplies were getting low; and if it had not been for the fish and oysters that were so plentiful, there might have been a "starving time" like that of Jamestown. Everybody had to work. Even Governor Winthrop worked with his hands, building and digging as hard as any of them. He knew how Plymouth had suffered, and he did not intend that Boston should have so hard a time.

By February all their food was gone, and there was so much ice that they could not get fish and oysters. It is said that just as Winthrop was giving a poor man the last handful of meal in the barrel, a cry went up that a ship bringing food was in sight. This saved the colony. Better times followed; and later one of the settlers wrote that they had "materials to build with, fuel to burn, ground to plant, seas and rivers to fish in, pure air to breathe, good water to drink, and cows, pigs, and goats for food."

So many colonists came from England that before the end of the first winter they had spread out and formed eight small towns. Many of them were men of wealth, and the king did not want these to leave England. He had not cared when the Pilgrims left, for they were poor working-people, but the wealthy Puritans were important and useful at home. But a few at a time continued to leave England quietly and added to the growing numbers of the Massachusetts colony.

How the Church controlled the People in the Massachusetts Bay Colony

We have already learned that the Puritans were much more strict than the Pilgrims. The church ruled men's lives more than it does today. The ministers were the most important people in every town. Only members of the Puritan church were allowed to vote. There was even less freedom than in England; the difference was that the people in the colony were Puritans and therefore were willing to obey all the laws of their church.

Very strict laws were passed. There was even a law against being merry and having a good time on Christmas Day. One man did not like to see the cross on the flag of England, so he cut it out with his sword. The king was very angry. If England had not been at war with another nation at that time he would probably have punished the colony severely. He never liked the people of Massachusetts Bay.

What happened to People of a Different Religion

What happened to the people who did not follow the same religion as the Puritans? One of them, Roger Williams, was driven out and founded the colony of Rhode Island. Another was a woman who held meetings in her house twice a week for other women who had not been able to go to church. At these meetings she told what the minister had said. Then she herself began to preach to them. The colony was divided over the "boldness of this proud woman" — some in favor of her and some against. The church at last decided that she would have to leave; so she and some of her followers moved into the wilderness and founded a colony of their own, near that of Roger Williams.

Shortly afterwards some Quakers came to Boston. They entered the Puritan churches in the midst of the services and told them that their religion was wrong. The Quakers were put into prison, and the windows were boarded up so that they could not talk to anyone outside. Their books were burned, and as soon as a West India ship came in they were put on board and sent away.

But they came back. Then they were whipped, were tied to wagons and dragged from town to town, and at last three of them were hanged. But this too severe a punishment, the Puritans thought. So their

Roger Williams escaping from Massachusetts
This is what happened to people who believed differently from
the Puritans

law was changed, and after that other people besides
Puritans were allowed to live in the colony. A little
later the right to vote was given to others than church
members.

A strange belief which the people had in colonial days
was the belief in witches. Certain persons, especially
very old women or queer-looking old men, were said to
have sold themselves to the Evil One and were therefore
called witches. They were supposed to be able to ride
through the air and to "cast spells" over other people;
that is, to make them do strange things or to hurt them.

Some poor old men and women were burned to death because their neighbors were afraid of them and said that they were witches; but the colonists soon stopped this cruel practice.

Growth of the Bay Colony

During the ten years that followed 1630 the Puritans in England came to Massachusetts in greater and greater numbers. Three hundred ships brought twenty thousand people. Twenty-two towns were built, with houses, roads, fences, and bridges. The more strict the king became, the more Puritans left England.

All the people in Massachusetts were English, and nearly all were Puritans. Few were poor, and few were white servants. Boston soon grew to be the greatest city in English America, though after Philadelphia was founded, that became larger than Boston. The Bay Colony was more thickly settled than Plymouth or Virginia or New Netherland. (Find the limits of the Massachusetts Bay Colony on the map on page 271.)

Laws about Schools

Many of the ministers in Massachusetts had attended the finest schools of England. They were afraid that in these "ends of the earth," as they called America, learning would die out. The colonists wanted their children to learn to read the Bible at least, and they themselves were too busy cutting down trees and plowing the soil to be able to teach them.

When the Bay Colony was only six years old a minister, John Harvard, gave to the colony all his books and half his wealth to start a college. The colony started it and named it Harvard College. Many who were very poor gave something to the college — either money, or silver plates, or wool, or dishes, or whatever they could. The assembly gave two thousand dollars.

A few years later the colony made a law that any town in which fifty families lived near together must establish a school for little children and must pay for it by a tax. Wherever a hundred families lived near together they had to build a school for older children also. Massachusetts was the first colony in which the people were much interested in learning; they established schools because, first of all, they wanted children to be able to read the Bible.

Town Meetings

At certain times in the year all the freemen who had been allowed to come to Boston gathered at the "meetinghouse." All the men were present: the minister, the teacher, the fathers of families, the young men. At this meeting they chose their officers. One of their officers was the man to take care of the cows of the village; another was the man to look after the pigs. They made rules about animals running in the streets; they decided whether or not to let new members stay in the village; they gave land to those who had not been given land at other meetings, and decided all important matters. This "town meeting" took charge of the government of the town.

There were now twenty-two towns, and each town had its own town meetings, made its own laws, and chose its own officers.   But there were some matters in which all the towns were interested. If a bridge were to be built over a river between two towns, which town should pay for it? If a fort had to be built far out in the Indian country, was it fair to ask any one town to pay for it? If war broke out, which town should furnish the commander of the army?   And should any one town be allowed to choose a governor for them all?

To settle such questions, the towns in Massachusetts decided to send representatives to meet together in an assembly, like the one in Virginia. After that each town took care of its own affairs in its *town meetings*, but its representatives decided matters that interested all the towns in the *assembly*.

Attempts to work Together

The colonists in New England had been living and working together for more than ten years when they heard that the Indians were planning to make a great attack upon them and drive them out of the country. They knew that England would not give them much help. They would have to depend on themselves.

There was another danger. Not far away, to the west of them, on the Hudson River, was the Dutch colony (for this was before the English had driven the Dutch away). The Dutch would not let the English trade along the Hudson River, and were taking all the fur trade away from the English settlers.

Then at the north of them were the French; and the French were trying to keep the English away from the best fishing grounds. There was danger too that the French and their Indian friends might come down and attack the English settlements.

In the face of these dangers four New England colonies — Massachusetts Bay, Plymouth, Connecticut, and a smaller one — decided to form a *league* to protect themselves. All four sent representatives to Boston once a year to talk over the Indian troubles and any other dangers that might have risen, and to tell the separate colonies what they should do.

The league lasted for about twenty years. During that time it fought some terrible Indian wars. It also helped to make the people of the four colonies work together.

After the Dutch had been driven away from the Hudson River and the Indians had been defeated, there was not much reason for such a league, and it died out.

Massachusetts Punished

The Massachusetts Bay Colony had been growing so much larger than its neighbors that it began to think they were of very little account, and to care little for their rights. They had complained to the king about this, and three times he had ordered the Bay Colony to send men to explain the matter. But no men had been sent.

Then some of the king's officers came out to Massachusetts to see if the complaints were true. After looking into the matter they returned to England and reported that Massachusetts Bay had been making its own silver coins, and that these coins did not even have the picture of the king on them! They also reported that in many cases only members of the Puritan church had been allowed to vote. Massachusetts Bay had also bought the territory called Maine, which the king had said they were not to have. And, last of all, they had been the leaders in forming that *New England league* and had not even asked the king's permission.

After thinking over these matters the king decided that he would take away the rights that had been given to the Massachusetts Bay Company many years before, and would take the government into his own hands. He would no longer let the people elect their governor; he would choose one for them.

One of the first changes that he made in the colony was to hold services for the Church of England in the Old South Church of Boston. After these services were over the Puritans might hold theirs if they wished.

Plymouth, which had always been smaller than the Bay Colony, was at this time joined to it. No longer were there separate colonies of *Plymouth* and of *Massachusetts Bay*. The two were joined and were given the one name *Massachusetts*.

A Memory Test

I. Read the questions over and decide whether you can answer them all. Say the answers to yourself. Then turn back in the story and test each of your answers to find out whether it was right.

1. For what purpose was the Massachusetts Bay Company formed?

2. How did this purpose change?

3. Did the Puritans allow freedom of religion?

4. Why were schools established in the Massachusetts Bay Colony?

5. What was the name of the first college that was established?

6. What law was made about education?

7. What was the town meeting?

8. How did the town meeting differ from the assembly?

II. If you could pass the memory test, this missing-name test will be very easy. Supply the missing words. They were used in the story.

1. The year in which Boston was settled was _____.

2. After the Bay Colony and Plymouth were united they were given the name of _____.

3. The laws for each little settlement were made by the _____.

4. Boston was settled by the _____.

5. Their governor was _____ _____.

6. The largest city settled by the Puritans was _____.

The Puritans settled in Boston.

They were better educated and had more wealth than the Pilgrims.

After a while Boston and Plymouth joined as one colony and were called Massachusetts.

Should you like to have lived among the Puritans?
Make a list of the things you would have liked. Make
another list of the things you would not have liked.
After you have read the story, correct your list or
add to it.

LIFE AMONG THE PURITANS

The Puritans lived very differently from the people
in the South. Instead of large scattered plantations,
they preferred small towns in which they might be protected from the Indians and in which the church could
be easily reached by all settlers.

Their little settlements were built on the seashore or
on the banks of rivers, so that they might get supplies
direct from England at the town wharves. At first
each village had only one street, with houses built close
together. In the center, around an open space called
the common, were the meetinghouse, the stocks, the pillory, a signpost, and perhaps a schoolhouse, a sawmill,
and a water mill for grinding corn.

Back of every house was the garden. The farms were
far away, outside the village. The men worked there
by day and came home at night. A farm was usually
scattered about in several parts, some sections near
enough to reach by walking, and others two or three
miles away.

The town meeting decided where each man's land
should be. A large farm was given to those who had

The town meeting

What are the white slips of paper held by each man? (From a painting
by Max Bohm)

large families, and a smaller farm to those who needed
less. Each man worked his own land. There were no
great plantations and there were few servants.

Outside the village were the meadows and the pas-
tures. These belonged to the town, so all the people
pastured their cattle on this "common" land. The
woods around the town also belonged to the town. The
town meeting decided that each family might cut from
the common woodland as much wood as it needed.

So each little town attended to its own business,
divided up its lands, governed itself, and depended very
little on the outside world. All the people were English;
they did not welcome people from foreign countries.

Houses

The houses in New England were also very different
from the great houses of the South. They were small
and square. The first ones were built of logs, with clay
and sometimes little pieces of wood between to keep

out the cold winds. Later they were built of sawed boards; some were two stories high and others one story and an attic. The attic was reached by a ladder and was used for storing corn as well as for a bedroom.

In the earliest days there was no glass; the windows were made of oiled paper. Even after glass had been brought from England it was very dear, and the windows were therefore small. Nails were made of wood, and hinges were made of leather. Roofs at first were covered thick with dried grass. Chimneys were made of sticks covered with clay, but so many of them caught fire that a law was made that they must be built of stone.

The first story of the earliest houses was one great room, in which the family lived, ate, and slept. There was a big fireplace at one end. Later the outside door was put in the middle of the house and made to open into a hall that ran through the house. On each side of this hall was a room. The floors were of rough wood and were generally bare, for few of the colonists had carpets.

The houses were not painted either inside or outside, and were built so loosely that the wind blew in and made the family draw close round the fire.

The father of the family usually built the house himself in a month or six weeks. Perhaps the carpenter would come and help out for a few days; the father would pay for this service by helping the carpenter in turn to build other houses.

Since the buildings were made of wood and the fireplaces had to be kept roaring all winter, fires were

Miles Standish's house

frequent. Every family had to have a fire ladder and some leather buckets. When a fire broke out the whole town came running with their buckets and helped to put out the flames.

Furniture

Only the simplest pieces of furniture were thought necessary, and most of these were made in the town itself.

The family sat in the kitchen in straight armchairs or on wooden benches. The table was a long narrow board around which the benches were drawn up at mealtimes. The children had to eat in silence and leave the table as soon as they had finished. Sometimes they had to stand while eating. The great fireplace not only was used for cooking, but it also gave light and heat to the room. There were no stoves, no matches, no lamps. Candles were used, but not every night, because it took too much time to make them. They were made of melted fat into which wicks were dipped and the fat allowed to harden, and dipped again and hardened, until the candle was large enough. A huge chest completed the furnishing of the room.

The brass pots and kettles sometimes cost more than any other articles in the house; they were always kept bright and shining. Dishes and cups were of wood. Often two people ate from the same wooden bowl. There was only one fork in Massachusetts, — that belonged to Governor Winthrop, — and there were only a few silver spoons. Governor Bradford of Plymouth had owned thirteen silver spoons, which was thought to be a large number. Most of the spoons were made of wood or horn. There was no china, and no glassware except bottles.

The bedrooms were cold. No wonder the Puritans slept on one feather bed with another over them. Woolen coverings also were needed. Sometimes the sheets were warmed at bedtime by passing quickly between them a long-handled warming pan full of hot coals. Even in the bedrooms in which there were fireplaces, water froze before morning.

Food

The New England colonists usually had enough to eat, such as it was, but they must have become very tired of corn meal boiled in water or milk. They had it three times a day almost every day in the year. Often they had nothing else.

Corn was the chief food, because it grew fast and required little work. The colonists planted it in the fields which the Indians had left, or they killed the forest trees by burning and planted it among the dead trees without plowing the soil. When it was ripe it was carried to the mill, where the man who ground it received one sixth of the meal for the work of grinding.

If the meal was not boiled in water, it might be baked as johnnycake; or it might be sweetened with maple sugar and boiled tied up in a bag; or it might be boiled with a piece of beef or salt pork.

Ears of corn were hung up all over the house to dry; the boys' work during the long winter evenings was to shell the corn. When a man needed to pay a debt and had no money, he often paid it with corn.

There was no way to keep meat fresh except in the winter, when it could be frozen. So the farmers killed their pigs and cattle in the fall and had fresh meat all winter. The rest of the time they had to eat the meat salted or smoked; they also had salted or smoked fish. They obtained the salt by drying up great quantities of sea water.

At certain times during the year there were plenty of wild deer and turkeys, which the colonists hunted. In this way they added to their food supplies. Turkey must have tasted good after months of salt pork.

There were many oysters and other shellfish, but the colonists did not seem to care much for these.

During the first years no vegetables were to be had;

but as time went on, many gardens were planted, and the colonists had sweet corn and peas and beans. Potatoes were few. Tomatoes were never eaten; they were thought to be poison, but they were grown sometimes in flower gardens because they were pretty to look at. We may think that the Puritans fared well with so many kinds of vegetables, but I am sure we should not like to have our vegetables all boiled together in one pot.

As the years went by many fruit trees were planted. The fruit was dried or made into preserves and kept in great jars for winter use. In season the children picked many wild berries, and these furnished a welcome change in the heavy fare.

Each family made its own supply of maple sugar in the spring, and sometimes they had wild honey from "bee trees" in the forest.

Almost all the food for the colony was raised by each family itself on its own farm. The only foods brought from other countries were sugar and spices. For many years no tea was used; then ships began to bring tea from China. At first the colonists did not know how to prepare it; they boiled the leaves and ate them, throwing the liquid away! Coffee was not used until the time of the Revolutionary War. Milk was used, but cider was the favorite drink. Some families put up from ten to thirty barrels of cider for use during the winter. A great deal of rum was used, both for drinking and for trading with the Indians.

Clothing

The clothing of the Massachusetts colonists in the early days was very different from that of the people in the South or in the middle colonies. It was much plainer, and few bright colors could be seen. Blue, black, and gray were the colors most used, with sometimes red for caps.

Usually each colonist had three suits of clothes — a very plain suit of homespun cloth for every day, a better suit for market or for going to town, and a fine suit of English cloth for Sunday wear. The poor were not allowed to dress like the rich, and there were laws against anyone's wearing large sleeves or ribbons or ruffles. Wigs were worn, as in the South; gentlemen were not allowed to let their hair grow long.

The men wore linen shirts, but the rest of their clothes were of wool. Their breeches reached only to the knee and were of heavy cloth or leather, their high woolen stockings came up over the knee, their shoes were of heavy cowhide, and their hats were of beaver. Shoes and hats were both homemade. In summer most of the men and children went without shoes.

The ministers wore long black gowns on Sundays.

The women wore very full, plainly cut dresses of homespun in dark colors. There were laws against the use of gold or silver belts or hatbands. Lace might be worn if it was not too wide. The clothes of each family were made at home by the women. They did not fit very well, were made over many times, and were often turned and patched.

As the people of New England began to trade with the outside world they dressed a little more like the settlers in the South. They began to wear bright colors, silks and velvets, great shoe buckles, and powdered hair. By the time of the Revolution the New Englanders were dressing as beautifully as the people of Charleston.

How the New England People earned their Living

The people of New England had to work very hard. Every man had to do all kinds of work. He had to cut down trees, pick up the stones on his land, dig out the stumps, build fences, guard his crops against wild animals, build his house and barn, make roads, and fight the Indians.

Nine people out of every ten were farmers; and even those who were fishermen, traders, or ministers worked their own land too. All the farms were small; and instead of only one crop, such as the tobacco or rice of the South, each farmer planted many kinds of crops. Wheat, corn, and hay were raised and enough potatoes to sell to the West Indies.

Often only one man in a town owned a plow, and he plowed for all the neighbors. Men who had large families put all their children to work; so a large family was a great help. There were few servants of any kind, and these few were paid regular wages. The white servants, such as were found in the South, whose time had been sold for a number of years, were very few. There were not many slaves; they could not learn to do the many kinds of work needed on the small farms.

A second great business in New England was ship-building. The New England coast was thickly covered with trees, "oaks fifty to sixty feet long and clear from knots, being straight and well-grained." The trees that would make good masts for ships were marked by a broad arrow and were kept for the king's navy. Those along the river banks were cut down and floated to the villages on the seashore, where sawmills made them into boards.

As many as a hundred and fifty ships were built in one year and sold to Europe or the West Indies. They were small but very well made. The first was built when the town of Boston was only one year old. It was called *The Blessing of the Bay*.

After many years the king made a law that no goods should be brought to the colonies except in ships built in England or the colonies. The Puritans were pleased at this, for then the merchants wanted more New England ships than ever.

The third large business was fishing. As soon as Boston was settled its people began to catch fish. The fishermen of New England were among the best sailors in the world. They ventured far out from shore, and their most important fishing was for cod. The best of their catch they sent to the Mediterranean countries; the poorest they packed in barrels and sent to the West Indies as food for slaves.

Catching whales, or whaling, as it is called, is perhaps a kind of fishing; though whales, as you know, are not fishes, for they have warm blood and come to the top of the water to breathe. Some of the earliest settlers had found the dead bodies of whales cast up by the sea and had cut them up to use for oil. Afterwards they had gone out after them in ships, all up and down the coast, until in fifty years' time no whales were left in those waters. Then the whaling ships followed the great animals into the cold oceans of the north and south, on voyages that often lasted three years.

Small boats would put out from the ship when a whale was sighted, and when it came to the surface to breathe the men would throw spears into it. Sometimes the whale would overturn the small boat with its tail, and sometimes it would even attack the ship. When the sailors killed it they would cut it to pieces and carry the bones and the fat on board the ship. They tried out the fat into oil and stored this in barrels. When the deck was covered with barrels they sailed for home. The whale oil from a single voyage sometimes brought as much as a hundred thousand dollars.

Trade was the fourth great industry of New England. Some of the many ships from there sailed to India and China ; some took lumber, fish, and naval supplies to the Mediterranean countries and brought back wine. Some sold corn and salt pork to other colonies up and down the coast. Some took lumber to England and brought back linen and woolen goods and iron and nails. Some carried lumber, barrels, and other wooden articles, candles, soap, and fish to the West Indies and took for their pay great pieces of silver and gold Spanish money— "pieces of eight," as they were called. Few other coins were to be found in the colonies.

There was a three-cornered trade which made much money for the colonists. They would take rum to

Whaling in New England
Can you see the back of the whale?

Africa and there exchange it for slaves. Then they would take the slaves to the West Indies and trade them for sugar and molasses. Then they would come home and make more rum out of their molasses. Boston was the chief trade center.

We have now mentioned the chief ways in which the colonists earned their living, but we have not learned about their homemade goods. Each family raised its own sheep, cut the wool, combed and carded it, spun it into thread, and wove the thread into cloth. They would then dye the cloth and make it into coats, breeches, and dresses.

They also tanned skins, and during the long winter days made the leather into shoes for themselves or into harness for their horses. They did their own carpenter work and made their own furniture, hats, candles, and soap. They picked feathers from the geese for their feather beds. With their knives men whittled bowls, powderhorns, plates, and ax handles. Every head of a household had his own blacksmith's tools.

The farmers' wives baked, made wine and cider, dried fruit, made dyes from roots, berries, and bark, raised chickens, and made butter and cheese.

Since each farm bought very little from the outside world, trade was very different from what it was in the South, where only one crop was raised and everything else was imported.

Sunday in New England

In New England the church[1] was the most important place in the village.

At first the fort was used as a meetinghouse, but as soon as possible a church was built in the center of each town. It was a plain, bare building, not painted. It served also as town hall and courthouse. All kinds of notices about sales, meetings, and village happenings were nailed to the outside door.

The inside of the church, too, was bare and plain. The high stand for the minister was at one side; the people sat in square seats, with walls so high that one could hardly see over the top. When they stood up during

[1] The Congregational church.

Puritans going to church
From a painting by Boughton

the long prayers the seats were turned back and made a great noise. As in the South, everyone had a certain place to sit, the best seats being given to the most important persons.

There was no heat. Women and children carried footstoves in winter. The boys all sat together, and those who made a noise were punished after church in the presence of all the members.

The morning service began at nine o'clock. Hours before that time people began to gather from near and far, wives riding horseback behind their husbands. In summer the people fastened their horses to the hitching rail and sat in the churchyard until time for the meeting. In winter they went to the special "Sunday House," which had been built for the purpose, and warmed themselves at the fireplace. At nine o'clock a drum or a horn was sounded, and they formed in three rows and marched to church with the governor and the minister at the head.

The minister read the sermon from his notes. Sometimes it lasted an hour, but it often lasted two hours. Prayers were three quarters of an hour long. Time was told by the use of an hourglass (see border, top of page 290). It took one hour for sand to run out from one part into the other. When the hour was ended, the minister turned the hourglass upside down and went on. The doors were closed when the sermon began, and no one was allowed to go in or out. If anyone went to sleep an officer of the church would tap him with a long rod to wake him up. People carried notebooks to church and took notes on the sermon. Sometimes they stopped the minister and asked him questions.

The only church music was singing. The leader would read one line of a song, and all the people would sing it; then he would read the next line, and they would sing that, and so on. One song might take half an hour.

At noon all went home or to the Sunday House to eat dinner; then they returned for the afternoon service. When it was over, the father of each family would come to the front of the church and give as much money as he could.

During the rest of the day one was not allowed to work or play, but was to think good thoughts or to read the Bible. Sunday began at six o'clock on Saturday night and lasted until six o'clock on Sunday night. Between those hours no work was done, and there was no travel. The inns were closed, and people did not show themselves on the street except when going to or coming from church.

We now have some idea of what it means when we read that the church ruled the lives of the Puritans.

New England Schools and Schoolhouses

Schools were not so important as the church, but every Puritan had to be able to read the Bible, and so he must be taught to read.

Very small girls attended a school kept by a woman of the town in her own home. While this woman was sewing or baking or doing other housework she taught them to read. Little boys were often taught by the minister, who kept school in his own house on week days.

There were a few schools where reading, writing, numbers, religion, and a little spelling were taught. These were private schools, and the parents of the children who went to them had to pay for the teaching. Girls were not allowed to attend, so they seldom could write or figure well. Even the wife of Governor Bradford could not write her own name.

The schoolbooks were not very interesting. The book from which most of the children learned to read began with this story:

> In Adam's fall
> We sinned all.

Should you care much to read the rest of it?

We have already learned of the beginning of Harvard College. Only boys who were studying to become ministers went there. The ministers and a few of the rich men were the only well-educated people. Most homes had no books except the Bible, a songbook, and an almanac.

After a while several printing presses were set up, and Boston had the first weekly newspaper in English America, the *Boston News-Letter*. But it told more news about England than about the colonies.

There were few trained doctors and no lawyers.

Good Times among the Puritans

Though the Puritans were sober people, they also had their good times. They hunted and fished, went skating, and had parties, though the parties were usually connected with their work.

When a man was ready to build a house or a barn he would often call in all his neighbors to help. They would come and work all day, log-rolling, barn-raising, or house-raising, and in the evening they would play games together. They were not paid for their work, but received only food and drink for the day, and stayed for the party in the evening. Corn-husking bees were parties at which all worked at husking corn and then played games and had a good time. Apple bees were parties where women met to prepare apples for drying.

Training day was a great time. Once a year men from all the country round about met in the towns, gave their names to the captains, formed companies, and practiced drilling. If war should break out, every man would then be able to take his place quickly.

When Puritans were married the party lasted two or three days, and guests from out of town often stayed a week.

Dancing was not allowed, nor horse-racing, nor playing cards, nor smoking in public places. There was no theater. Thanksgiving was the great holiday of the year. Then the families gathered in the churches and afterwards feasted in their homes.

You must not think that they had no good times. Boys owned balls, marbles, and tops, and played tag, and girls had their dolls as they do today.

Punishment

The Puritans were very strict about obeying the laws. Stocks, pillory, and whipping posts were seen in every town and were often placed directly in front of the church. Fifteen different crimes were punished by death. For less serious crimes the punishment was to pay a fine or to be put in prison or to be sent out of the colony. For swearing, a man sometimes had a hole bored through his tongue with a hot iron. For scolding, a woman was made to sit in her doorway with a cloth bound round her mouth. For lying, people were put in the stocks. If a man was often drunk he had to wear the red letter D around his neck for a year. (What did the D stand for?)

We probably should not like to have lived among the Puritans; yet they were strong and earnest men and women — the strongest and most determined of all who had yet tried to make colonies in the New World.

Are you Ready?

Are you ready to take a test on the Puritans? Try yourself out on these questions:

1. Why did the Puritans prefer to live in towns?

2. How did each family get its land?

3. What was the "common"?

4. What was the chief industry in New England? What was the second industry? the third? the fourth?

5. In what ways did the church rule the lives of the Puritans?

Using New Words

You found the new words **stocks**, **pillory**, and **hourglass** used in the story. Make a sentence for each one, beginning

$$\text{The } \underline{\quad\quad\quad} \left\{ \begin{array}{l} \text{is a} \\ or \\ \text{are} \end{array} \right\}$$

The Puritans lived a very simple life.

They lived in towns rather than on plantations.

They manufactured most of their goods at home.

The church ruled their lives.

Have we heard of Catholics coming to any of the English colonies? Why might they also wish to come to America? Where do you suppose they might go? The story will tell you.

A HOME FOR CATHOLICS

We have now read of the English who came to Virginia to make a better living for themselves, and of the Pilgrims and Puritans who came to New England because they wished to attend their own churches. But Pilgrims and Puritans were not the only people who were badly treated in England because of their religion. The Catholics suffered even worse.

A Friend of the Catholics makes his Plans

A noble in England, Lord Baltimore, became interested in finding a region where Catholics might be as free as the Puritans were in New England. He was a man of wealth and good education, had traveled in Europe, and had been a member of the Virginia Company.

The Beginning of Maryland

If Lord Baltimore had told the king that he was trying to make a colony for Catholics, the king would surely have refused to give him land, even though he was Baltimore's friend. For the laws of England at that time said plainly that the Catholic Church was to be driven out of the kingdom. Baltimore therefore planned a colony in which all Christians were to be given freedom to attend whatever church they chose. His was to be the first colony to which any Christians of any church would be welcome. (Rhode Island was not founded until two years later.)

The king let him choose any part of Virginia that had not been given to others, and called the new land Maryland after his own wife, whose name was Mary. He gave to Lord Baltimore not only the land, but also the right to tax the colonists, to coin money, to make war, and to try cases at law in his own court. Laws made in Maryland did not need to be approved by the king, and England was not to tax the colony. These were greater powers than any English king had ever before given to any English subject. Lord Baltimore was called the *proprietor* of the colony. He chose land north of Virginia.

The only check on his powers was that his laws must be approved by the free men who lived in the colony. We shall expect, therefore, to find an assembly in Maryland like that in Virginia. But to show that the king was still ruler of the colony Lord Baltimore had to send him two Indian arrows every year and give him one fifth of the gold and silver that might be found. None was ever found.

Lord Baltimore died just before the colonists were ready to leave England, and his son, the second Lord Baltimore, carried out the father's wishes. The second Baltimore never even saw his land, for he had to stay in England to defend himself against his enemies at court. A younger brother went out in charge of the colony.

The First Colonists set Sail

At last all was ready, and the colonists set sail — twenty gentlemen with three hundred common people to do the work. There were women and children among them and two priests, one of whom wrote a very full account of what happened in the new colony.

Most of the gentlemen were Catholics, and the common people were Protestants. From the beginning there were more Protestants than Catholics, but there was very little quarreling.

They went to Maryland in two ships, the *Ark* and the *Dove*. Every man who paid for his passage was to be given one hundred acres of good land. But some could not pay for their passage and also buy the necessary supplies. They were given supplies. Each person was expected to have eight bushels of meal, a gallon of oil, sugar and spices, two hats, three shirts, four suits of clothes, three pairs of stockings, six pairs of shoes, and his own bedding, guns, tools, pots, and pans. On board ship he must also supply his own flour, fruit, butter, cheese, and chickens or other meat. Making a voyage in those days was not so easy and pleasant as it is today.

The voyage, by way of the West Indies, took three months. The colonists had a fine passage, ran races with other ships, and saw flying fish and many other interesting sights.

In the West Indies, where they stopped to buy seed corn, they were as much surprised to see the natives using hammocks as Columbus had been. They saw pineapples for the first time, and called them the "queen of all fruits"; they saw a bunch of bananas, which they said looked like "a hundred cucumbers together."

Setting sail again, they soon reached Virginia, where they bought more supplies. Then, sailing farther north, they entered a bay which the priest said was the most delightful water that he ever saw. He said the Potomac River, which emptied into it, "made the rivers of England seem but a little finger to it." Along the shores were beautiful trees with no underbrush. The soil was "as good ground as in all Europe." Even in winter the cold was not great. There were many kinds of fish, fruits, berries, and wild animals and birds. One bird was all black and gold, the colors of the Baltimore family; today we call it the Baltimore oriole.

The vessels stopped at an island which was too small for a settlement, but the colonists built a fort upon it. Farther on they stopped at a small Indian village to trade colored cloth, knives, and axes for supplies which the Indians had. The village was high on the bank, and the river furnished a good harbor for ships. This seemed to be a good place for a colony.

The Indians, who at first were afraid, came out after a while to the ship, which they thought was made of a single tree as their boats were. They wondered where such a huge tree could have grown.

They were planning to move away from this land soon and were therefore glad to sell it. This was fortunate for the colonists, for the fields were already cleared, crops planted, and houses built. Baltimore paid the Indians for their land, and they promised to stay long enough to teach the English how to live in the wilderness.

The Landing in Maryland

Why are the Indians present? (From a painting by Howard E. Smith)

Baltimore set up a great wooden cross and took possession of the place. He called the village St. Marys (find St. Marys on the map on page 315). First a storehouse was built, and then the English flag was brought from the ship. The largest wigwam was used as a church until a church could be built. The fort was already finished. The whole town was planned before any houses were built.

As the colonists had arrived in early spring, they had the whole summer in which to prepare for the hard times that winter in a new land always brought. They planted seeds of all kinds, and the Indians taught them to raise corn and tobacco. Indian women showed them how to make corn bread and hominy. From their English neighbors farther north they bought fish, and from those at the south they bought pigs and cattle.

Maryland had no "starving time" like Virginia's, no sickness like Plymouth's, and no Indian troubles like those of Massachusetts. From the beginning it grew rapidly. When the Indians moved out in the fall the colonists had not only enough to live on during the winter but also a whole shipload of corn to sell to New England in exchange for fish.

Maryland Grows

In six months Maryland was in better condition than Virginia had been at the end of six years. The winters were not cold. The location was better than that of Jamestown. The peace with the Indians was never

Maryland and Pennsylvania

broken. The soil was good, and all men were allowed
to attend whatever church they pleased.

The first year there was no trouble of any kind.
There was a good corn crop, and there was much tobacco. Along the rivers and the bay were scattered
plantations like those in Virginia. Travel by water was

easy.   The work was done by white servants, most of whom became free in four or five years.   Black slaves were not used until many years later.

During the first year the assembly met; all free men came to help the governor make the laws.   But in a very short time there were so many settlers that they could not all crowd into the assembly room.   Some of them, too, had to travel a very long way.   So they began to elect representatives, as the Virginia colonists had done.   (Find the limits of the colony of Maryland on the map on page 315.)

Maryland tries to give the New World Freedom of Religion

From the beginning of the colony Lord Baltimore had allowed all Christians to come in, whether Catholic or Protestant.   The reason was partly that the king would not have permitted him to make a colony for Catholics only, but also that Baltimore was a fair man.

So Catholics and Protestants lived side by side in peace for many years.   Because freedom of religion was allowed in Maryland and not in Virginia, many Protestants from Virginia came and settled in Baltimore's colony.   Soon there were many more Protestants than Catholics, but Baltimore treated all alike.

Then came the great revolution in England, a revolution by which the Protestants, or Puritans, came into power.   Lord Baltimore was afraid that if the Puritans should win power in Maryland too they would treat the Catholics cruelly.   He had the assembly make a law that all people who believed in Christ were to be allowed to follow their religion in peace. No one was allowed to call another hard names because of his religion. Thus Maryland was one of the first colonies to make a *law* about freedom of religion. There was nothing new about this law: it was what Maryland had been doing from the beginning. But Baltimore thought if the *custom* were written into a *law*, perhaps it would not be an easy matter for the Puritans to change it if ever they should come into power in Maryland.

Things turned out just as he feared they might. When the Puritans came into power in England they came into power in Maryland also. They drove Lord Baltimore out and did not waste much time in changing the Maryland law about freedom of religion. The Puritans took away the rights of the Catholics; they would not allow them to vote nor to hold office.

After a long time Lord Baltimore was given his colony back again, but trouble continued for many years. At last one of his grandchildren became a Protestant and was made governor. The old rules against Catholics were put in force once more.

Thus ended the attempt in Maryland to allow freedom of religion to all Christians. Rhode Island remained the only English colony in which freedom of religion was allowed. Baltimore's plan had failed.

Yet Maryland continued to grow. Its plantations produced wheat as well as tobacco; its trade in furs, meat, and tobacco made the planters rich. Farming was the most important industry.

To test the Class

After you have proved that you can answer all these questions, choose one to ask of the class:

1. Why did Lord Baltimore not dare to tell the king that his colony was to be for Catholics?

2. Why did he grant freedom of religion to all Christians?

3. Why did Maryland have an easy time the first year?

4. What law was made about religion? Why was it necessary?

A Choose-One Test

Make a list of the right words for each sentence below, and show your list to your teacher:

1. Lord Baltimore wanted to make a home for the

    Pilgrims   Puritans   Catholics

2. He made a home in

    Carolina   Maryland   Virginia

3. In the new colony he was the

    proprietor   patroon   prince

4. Maryland was settled by

    Lord Delaware   Lord Baltimore   Lord North

5. No man in the Maryland colony found that his religion was made the cause of his

    celebration   officeholding   persecution

Lord Baltimore founded Maryland as a home for persecuted Catholics.

He allowed all Christians to come and settle there.

Do you think "Friends" is a good name for a society? What kind of people must they have been to choose such a name for themselves? This story will tell you about them and about their colony in America.

THE SOCIETY OF FRIENDS IN THE NEW WORLD

We have now read of how the Pilgrims, the Puritans, and the Catholics found homes in America. In England there was still another group who suffered for their religion. They were the Society of Friends, sometimes called Quakers.

The Friends had no paid ministers and no rules. They believed that all men are equal; therefore they would use no titles and would not take off their hats as a sign of respect, even in the presence of the king. They called everyone by his first name. They thought it wrong to fight, even in a war to protect their homes. The "inner light"[1] would tell each man what was right if he would follow it. At their meetings they worshiped in silence, listening to the voice of God in their hearts.

The rulers in England did not know how to deal with people who would not fight in the army, nor swear in the law courts that they would tell the truth. Some were put in prison, and some were put behind iron bars and left where the cold winds and the rain would beat upon them. But nothing could make them change their simple ways of living.

[1] The conscience.

Penn's Interest in the New World

At this time there lived in England a young man named William Penn, the son of an admiral in the English navy. His father, the admiral, was rich and a friend of the king. But young Penn, instead of being interested in court life, attended the meetings of the Quakers and thought deeply about what they believed.

When Penn was about thirty years old he was one of a company of Quakers who bought land in New Jersey and sent out settlers. In this way he became interested in America as a place to colonize. He began to think that it might be easier for Quakers to practice their ways of living in a new land where no one could discourage them.

About this time Penn's father died, leaving his wealth to his son. The king owed the admiral a large amount of money, but he did not like to pay his debts, and young Penn was not sure of ever receiving the money. So he went to the king and asked for land in the New World instead.

The king was glad to please the son of his old friend and at the same time find an easy way of paying a heavy debt. He gave Penn a country north of Maryland, crossed by creeks and rivers, covered with tall trees and sweet flowers, and full of game and fish. To show that the king was still ruler of it, Penn had to agree to send back every year one fifth of all the gold and silver found and two beaver skins. The king had not yet given up hope of finding rich mines, though almost two hundred years had passed since Cabot sailed along this coast.

The Landing of William Penn

The king called the land Pennsylvania, which means "Penn's woods." Penn objected, saying that people would think he was vain, to give the land his own name. The king replied that the honor was for Admiral Penn and not for the son; so there was no more to be said.

Penn then had a paper printed, telling the kind of colonists he wanted: farmers, carpenters, weavers, shoemakers, and men who understood government. He said that in this new country "an example might be set to the nation," and he promised that at least the colonists would not be at the mercy of a governor who came out to make a great fortune for himself. The colony was to be "for the good of the people." (Find Pennsylvania on the map on page 315.)

Settling in Pennsylvania

About five hundred settlers were already in Pennsylvania, carrying on the fur trade with the Indians. Penn allowed these to stay. Then in 1682, a *half-century* after Maryland had been founded, he set out in his ship *Welcome* with about a hundred more and with a large sum of money given by rich Quakers.

When the ship arrived, the people who were already there gave Penn the key to the fort; also a piece of soil with a little tree on it and a cup of water to show that he was owner of the land and the water. He sailed on until he found a high place where two rivers came together and where there were two miles of water front where boats could land. There he laid out a city and called it Philadelphia, which means "Brotherly Love."

All the streets running one way were called First Street, Second Street, Third Street, and so on, and all the streets running the other way were given the names of trees, such as Pine Street, Chestnut Street, and so on. (Find Philadelphia on the map on page 315.)

There were so many colonists who wanted to settle there that they could not build houses fast enough. Some had to live for a time in caves along the river banks and in log huts. At the end of the first year three hundred and fifty-seven good houses had been built. Penn's own home was a square brick house with a large back porch where he received his guests. It was surrounded by a beautiful garden.

Many Germans came to Pennsylvania and built a city of their own at Germantown, where the first clocks were made in the colonies. Pennsylvania had a larger number of Germans than any other American colony.

Penn and the Indians

The people who came to Pennsylvania found the Indians friendly, because the Dutch who had lived there before Penn came had been fair to them. The Indians sold as much corn as they could spare to the newcomers. Penn made many treaties of friendship with them and many treaties for the purchase of lands. He paid the Indians for all the land that he took, as the Dutch and the Puritans had done.

The treaties were made with the chief of the tribe and his council. All the old men would sit in a circle, with the younger men back of them. First one would speak and then another, while all the rest listened. At last the Indians and the English would agree to "live in love as long as the sun gave light." The chief would warn his people to keep peace, and at the end of his speech they would all shout. A woman who said she once saw Penn make a treaty with the Indians, wrote that he sat on the ground as they did and ate roasted nuts with them. When they began to show how far they could hop and jump, he got up and jumped with them.

In his treaties Penn paid at different times a quantity of lead, bells, cloth, guns, kettles, combs, axes, shoes, and some beads and caps. In return the Indians each time gave up a certain amount of land — sometimes as far back from the river as a man could ride on horseback in two days, sometimes as far as a man could walk in two days. Sometimes the boundaries were marked out on trees by carving them with the letter *P*.

Penn treated the Indians fairly, and they kept peace with him; so Pennsylvania had very little Indian trouble.

Land Troubles

Penn's land was directly north of Maryland, and for many years the two colonies quarreled over their boundary. The trouble was that Penn's colony had no seacoast. He first tried to take from Lord Baltimore some of the land on the bay and later he tried to buy it. For three quarters of a century these men and their children after them fought over the matter.

At last two surveyors were sent from England to draw the boundary line between Pennsylvania and Maryland.

Their names were Mason and Dixon, so the line they drew was known as Mason and Dixon's line. It was marked by a row of stones with the arms of Penn on the northern side and those of Baltimore on the southern side. Years afterwards it became part of the line which divided free states from slave states.

Pennsylvania at last received its seacoast, through Penn's buying land, which he called "the lower counties," along Delaware Bay. What we today call the state of Delaware belonged to the Penn family almost up to the time of the Revolutionary War, and its history is much the same as that of Pennsylvania.

Growth of the Colony

Pennsylvania grew rapidly. In the first year twenty-three ships arrived bringing settlers. In three years there were seven thousand people; soon fifty little villages grew up outside Philadelphia.

There was very little sickness and no "starving time." Colonists could easily buy supplies from their neighbors, and in ten years they were selling food to the West Indies. Each man owned and worked his own land with the help of a few slaves, some free negroes, and many white servants.

All who believed in God were allowed to enter the colony, and it was free from such religious troubles as Maryland suffered. Its prisons were clean, and the prisoners were taught how to earn an honest living.

The government was made up of the governor, a council to help him, and an assembly elected by the people. One third of the men in the council were chosen one year, one third the next, and the last third the following year. Thus most of the men in the council were always used to the business and knew how to proceed.

Helping Yourself

I. Answering these questions will help you to complete the sentences following them:

1. What were some of the beliefs of the Quakers?

2. How did the English king happen to give William Penn land in the New World?

3. What trouble did Pennsylvania have with Maryland?

4. How did Penn secure some seacoast for his colony?

5. What was one good plan used by the government of Pennsylvania?

II. Complete these sentences with words you found used in the story. Show your list of words to the teacher.

1. The man who founded Pennsylvania was _____ _____.

2. The _____ believed that the "inner light" would tell them what was right.

3. The chief city of Pennsylvania was _____.

4. _____ was the colony founded by Quakers.

5. Pennsylvania was founded a _____ _____ after Maryland.

6. Penn made a _____ with the Indians.

William Penn founded Pennsylvania.

The Quakers got along well with the Indians.

Unit Four

How England came to own Most of North America

━━

TITLES OF STORIES

Unit Four

*How England came to own Most
of North America*

In one of our stories we learned that a single ship took
back to the Old World eight thousand skins of animals.
Who do you suppose caught so many wild animals? This
story tells how the fur trade in America was carried on.

THE FRENCH FUR–TRADERS

We have followed the story of the English while they
were settling along the coast and beginning to spread
into the back country. Now let us see what the French
were doing.

We left them at the time that Champlain had founded
the city of Quebec and had explored two of the Great
Lakes. All New France was then busy with the fur
trade.

The Great Fair

Every year, early in the spring, line after line of Indian canoes might be seen gathering in Green Bay or at Mackinac. In each canoe there were from two to ten Indians, and each boat was piled high with packs of furs, the result of the winter's hunting.

After hundreds of canoes had gathered, a group of white men dressed in the same way as the Indians gave the signal to start. These men were called *woodrangers* because they spent their lives in the forests, meeting Indians who had furs to sell and guiding them to the French markets. They were usually young men of good families, with some experience as soldiers. They had come to New France as officers but, soon tiring of this life, were drawn to the wilderness. At the end of the seventeenth century there were said to be as many as eight hundred woodrangers in New France.

When these woodrangers gave the signal all the canoes pushed away from the shores at once, and the thousand-mile journey began. By the middle of the summer they reached the cities along the St. Lawrence River. All the townspeople turned out to see the fleet, for the fur trade was the life of the settlement. The Indians set up their skin tents outside the town and unpacked their pots and kettles. They meant to stay for some time.

A great council was held at which white men and red men smoked the pipe of peace and promised to be friends during the coming year. The governor was present, splendid in his velvet coat and his red hat with a long feather.

The great fair

Can you see what the Indians have for exchange?

Then came the trading. Along the shore the French merchants put up their shops and showed the latest goods from Paris: guns, ammunition, many-colored blankets, knives, axes, kettles, needles, and all kinds of trinkets — rings, chains, bells, combs, and tin looking-glasses. What the Indians liked best of all was liquor. Often merchants who were not honest waited until the Indians were drunk, and then paid them such a small price for furs that they received almost nothing for a whole year's work.

The fair lasted two weeks. The price paid for furs depended on two things. The first was the fashion in

France. If men in France were wearing large beaver hats, much fur was needed, and the price rose. If hats were small, not so much fur was needed, and the price fell.

The second thing on which the price depended was the feeling of the Iroquois (you remember that the Indian friends of the French were the Algonquins and their enemies were the Iroquois). If the two were at peace, the Iroquois allowed the Algonquins to carry their furs to the French without troubling them. If they were at war, the Iroquois would stop the canoes, take away the furs, and kill as many Algonquins as they could. Then the price of furs in the French cities would be very high.

Beaver was the fur that the white people liked best. The skins were soft and warm and wore very well. Furs taken from animals killed during the winter were the finest. In a good year the Indians would sell a hundred thousand of them.

Skins of otter, mink, bear, and deer were also sold, but did not bring such high prices. Buffalo hides could also be had, but they weighed so much that it did not pay the Indians to carry them very far.

When all the furs had been sold, the woodrangers gathered a stock of goods with which to do a little trading on their own account; and they took charge of the presents from the king to the western chiefs. Then they would give a signal, and all the canoes would begin the journey back to Mackinac and Green Bay.

There the parties would break up, each Indian returning to his own home to show his new gun or his blanket or, perhaps, some new tin looking-glasses.

Fur-Trading Posts

The French claims extended from the mouth of the Mississippi to the mouth of the St. Lawrence, and the traders traveled from Mexico to the northern ocean.

The fur-bearing animals in the east had been quickly killed off, and it became necessary to travel ever farther and farther away to find tribes that had furs to sell.

Because the woodrangers had to travel so far, they could not go back to Quebec whenever they ran out of supplies. Therefore *trading posts* were built at the mouths of rivers, at portages around the Great Lakes, and at meeting places on the important Indian trails.

These posts centered around log forts which were held by a few soldiers, in order to make the Indians respect the force of the French; but the soldiers did not often have to fight. Around each fort thirty or forty woodrangers had their homes, with their gardens and cattle. One of the houses served as a storehouse for the goods that the woodrangers needed in their journeys: coffee, sugar, salt, and flour, guns and ammunition, and liquor. These goods were not to be sold to the Indians, but were for the traders' own use. At a little distance from the fort was the Indian village.

The business of the woodrangers was to travel to all parts of the country, especially those parts never before visited by white men, and to persuade the Indians to bring their furs to the French posts. They were not allowed to trade for furs on their own account. The king kept that trade for himself, or gave it to a company of men or sometimes to a city.

From the way they lived it is easy to see that the woodrangers themselves were poor; they gained little from the fur trade. Nor did the boatmen who managed the boats, nor the clerks in the trading posts, nor the Indians become wealthy. But the merchants in the cities of New France and the governor and high officers made great sums of money. Often, after a few years in the wilderness, they went back to France very rich.

How the Plan Worked

At first this plan of carrying on the fur trade worked as the king had intended. Then, for several reasons, it began to work badly.

The chief reason was that when officers and traders saw how much money could be made in furs they began to buy on their own account. The trading posts began to sell the coffee, tobacco, gunpowder, and liquor which the king had sent as supplies for the woodrangers. The Indians would bring in their loads of furs, and the traders would sell them the king's goods. For days there would be constant drinking and fighting. The Indians would sit on blankets before a bonfire and gamble away their furs, their horses and guns, and even their clothing. So long as their money lasted they remained; but sometimes a trapper would spend in a few hours all that he had earned in a year of hard work.

When spring came and it was time to lead the canoes to the cities of the St. Lawrence, not so many Indians gathered, for they had already sold their furs at the trading posts.

A second reason was that the woodrangers themselves began to learn from the Indians how to trap for furs. They used canoes which would float in six inches of water, or they took two or three horses, riding one and using the others as pack horses, until they reached lands very far away. Arriving at the trapping grounds early in the spring, they would go up and down all the rivers looking for signs to tell them where to place their traps. They did not dare to fire guns for fear of driving the animals away.

After placing their traps, the trappers had to visit them about twice a week to see if they had caught anything. On their return to camp they had to skin the animals, stretch the skins over branches of trees, and clean the under sides. When well dried, the skins would be packed with all the others in the canoes or on the horses.

So we may see that not only were the officers buying furs for themselves, but the woodrangers were trapping for themselves instead of trying to find Indians with skins to sell.

A third reason why the king's plan did not work well was that the Indians were finding out that they could buy their goods from the English at a cheaper price than from the French. The English made such goods as the Indians wanted — rum, blankets, iron goods, and coarse woolens — and the French did not.

If an Indian wanted a gun, he could buy one from the English at Albany for two beaver skins, but at Montreal he had to give five beaver skins to the French. He could buy eight pounds of powder from the English for one beaver skin; the French charged four skins. The English charged one beaver skin for a blanket and the French charged two. For other things there was about the same difference.

It was surprising that the French were able to get any trade at all. They did so for nearly a century by keeping the English away from the fur-bearing regions. Then too the French treated the Indians kindly, learned their language, and lived among them. Some spent their lives with the Indians, were made members of Indian tribes, married Indian women, and went on the warpath with their red brothers. In this way they knew of rivers and trails that no Englishman had seen, and they found it easy to explore the heart of the continent.

The English, on the other hand, paid higher prices, but they always showed plainly that they thought themselves better than the Indians, and did not try to please them.

Effect of the Fur Trade

The fur trade had a bad effect on the Indians. Some of the worst of the white people came to live among them and taught them evil ways. They taught the Indians to drink liquor. Some of the French thought that the sale of liquor ought not to be allowed, but they knew that the Indians would get it from the English if not from them. So the sale went on. Liquor did even more harm to the savages than it did to the white men.

The fur trade also had a bad effect on the French in spite of the fact that they made so much money from it. It took the strong young men out into the wilderness instead of keeping them in the settlements to cut down trees, make homes, and build towns. Even the officers did not try very hard to settle their new lands, because if they did the fur-bearing animals would leave, and furs were more important to them than anything else.

France, then, had less chance of holding the continent than the English, because the English took up land, cleared it, and made farms, while the French roamed over vast stretches, few of them settling down and building homes.

Testing your Neighbor

Ask these questions of your neighbor.

1. Who were the woodrangers?

2. Where was the fair held?

3. What classes of people made money from the fur trade? What classes did not?

4. For what three reasons did the king's plan fail?

5. Why could the English sell their goods more cheaply than the French?

6. What effect did the fur trade have on the Indians? on the French?

Sentences to Finish

Tell the class how you would finish these sentences.

1. Mackinac was the place from which

2. Fur-traders were people who

3. Trading posts were places where

4. Woodrangers were men who spent their time in

The woodrangers explored far into the forests.
They made many of the Indians friendly to the French.

What is a missionary? Do American churches today send missionaries to foreign lands? Who do you suppose the "Black Gowns" were? This story will tell about the hard times the "Black Gowns" had among the Indians.

THE COMING OF THE "BLACK GOWNS"

Columbus had said that one of his reasons for seeking the Indies was that he wanted to make Christians of the Indians. The French king had the same wish.

Soon after Champlain became governor four missionaries had come to Canada from France. They worked for years in the wilderness among the Indians, but there were not enough of them to do much good.

Then Jesuit missionaries were asked to undertake the work in New France. Their society already had mission stations in Asia, Africa, and South America. They had had long experience among savage peoples, and they were brave and willing to give up their lives, if necessary, to spread their religion. They wore long black gowns, with chains of beads hanging from their waists, so the Indians called them the "Black Gowns."

The Jesuits in America

In America the Jesuits endured great hardships, living like the Indians and eating the Indians' food, traveling through the wilderness on snowshoes in the middle of winter, and paddling their canoes to the farthest reaches of the foaming rivers. For months at a time

The "Black Gowns" and their church

Why do you suppose the Indian is bringing his children to the priest?

they did not see any other white men; and they were
likely at any time to be captured and put to death, by
their savage enemies.

They had to live in bark houses so full of cracks that
the cold winds blew through and almost froze them.
The smoke from the fire hurt their eyes so badly that
they could not read their prayer books. Indian dogs
stole their food. The Indians made fun of them, and the
medicine men tried to drive them away. Still they kept
on, and a few more came on almost every ship.

The Huron Mission

The missionaries decided that they could teach their
religion most successfully to those Indians who had settled down in one place. Among the great Indian families
in New France was one which had built permanent villages and had planted fields of corn. These were the
Hurons. Among the Hurons, then, the Jesuits planned
to begin their work.

The next spring, when the fur fleet came down to
Montreal, Champlain called a great council. He told
the Hurons that the fathers in the black gowns wanted
to settle among them and teach them a better way of living. The Indians were not eager to learn, but they did
not like to refuse what Champlain had asked. So they
said that the Jesuits might come with them when they
returned up the Ottawa River to the shores of Lake
Huron.

It was a hard journey. For weeks the missionaries
had to paddle their canoes every day from sunrise to

sunset. Their food was only a little corn. Thirty-five times they had to carry the canoes around falls. Fifty times they had to get out and push them along the shore through the icy waters of rapids.

When at last they reached the Huron country the Hurons helped them to make a large wigwam. They divided it into three rooms, one of which was to be used for a church. The church bell was hung on a tree close by.

Before the missionaries could begin to teach the Christian religion they had to learn the Indian language. That was a hard thing to do. They found an Indian who had once been taken to France, and they paid him to be their teacher. Whenever he lost interest in the lesson they would give him tobacco. Did you ever before hear of pupils giving the teacher a present in order to make him pay attention? But at last they learned enough to give the church services in the Indian language.

But even after they had learned the language they found it hard to make the Indians believe the Christian religion. There were no such words in their language as *faith* or *salvation*. They could not understand about heaven. Some did not want to go to heaven because they could not carry on war there; some did not want to go anywhere where the Iroquois would be allowed.

They came to the missionaries asking for charms of all kinds to help to kill their enemies or to kill the animals which ate their corn. They thought the Christians' God ought to help them in war or to give them anything they wanted. And he did not. They were surprised and angry when the missionaries told them that they should not carry on their dances, games, and feasts as their fathers had before them.

When the Jesuits found it so hard to get the grown people to listen to them, they decided to begin with the children. Every day a missionary would stand at the wigwam door ringing a little bell. When a crowd of children had gathered he would ask them to come in, would teach them a prayer and a song, and before they went away would give them something to eat so that they would want to come again the next day. A few grown people came to the services, but not many.

The Indians were interested in the mission clock, which they called "the Captain." When the clock struck they wanted to know what "he" was saying. Writing seemed to them very wonderful; they thought the white men could make paper talk.

One missionary always had to stay in the house, for the Indians would steal whatever they could lay their hands on. The other missionaries spent their days going about from wigwam to wigwam teaching the people and taking care of the sick. Each missionary had about four hundred families to visit.

When winter came on a terrible disease broke out. The Indians decided that the Jesuits had brought it, and began to treat them very badly. They would not give them guides for their journeys, and sometimes they shut the doors of their wigwams in their faces. After several years of hard work the Jesuits had persuaded only sixty Hurons to become Christians. The rest could not understand the new faith.

Every year the Jesuits had to write a full account of their work to send back to France. The reports were printed in books, and it is from those books that we have learned the story of the Jesuit missions.

The Suffering of the Jesuits

But the Hurons were not nearly so cruel to the Jesuits as the Iroquois were. When the missionaries fell into the hands of the Iroquois they were made to suffer dreadfully.

Once when the Huron mission had used up all its supplies, a Jesuit with several companions was sent to Quebec for help. On the way the whole party was captured by Iroquois. The missionary might have escaped, but he would not leave his friends.

The Iroquois made him suffer terribly, burning his body with hot irons and pulling out his finger nails. Then, while he was still suffering, they made him carry heavy loads. His only food was wild berries. From village to village the savages traveled, showing their captive.

Whenever he found a chance, even while on the march, he taught the Christian religion to his fellow prisoners and received them into the church.

So time passed. At last the Iroquois visited their friends, the Dutch, at Albany, and the Dutch helped the missionary to escape to France, where he was treated with the highest honor. The queen herself kissed the stumps of his poor fingers, which the Iroquois had hurt.

But even in the court his one wish was to return to the mission field. He went back to Canada and again went out to the very savages who had treated him so cruelly. When he came to them they invited him to a feast. As he was about to enter the wigwam in which it was to be held, someone from behind struck him dead.

Result of the Jesuits' Work

When the Huron missions failed, the hope of making Christians of the Indians failed also. A few missionaries still worked among the tribes farther west, but they were not very successful. After a few years Canada was no longer a mission field. Every village had its church; but the work of the missionaries was now mainly for the French, not for the Indians.

The chief results of the work of the Jesuits among the Indians were (1) exploration of the Indian country; (2) the bringing about of a friendly feeling between the Algonquin Indians and the French, which helped to establish a rich fur trade; (3) a change in the manners of the Indians (they became a little less fierce and no longer ate their enemies or treated them so cruelly); (4) when wars against the white people were being planned, the Jesuits usually heard of them and often sent warnings to the French colonists.

The evil done by some of the traders was in many cases greater than the good done by the Jesuits. The missionaries had sent back to Quebec asking the officers not to allow the sale of liquor to the Indians, but the traders kept on selling it. The Jesuits taught that

Christians must not lie nor steal, and that they must live pure lives. The traders did everything that the fathers preached against. Thus the work of the missions was hindered.

If the Jesuits had succeeded in their plans, all the Indians in New France would have been settled in permanent homes, on farms, and in villages. They failed, but they had worked hard and had made a brave struggle.

To Test your Reading

Test how well you remember what you read, by answering these questions:

1. Why were the Hurons chosen for the first mission?

2. Why was it difficult to learn the Indian language?

3. Name four results of the Jesuits' work.

4. In what way did the traders harm the work of the Jesuits?

A Missing-Name Test

In the story you will find the names needed to fill these blanks:

1. The _____ missionaries came to make Christians of the Indians.

2. The settlements they built were called _____.

The missionaries went into the interior with the fur-traders.

They explored for France.

Do you know what river the Indians called the "great water"? Your teacher will show it to you on the map. Should you like to go with two Frenchmen on an exploring trip to find it?

REACHING THE "GREAT WATER"

During the years that fur-traders and missionaries had been exploring the interior, France had not given up her hope of finding a passage to the South Sea. Champlain had heard of a great water to the west, but his duties as governor had not allowed him to seek it.

Who should be sent out to Explore?

The new governor who followed Champlain began at once to look about for someone to send out in search of the "great water." He soon heard of a young fur-trader and explorer who knew the life of the wilderness as well as any Indian. He had already come very near to this great river and had explored as far as the shores of Lake Superior. His name was Joliet. Joliet was made the leader of the new expedition.

Every important exploring party had a missionary with it, so the governor asked the Jesuits to choose one of their number for this purpose. They chose one who had been a friend of Joliet's in Quebec. He had worked in three missions on the Far-Western frontier, and had heard from the Indians of this great river which, he

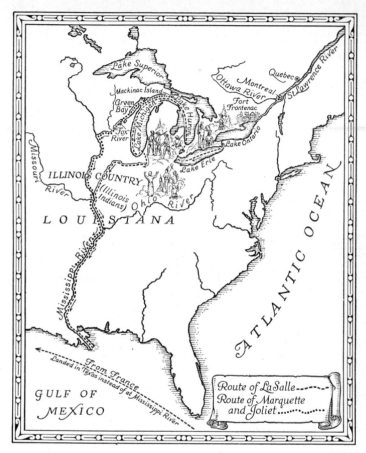

The French on the Mississippi

believed, flowed into the Pacific. The Indians had promised to make him a canoe and to guide him there. He had learned six Indian languages in preparation for his journey and had begged for years to be sent *to found a mission* among the Illinois Indians. This missionary was called Father Marquette.   Joliet and Father Marquette, then, were chosen to undertake the work. Father Marquette was already at Mackinac.

From Quebec to Green Bay

Joliet set out from Quebec alone.   (Find Quebec on the map on page 347.)   It was late in the fall before he finished the journey of a thousand miles to Mackinac, where he found a fort and a log mission with a bark roof.   Marquette was at work there.   Joliet gave Marquette the letters from the governor telling him to join the expedition, and eagerly the two friends began to make ready.   (Find Mackinac on the map on page 347.)

This took all winter.   They gathered supplies of Indian corn and smoked meat.   They sent far and wide for Indians, fur-traders, and missionaries who knew about the river ; and all together drew up a map of the country, with the names of the lakes, rivers, and Indian tribes that the explorers would pass.   They had two bark canoes with five Frenchmen to help in paddling them.

As soon as spring came they set out, all seven taking turns kneeling in the boats and paddling.   Their first stop was among the wild-rice Indians.   Marquette had preached among them, so they treated him kindly ; but at the same time they tried to persuade the party not to go any farther.   They told of the savage Indians, of the danger of the great river itself, and of the terrible heat that they should find as they went farther south.

Indians do not make exploring trips; they go to strange countries only to hunt, to mine, to trade, or to make war. So the wild-rice Indians could not understand why Joliet and Marquette were risking their lives for nothing at all. But they could not stop the explorers.

From Green Bay to the Mississippi

Leaving Green Bay, the little exploring party paddled up the beautiful Fox River. (Find Green Bay and the Fox River on the map on page 347.) At first traveling was very easy, but later they found many rocks and rapids. They had plenty of food, for wild ducks came to feed on the rice along the river banks.

The explorers soon reached the lands of the Fire Nation, which was as far as Frenchmen had gone up to that time. These Indians gave them two guides, without whose help they could never have found their way. They had to cross many swamps and lakes to find the river which emptied into the Mississippi. After carrying their canoes about two and a half miles, they reached its banks, offered up a prayer, and floated down with the current. (Find their route on the map on page 347.) The place across which they carried their canoes was called a *portage*.

They passed through a beautiful country full of deer and buffalo. Then, just one month after leaving Mackinac, their canoes drifted out upon the "great water." The first part of their search had ended.

Down the Mississippi

The Mississippi was almost a mile wide at the place where the explorers entered it, but soon it became narrower and deeper. There were no longer forests and hills; all the land about them was flat. Huge fish struck against the canoes and nearly turned them over. Every day the boatmen killed game; sometimes they saw herds of buffalo numbering as many as four hundred. Every night the party landed to make a fire and cook their food, but they slept in their canoes in the middle of the river, and one of them always kept guard.

For a long time the only signs of life were wild beasts and birds, but one day they found the prints of men's feet in the sand. The footprints led them to an Indian village. The chiefs came forth to meet the strangers, bringing the pipe of peace, while the rest of the people watched in silence. These were the Illinois Indians.

A great feast was held, with many speeches and many gifts. The feast consisted of corn meal, of fish, from which the chief removed the bones for his guests, and of a roast dog — which the Frenchmen did not eat.

The chief told the explorers that their visit made the sky more beautiful, the river more clear, and even the tobacco stronger. But he warned them of bad Indians and evil spirits farther south, and begged them to remain among the Illinois. They said that they must go on, however; and the next morning six hundred Indians came down to the river to say good-by to them.

Marquette and Joliet reach the Mississippi
Which one is Marquette? Which is Joliet?

Farther down the river, Marquette and Joliet passed high rocks with such frightful figures painted on them in red, green, and black that even the bravest of the Indians would not look at them. Then they reached the point where the Missouri River empties into the Mississippi, its water thick with mud. Here the force of the current was so great that their canoes were nearly overturned. Trees floating swiftly down the river made the danger still greater. Marquette hoped that some day he would be able to explore the Missouri also, but he could not do it then. (On the map on page 347 find the point where the Missouri empties into the Mississippi.)

A little later the expedition arrived at the point where the Ohio River empties into the Mississippi. The mosquitoes were so troublesome that the men had to roll themselves up in the sails to protect themselves. When they tried to land they were attacked by a tribe of fierce Indians. (On the map on page 347 find where the Ohio River empties into the Mississippi.)

By this time the travelers were beginning to see that the Mississippi must empty into the Gulf of Mexico rather than into the Pacific Ocean. Indeed, the natives told them that it was only ten days' journey to the mouth of the river. They were also told that the savages at the mouth of the river would certainly capture them if the Spaniards who lived there did not, so they decided to return. It was a great disappointment to them to find that the "great water" was not, after all, a passage to China.

The Return

Paddling up the river against the current was very hard work and took a long time. The party was at last quite worn out by the constant toil, by poor food and lack of rest, and by being out in all kinds of weather.

When they reached the land of the Illinois the Indians guided them by a short cut from the Mississippi to Lake Michigan. (On the map on page 347 find the land of the Illinois Indians.)

Marquette had suffered even more than the others, and was eager to reach the mission. Yet he stopped three days to preach among the Indians, and promised that some day he would return to found a mission.

When the explorers arrived at the mission on Green Bay, Marquette and Joliet separated. In their journey of four months they had traveled twenty-five hundred miles.

Joliet set out for Quebec by way of the Ottawa River. When he was almost at the end of his journey he tried to shoot the rapids, and his canoe was overturned. All his records, papers, and maps were lost. His young Indian guide was drowned.

Joliet reported his journey to the governor of Canada and drew from memory a map of the Mississippi region. He asked to be sent back to found a fur-trading post, but the governor did not think it best; so nothing came of it. Years afterwards he was given a little island in the Gulf of St. Lawrence as a reward for his discoveries.

Marquette was ill for more than a year, but he did not forget his promise to the Illinois Indians. As soon as he could, he returned to them. Cold weather quickly made him ill again, and all winter he had to lie in a poor hut, depending on the friendly Indians for his food.

In the spring he used the last of his failing strength to begin the mission for the Illinois Indians. A building was put up and a few services were held. Then it became clear to all of them that he had only a short time to live. He set out for Mackinac, but died on the way, and was buried on the shore of Lake Michigan. Later some friendly Indians took up his body and buried it in his mission.

Marquette's records and reports of the Mississippi region were saved; they carried the news of the expedition to far-away France. He himself did not know that he had become famous; he only knew that he had been able to do God's work among the savages.

Results of the Journey

The most important result of the journey of Marquette and Joliet was that New France learned that it was possible to travel up the St. Lawrence, across the Great Lakes, and down the Mississippi. Soon forts were built along the route, and the fur trade was established. So it may be said that Marquette and Joliet were the real discoverers of the Mississippi. De Soto, who had seen the river a century and a quarter earlier, had only explored the lower part of it, and his discovery had not been followed by settlements.

Something to Explain

1. What preparations did Joliet and Marquette make for their journey?

2. What did they see at the mouth of the Missouri?

3. Why did they turn back?

4. What was the most important result of their journey?

5. Why are they called the real discoverers of the Mississippi?

Choices to Make

1. The missionary who tried to find the passageway to the Far East was

    Champlain   Marquette   Joliet

2. The fur-trader who was in charge of the expedition was

    Marquette   Joliet   Cartier

3. Marquette and Joliet paddled their canoes from Mackinac across the end of

Lake Michigan   **Lake Erie**   **Lake Ontario**

4. A place where boats are carried from one stream to another is a

mission station   gap   portage

5. When the Indians wanted to show that they were friendly they offered the

pipe of peace   scalping knife   tomahawk

Marquette and Joliet were looking for a passage to the Indies.

They were the first to discover the middle part of the Mississippi River.

What do we mean when we say that a person has a strong will? Then what would an "iron will" be? Do you think you would like a man with an iron will? You can answer the last question better after you have read the story.

THE MAN WITH THE IRON WILL

We are not surprised when we hear of Indians enduring all kinds of suffering; we know that they were trained to it from their youth up. But when we hear of a wealthy Frenchman, born of a proud old family, well educated, and used to ease and riches, who of his own free will walked overland through melting snow for a thousand miles, with only dried corn to eat and with no covering at night to protect him from the icy winds, we are forced to wonder and to admire.

Such a man was La Salle. He belonged to a proud and wealthy French family, who expected that he would become a soldier. Instead of that, he studied to become a Jesuit missionary; but after some years he decided that he did not want to live a life in which he would always have to obey others. An older brother had already gone out to Canada; and La Salle, while still a young man, followed him.

When he arrived in Canada he was given land along the St. Lawrence River. There he built a house and some barns and at once began to study the Indian languages and the Indian ways of living. Why? No one

356

knew. He had few friends, this silent, stern man whose iron will drove him in spite of every difficulty to do whatever he set out to do.

The Iroquois Indians often visited his farm, for by that time they had made peace with the French. They told him of a great river to the south which we today call the Ohio. La Salle decided to explore it, with the old hope of finding a passage to China. He sold his lands, and with the money that he got for them he bought four canoes and supplies for fourteen men for a long journey.

Joining some missionaries who had already started, the party set out. The Iroquois served as guides. At night the explorers slept on the ground or under shelters made of bark. In the Indian villages through which they passed, feasts were given to them. Slowly they followed along the southern shore of Lake Ontario and in time reached Lake Erie.

There they met Joliet coming home. His report of the Indians of the upper Great Lakes made the missionaries change their minds and decide to go north instead of south.

La Salle, however, had set out to find the Ohio River; and he determined to go on, no matter if his companions did desert him. Just what he did in the next two years is not clear, but it seems that he succeeded in reaching the Ohio and exploring it as far as Kentucky. His men left him, and he made his way back alone.

Building Forts

During the following years La Salle's plans took shape: he would leave Canada, which was shut in by ice more than half the year, and would lead his followers into the heart of the country along the Mississippi River. The rich fur trade of the interior would pay all the expense of such a movement.

As a first step in carrying out his plans, he intended to build forts along the Great Lakes and thus secure for France the fur trade, which the English were every year winning away from them. It was necessary to get the governor's permission to do this, but the governor believed in La Salle and liked his plan.

Together the governor and La Salle set out on a great expedition to the Iroquois lands to build the first fort. They had one hundred and twenty canoes and two large flatboats, which they painted red and blue to please the natives. The boats struggled through the many rapids of the St. Lawrence, past the Thousand Islands, to Lake Ontario. There a great body of Iroquois had met, whose chiefs made another treaty of peace with the governor. La Salle gave guns to the men and raisins to the women and children, so that they might feel more friendly toward the French. (On the map on page 347 find the French fort on Lake Ontario.)

The soldiers began work on the fort. Some cut down trees, some dug ditches, and some rolled the logs into place. Soon the fort was finished, and La Salle was put in command. Then he made a voyage to France with letters from the governor asking the king to let

La Salle, alone, have the fur trade at the new fort. The king was pleased, granted the request, and made La Salle a noble. No one else was to trade in furs on Lake Ontario. Another piece of good fortune which La Salle met on this journey was worth more to him than his fort or his fur trade. A young Italian joined him, and for years was his most faithful helper.

When they returned to Canada they set about making a village round the fort. The log building was torn down and a stone fort put up in its place, ground was cleared, and French and Indian villages were begun. Cattle, pigs, and chickens were bought. Nine cannon were mounted on the walls, and some vessels were built on the shores of the lake.

A mission was started. All this work La Salle did at his own expense. When all his money had been used, he borrowed from his friends.

Then the fur-traders whose trade he had taken away began to plot against him. They charged him with trading outside the region which had been granted to him (which was true), and they even tried to poison him.

La Salle made a second voyage to France. Indeed, during these years he was constantly traveling from the Ohio to Mackinac, to Quebec, and back to France, in spite of the hard work at the forts and the dangers of the journeys. On this second voyage his purpose was to ask the king for permission to build still more forts in order to hold the Mississippi region against the English. He showed that it would be possible to send furs down the Mississippi and across the ocean to France without passing through Canada. The king granted him permission to build as many forts as he liked, but gave him no money and would not allow colonies to be founded along the Mississippi.

Returning, La Salle built a second fort on the shore of Lake Erie, though it was so late in the fall that he had to use hot water to make the frozen earth soft enough to work. The Indians were not pleased when they saw another fort rising, but they did not prevent it. Indeed, La Salle always had less trouble with the Indians than with his own people.

The ship which was bringing supplies for the new fort was wrecked, and the supplies were lost. At this the people from whom La Salle had borrowed money seized all his goods. Probably most men would have given up the plan in the face of so many difficulties, but not La Salle.

The First Attempt to reach the Mississippi

La Salle decided that a sailing ship should be built on the shores of Lake Erie, for a canoe could not hold enough trading goods and furs to set up trading posts in the West. Shipbuilders went to work cutting down trees, and La Salle traveled on foot two hundred and fifty miles to get supplies for his vessel. The last two days of his journey he was entirely without food.

By August the ship was finished, the first sailing vessel on the Great Lakes. It was called the *Griffin*. The Indians had intended to burn it, but did not have a chance to do so, and it set sail.

La Salle building the _Griffin_

Why did La Salle want so large a ship? (From a painting by
Stanley M. Arthurs)

The *Griffin* passed Detroit, and reached Mackinac just six years after Marquette and Joliet had set out on their journey. The Indians wondered greatly at the "floating fort," as they called it. La Salle learned at Mackinac that the traders whom he had sent on ahead in canoes had used up all his trading goods and had left him no furs. So he went on to Green Bay, where he found furs and took on a rich load of them.

Then he sent the *Griffin* back to the settlements with furs to pay his debts, but no one ever heard of it again. Perhaps it went down in a storm.

Knowing nothing of what had happened to his vessel, La Salle paddled down Lake Michigan through heavy weather, dragging his canoes on shore every night. At the mouth of a river in Michigan he built a fort and waited for the *Griffin* to return with supplies and goods for trading. As we know, it had already been lost. After waiting for some time in vain, he traveled overland to the country of the Illinois, where Marquette had begun his mission. (Find the Illinois country on the map on page 347.) The weather was getting so cold that his men had to build fires inside the wigwams to keep warm, and once they were almost burned to death. In Illinois they built another fort, the French name of which means "Heartbreak." Many times La Salle must have felt that his heart was breaking because of his disappointments. Most of his men deserted because of the hardships that they had to suffer, and again someone tried to poison him.

It was clear that without supplies no more forts could be built and no trade begun, so La Salle set out to go on foot all the long way to his fort on Lake Ontario. He left most of his men at Fort Heartbreak, ordering one party under his Italian helper to build a ship and be ready to sail down the Mississippi when he should return, and the other party to explore its upper waters.

A few men went with him on his journey through the deep snow. Trees and bushes tore their faces cruelly, and they were soon so covered with blood that they hardly knew each other. Each man carried his own blanket, pot, ax, gun, powder, and lead. For days they marched through melting snow sometimes waist-deep. Their clothes froze hard on their bodies. It was the hardest journey ever undertaken by Frenchmen in America. At last, after great suffering, they reached the fort on Lake Erie. There La Salle learned that the *Griffin* had been sunk and that another vessel coming from France with supplies had also been lost.

Meanwhile his Italian helper back in the Illinois country had succeeded in building a fort on top of a high rock, but most of his men had deserted, the Iroquois had attacked him, and he had barely escaped with his life. With great difficulty he managed to reach Green Bay, for he had not even a compass, and his canoe had broken into pieces under him.

The Second Attempt

At this, one would think, La Salle must surely give up. The number of his enemies grew greater and greater. He was deeper in debt than ever, and would have to begin all over again.

But he had no thought of giving up.   In some way he succeeded in borrowing more money.   Again he set out for the Illinois country, but found no one there, for his Italian helper had been obliged to escape, and all the forts had been destroyed.   La Salle searched as far as the Mississippi, walking in front of his men to break a path for them through the snow.   Then word was brought to him that the Italian was at Mackinac. Back to Mackinac he went ; and then the two friends returned sadly to Lake Ontario.   The seventeenth century was nearing its end, and the French had taken no advantage of the claim to the Mississippi which had been given them by the journey of Marquette and Joliet.

Down the Mississippi

No sooner had La Salle returned to his fort than he set out once more over the route he had followed so many times to failure.   At the end of Lake Michigan his men made sleds to carry their goods across the Illinois portage.   They gave up the idea of building a ship and decided to use only canoes in their exploration of the great river.

The journey began well.   The party entered the Mississippi and soon passed the mouth of the Missouri, which they thought more like "clear mud" than river water.   Every day they stopped to fish and hunt. Then they passed the mouth of the Ohio.   Every day grew warmer. At last they reached the three mouths of the Mississippi. (Find La Salle's route on the map on page 347.)

At one of these mouths they took possession of the river, and of all the land drained by it, for the king of France. On the shore of the open sea they set up a cross and a wooden post with the king's arms, and buried in the mud a lead plate with the names of those who had made the discovery. La Salle named the country Louisiana in honor of King Louis.

He had had no trouble with the Indians, but his food was almost gone. The country was full of sickness. La Salle lay ill forty days with a fever, and even four months afterwards he was so weak that he could hardly write a letter.

The return journey up the river was made slowly. The travelers enjoyed the beautiful country. They saw many kinds of trees for shipbuilding and learned that three or four crops of corn could be grown each year.

The expedition reached the Illinois country without having lost a man. They had met with success; but they had no furs, and the cost of the journey had been very great. Iroquois Indians were about to attack the Illinois, and the governor of Canada would send La Salle no help.

The brave explorer hurried back to Quebec and found that there was a new governor. The new governor hated La Salle and took the command of all the forts away from him.

There was nothing for La Salle to do but to return to France and lay his case before the king. He did so, and to his surprise found the king ready to listen to him. He had asked once before for permission to build a colony at the mouth of the Mississippi and had been refused.   But this time France and Spain were at war, and it would be a great advantage for the king to have a French colony on the Gulf so near to the rich mines of Mexico.   Whoever held the mouth of the Mississippi could control the continent.   La Salle was given permission to found colonies in Louisiana and was appointed its governor.

The Expedition to the Gulf

With four ships and nearly four hundred men, La Salle set sail for the Gulf of Mexico.   It seemed as if his evil fortunes were now ended and as if his great plan of holding the heart of the continent for France was about to succeed.

The expedition went by way of the West Indies, where they secured cattle for the colony.   The heat and the bad water made La Salle very ill again, and they had to stay in the islands for weeks.   At last they started on, but one of the ships did not appear with the others. It had been taken by the Spaniards.   Many tools and supplies were on board.   La Salle knew that the loss of these was a deathblow to the colony.

The other three ships sailed slowly on, trying to find their way without charts or maps, for the Spaniards had never allowed their sailing charts to fall into the hands of other nations.   They went far past the mouths of the Mississippi, and at last two of them stopped in a bay in Texas.   (Find their route on the map on page 347.)

One ship was wrecked.   The supplies ran out and the colonists had to land.   Some of them were captured by the Indians. The captain of the largest vessel thought he had stayed as long as he could, and so returned to France; and the little colony was left to itself. Sickness broke out among them; five or six died every day. They had no tools, and the grain that they planted would not grow. They lived in tents, made clothing from sails, and suffered from bad water and snake bites. Disappointment made La Salle more silent and strict than ever.

After much suffering twenty men set out on foot to find the Mississippi. They crossed rivers on logs, cut their way through the cane with axes, and fought constantly with the Indians. When only eight men were left they returned to the colony, bringing with them five horses that they had succeeded in buying from the Indians. La Salle then set out with a small party and the five horses to try again to find the Mississippi. After many days of hard travel and great suffering, some of his own men killed La Salle. They stripped off his clothes and threw his body into the bushes.

The colony on the seashore was soon destroyed by Indians, and the men who had killed La Salle quarreled among themselves. Most of them were killed also. Only a few of his friends succeeded in making their way to Quebec with the story of what had happened.

Thus La Salle died, thinking that his life was a failure. But it was he who gave the whole vast Louisiana country to the French.

Getting Ready

You cannot do the exercises below unless you know the story well.   Test your knowledge by these questions:

1. Did La Salle reach the Ohio?

2. Where did he build his first fort?

3. Why did he decide to build a sailing vessel?

4. Why could the ships from France not find the mouth of the Mississippi?

5. Was La Salle's work a failure?

Something to Do

You may make sentences of your own, using the following words.   Read your sentences to the class.

Name of Person

1. La Salle

Names of Places

2. Mouth of the Mississippi River

3. Great Lakes

4. Louisiana

Date

5. Near the end of the seventeenth century

Word

6. The *Griffin*

La Salle went down the Mississippi River to its mouth and claimed the land for France.

He built some forts along the river.

He wanted to found a colony at the mouth of the Mississippi, but failed.

What are pioneers? Do you like stories about pioneers and about being captured by Indians? This is that kind of story.

THE ENGLISH MAKE THEIR FIRST MOVE
TO THE WEST

While the French were making their explorations to the north, the west, and down the Mississippi River, the English colonies along the east coast were steadily growing. By the middle of the eighteenth century (about 1750) all the thirteen English colonies had been settled. Along the coast, and up those rivers on which boats could travel, the best land had already been taken. There were still many miles of wilderness in which not a single house could be seen, but either the soil was not good or else there was no way of sending the products of such regions to market in the coast cities. Yet great numbers of people continued to arrive from Europe. Where could they find free land which was also good land?

Interest in the Land beyond the Mountains

Men's thoughts began to turn for the first time to the vast regions away from the seashore. What kind of land lay hidden there? All sorts of stories were told about it. Some described huge mountains covered with trees; others reported great rivers with rich soil along their banks; still others said that the land was a flat plain with no trees but with tall grass; and a few told tales of lakes as large as seas.

Were these stories true? The only persons, except the French, who had traveled far from the coast were a few hunters, some fur-traders, and a small number of cattle-men. Even they had gone only a little way, some of them not even reaching the mountain tops. The governor of Virginia had once gathered together a band of his friends to go exploring westward. They had reached the summit of the mountains but had not gone beyond. (Find the Appalachian Mountains on the map on page 375.)

Those who were most eager to learn about free land were (1) farmers' younger sons who had no land of their own, (2) white servants who had served their time and were free to work for themselves, (3) men who were no longer satisfied in their own villages or counties, and (4) foreigners who continued to pour in from Europe.

Many Germans came because of the wars which were fast laying waste their own country. They arrived in Pennsylvania, traveled as far west as the mountains, and then spread out in all directions. Others who came were the Scotch-Irish; they were not very well received by the settlers already in the colonies, and were sent far out on the frontier. Some of them followed the valleys between the mountains as far as North Carolina. From this group came the family of Andrew Jackson.

Not all these pioneers were farmers; some wanted to go beyond the mountains into the interior because of the rich fur trade with the Indians. They could exchange guns, powder and lead, knives, kettles, blankets, axes, and liquor for skins and furs.

Building the new home in the West

What tools does the man have to work with? (From a painting by
Stanley M. Arthurs)

Routes to the West

How could the country beyond the Appalachians be reached? To climb straight up one mountain, down its other side, up the next, and so on was such hard work that no one even tried to do it.

Part of the way were paths, or trails, which the feet of animals had beaten out. Such paths usually lay along the tops of the mountains, where there were few trees and where the wind in winter blew the snow away. The Indians had followed these tracks for years in bringing furs to the settlements.

Another way was to go up the rivers as far as boats could be used. If we look at a map of the settlements in the middle of the eighteenth century we shall see that they lie closely along the coast and that they reach up, like long fingers, along the rivers into the interior.

George Washington knew more about the interior than any other important man of his time. He had explored much of this land on foot. He knew that sometime people would go up the rivers as far as their beginnings; that they would then carry their goods over to the beginnings of rivers that ran down the other side of the mountains, and thus travel from the Atlantic to the Ohio River, the Mississippi, and the Great Lakes. They could send back their farm products to the coast by the same route, and the coast towns could send them the things they were not able to make for themselves — guns, powder and lead, axes, sugar, coffee, and tea. In this way trade could be set up between different parts of the country.

Daniel Boone, One of the Greatest Pioneers

Daniel Boone was one who did more, perhaps, than any other man of his time to make such trade possible. At least he is better known than the others who went out into the West.

Boone was three years younger than Washington. He was born in a log house in the middle of a Pennsylvania clearing. His father had to do the work of all frontier farmers: cutting down trees with his ax, burning the brush, pulling out the stumps and setting them up side by side to serve as a fence round his fields. Boone and his six brothers helped to plow and plant and take care of the horses. They had to search for their cattle in the woods and bring them home every night. They picked nuts and berries for food. As soon as they were old enough, they learned to hunt. Daniel had a little hut of his own where he used to live by himself when hunting. His gun was more than five feet long and weighed eleven pounds. Should you like to carry it?

The mother took care of the house, made all the clothing for the family, and prepared all the food, even to drying meat for winter.

The family were very near to the Indian country and saw many Indians who came to the settlement to trade. Most of the stories they heard were of wars and of settlers protecting themselves against the savages.

When Daniel was about fifteen years old the family moved to North Carolina. They had to cross wild sections of Maryland and Virginia; thus Daniel had his first taste of travel. In North Carolina he spent his time for some years hunting and farming. Then he married and moved farther back toward the mountains.

Exploring the Land beyond the Mountains

Settlements soon began to spring up. It became necessary to use fences to mark off each man's fields. At night one could hear the barking of his neighbor's dogs. Town life began, and with it came quarrels. Boone was not happy.

Stories of the land beyond the mountains interested him. The Indians described it as a "dark and bloody ground," a land of death. No tribe lived there, but all used it as a battle ground. One day there appeared at Boone's log house a man who had seen the land while on a hunting trip. Daniel listened eagerly to his tales and decided that the time had come for him to go there and see for himself. (Find Kentucky on the map on page 375.)

It would not be wise to move until he knew more about the country, so Boone and four of his neighbors set out on foot, hoping to get furs enough to pay their expenses. Their clothing was of deerskin. In a leather belt round the waist were carried a small ax and a knife. Over the left shoulder hung a bag filled with bullets. They took with them little food, expecting to live by hunting, fishing, and finding wild fruits.

They set out in the rain, and for a while had to dry themselves every night by the heat of the camp fire. For five weeks they climbed mountains and at last

Routes into the interior

stood upon the top of the range, from which they could see down on the other side. When they reached the lowlands beyond the mountains, they found more game than they had ever dreamed of: turkeys, deer, bear, and buffalo — sometimes hundreds of them together in one place.

For months they wandered about, exploring and gathering a great stock of furs. They had met no trouble, for no Indians lived in the land. But at the end of eight months a party of warriors passed that way, and one day Boone and his companion were captured while hunting. The Indians hurried away with them, guarding them closely and watching every move. But the white men did not try to escape. Instead they seemed to like the new life very well.

After a week the Indians no longer guarded them so closely. Then one night when all were sleeping soundly after a feast of roast buffalo, the two white men rose silently, crept over and got their guns, and escaped. They went back to their camp, but their two other companions and all the furs had disappeared. Boone never heard of them again.

Boone and his friend could not return to the settlement without furs, for they were in debt. So they began trapping again. Within a month they met two men in the woods. One was a younger brother of Boone's, who had come out to search for him. It was only by good fortune that he managed to find Boone's camp in that great wilderness.

All four men stayed in the wilderness during the winter. In the spring Boone's brother returned to North

Carolina with the furs, but Daniel explored still farther. So little powder and so few bullets were left that he could use them only in hunting for food; to get furs he had to use traps. He kept traveling, changing his camp often for fear that the Indians would find him.

Boone's brother made two more trips to and from the settlements before Boone was ready to go back. He had been away from home two years.

The Attempt at Settlement

Back in North Carolina, Boone talked to his friends and neighbors for two years more, trying to persuade them to go to Kentucky to settle; but settling in an Indian country is a much more dangerous thing than exploring it. He led several parties over the mountains, and they marked off farms for themselves by cutting the bark on the sides of the trees, but they were a little afraid to make homes there.

It was only three years before the Revolution began that Boone, his brother, and some of their neighbors at last decided to make the attempt. Forty men set out bravely, with the horses, cattle, seeds, and tools that were needed to begin a settlement. They followed the route that Boone had chosen earlier, going up one of the North Carolina rivers, passing through a great gap in the mountains, and then following a river that flowed down the other side into Kentucky. (Find the great gap in the mountains on the map on page 375.)

On the way, even before they reached the gap, they were attacked by a party of Indians, and one of Boone's sons was killed. Everyone was surprised, for the Indians did not often make attacks on the eastern side of the mountains. They stopped until they could find out the cause of the trouble, and they soon learned that a great Indian war was about to begin.

The governor of Virginia asked Boone's help. He had sent surveyors to Kentucky to measure off the land, for Virginia claimed all of it. Now he asked Boone to go and warn the surveyors of their danger, and Boone did so.

He was just in time, for the great Indian chief Cornstalk had sent his men on the warpath. All the frontier settlers gathered in the nearest forts and did not dare to go out, even to work their fields. Boone was made a captain and was given the duty of defending these forts while the army went out and fought the Indians.

In the war which followed, Cornstalk's men were defeated. They had to ask for peace. The governor of Virginia made them give up all claim to the lands south of the Ohio River. Thus a great danger was removed, and the settlement of Kentucky was made easier.

Boone's Settlement

After the war Boone started out again with thirty men. This time they cut a road called the Wilderness Road, following buffalo paths, Boone's own earlier trails, and an Indian road called the Warrior Path. It was only a trail for pack horses. At each mile they cut the bark from the trees to show where the track lay. (Find the Wilderness Road on the map on page 375.)

An attack by Indians
Can you see the pack horses?

In ten weeks' time they had reached the Kentucky River, from which they pushed on to a place that Boone had chosen on his first journey. There they built houses and began a stockade. But hunting was much more interesting than building, and as they felt quite safe from the Indians the men were very slow with the work. They were soon hastened by an attack by Indians who did not belong to Cornstalk's tribe and who had not made peace with the white men. After this they set to work in earnest, and the fort was soon completed.

Several others came out and joined the settlement, and soon there were eighty settlers. Some were directed to hunt, some to act as guards, some to cut down trees, and some to plant corn. The stockade contained thirty houses built around a circle. Their backs made part of the stockade wall. In the stockade there were several square towers from which the settlers could shoot down on an enemy. Some of the men had farms outside and lived on them, but they came into the stockade when there was danger.

Boone then went back to Carolina to bring out his family, for there were yet no women in Kentucky. A number of other families joined him, and all set out together for their new homes, with their cattle, horses, dogs, food supplies, seeds, plants, and tools. They moved slowly across the country, the older boys driving the cattle, and the little children sitting among the bedclothes on the horses' backs. The journey was hard, and all were glad when it was over.

When they reached the end of their journey they at once planted fruit trees and began working on their farms.

Adventures in the Wilderness

One Sunday, seven months after the families from Carolina had begun life in their new homes, Boone's daughter and two other girls were out paddling in a canoe. They ran upon a sand bar in the river, and while they were trying to get off they were suddenly seized by five Indians and were hurried away.

Hours went by before they were missed at the settlement. Then the empty canoe was found, and the marks on the bank showed what had happened.

A party of settlers headed by Boone set out at once to follow the Indians. The girls had left as plain a trail as they dared by dragging their feet, breaking branches, and dropping leaves when the Indians were not looking. The men followed this trail and soon came in sight of the Indians' camp. They had to be very careful, for if they were seen the Indians would probably kill the girls at once and run away.

Boone and his men crept nearer and nearer; then all fired at once. The Indians ran off into the woods as fast as they could go, and did not even have time to pick up their knives before they went. So the girls were saved.

Later in the year the settlement ran out of salt. There was no way to get more except by boiling down the water from the salt springs near by. Boone undertook the task. Five hundred gallons of water made only one bushel of salt, so the work was very slow. One day while Boone was at work he was suddenly surrounded by Indians and captured again.

The Indians felt proud of this, for they considered Boone the greatest of all Englishmen. They journeyed from village to village, showing their prize, even to far-away Detroit. On returning to the Ohio they made Boone a member of their tribe and gave him an Indian name.

Again he did not show that he wanted to escape. After a while they began to send him out hunting, carefully counting the bullets that they gave him each time. He soon found that if he came close enough he could kill game with only half a bullet, so he began cutting the bullets in two and saving the other half of them for the time when he might be able to escape. Thus four months went by.

The Indians north of the Ohio then began to plan a great attack on the Kentucky settlement. Five hundred men were gathered, and the supplies were ready. Boone knew that he must warn the settlers or they would be killed. So the next time he was sent hunting he took all the little store of bullets that he had been saving and set out for Kentucky.

The Indians were very angry when he did not return. They followed him, and it took all his skill to keep out of their way. For five days he did not dare to stop for sleep or rest or to cook food. On the banks of the Ohio he found a leaky old canoe in which he crossed the river. After that it was easy to reach the settlement.

Defending the Settlement

Boone's family had all returned to Carolina, thinking that he was dead. He could not follow them, for he had to help to get the fort ready for the attack. It came soon and lasted nine days. During all that time the men in the fort had to be constantly at the walls, getting a few minutes' sleep whenever the firing stopped. The Indians knew that the water supply in the fort was almost gone, so they shot burning arrows upon the roof and built fires against the stockade. It seemed as if the fort could hold out no longer, when a sudden rainstorm came and saved it.

Then the Indians began to dig a tunnel by means of which they might come up inside the fort. They drew so near that the sound of their digging could be heard plainly through the earth. Again the pioneers almost gave up hope, when another rain made the earth so soft that the tunnel caved in. Quite discouraged, the Indians then gave up the siege.

Boone joined his family in Carolina, and for a time lived in peace. But a longing for the wilderness came upon him again, and he returned with some more of his neighbors. One of these men was the grandfather of Abraham Lincoln.

By this time laws had been made about taking up land. The laws were hard to understand, and many of the pioneers did not do as they were directed. They did not think that anyone would question their right to the land they had worked so hard to win. Daniel Boone was one of these. Most of the settlers lost their land, but the assembly of Virginia voted to give Boone a thousand acres because he had served them so well. He was not able to hold even this.

Boone's Last Years

Very angry, and feeling that his services had not been valued, he went still farther into the wilderness, this time into the land held by the Spaniards. The Spanish governor heard of his coming and gave him a thousand acres of land even before he arrived.

The years in this new country were happy. Boone spent much time in trapping and hunting, for at seventy years of age he was still a wonderful shot. He even made a journey to the far-away Yellowstone River.

Then the United States bought this territory, and again Boone's right to his land was questioned. The United States Congress voted that the land which the Spanish governor had given to him was his and that no one might take it away from him. This did not help him much, for he was then a very old man, but at least it showed that his work had been appreciated.

At the age of eighty-six he died, firmly believing that God had chosen him for the work of opening up the wilderness.

Effect of Frontier Life

By 1750 the country from Maine to Georgia had been settled as far back from the coast as the mountains. Growth beyond the mountains was very slow. Daniel Boone's settlement was not made until the time of the Revolution. The people along the coast were mainly English, but in the back country there were many foreigners.

The pioneers were poor, they lived hard lives, they did their own work, and they had few servants or slaves. Every man could own land, so why should one work for another? There were few who worked for wages. All were equal.

Since they had to fight against the French and Spanish settlers and the Indians, they had learned to depend upon themselves. They did not ask help from others.

Thus the qualities we are used to thinking of as qualities of *all Americans* are those that were kept for us by the pioneers and handed down from father to son.

A Memory Test

1. Why did people wish to go into the interior?
2. By what two ways could they travel into the interior?
3. What is a gap through mountains?
4. What was the Wilderness Road?
5. How far back had settlements been made by 1750?
6. Why were all men equal in the backwoods?

A Matching Game

In the right-hand column are descriptions of the names given in the left-hand column. On a sheet of paper copy the words in the *right-hand column* and put the figure 1 before those that describe Daniel Boone (No. 1 in the left-hand column); and so on.

1. Daniel Boone	part of a country far from the sea
2. Kentucky	the highland that kept the early settlers near the coast
3. Appalachian Mountains	the earliest explorers or settlers in a country
4. eighteenth century	the time during which the states were colonies of Great Britain
5. colonial period	the " dark and bloody ground "
6. pioneers	all the years beginning with 1700 and up to 1800
7. interior	the man who made a settlement in Kentucky

Some colonists went far away from the sea because they wanted cheap land.

They had a hard time going over the mountains.

Why did both the English and the French build forts?
Do you suppose the reason was that war between these
nations might be coming soon? Let us find out.

FORT AGAINST FORT

The French were greatly concerned when they heard
from their woodrangers and from friendly Indians that
the English were spreading from Virginia, Pennsylvania,
and New York out into the West. One of their officers
wrote that Canada would be threatened "if the English were once settled at the heads of these Western
rivers."

A company was formed by English settlers in Virginia to settle the lands along the Ohio River. This
was known as the Ohio Company. Soon after it was
formed, a party of French surveyors was sent out to
examine and measure the land along the Ohio River
and to drive the English traders away. It took them
forty-four days to travel from Canada to the river,
but at last they reached it, turned their canoes down-
stream, and floated easily with the current.

Every time that they passed the mouth of a smaller
river which flowed into the Ohio, they stopped and
shouted in a loud voice that this river and all the land
drained by it belonged to France. Then they took out
of the first canoe a lead plate about a foot long and seven
inches wide, on one side of which was writing that
claimed all the surrounding land for France. Very

386

carefully they buried the lead plate in the earth along the river bank, and to a tree close by they nailed a sheet of tin having on it the arms of France. Six times they went through this form of taking possession of the land.

In almost all the Indian villages they found English traders — sometimes as many as five or six in one place. They drove these traders out and sent warning letters to the colonies from which they had come. They also told the Indians not to receive English traders, but the Indians answered that they needed English goods and they needed blacksmiths. The French had no blacksmiths to send them.

The surveyors returned to Canada with the news that the English had already entered the Ohio valley and that without doubt greater numbers would come soon.

The Line of French Forts

The French had two routes for reaching the interior — one by way of the St. Lawrence River and the Great Lakes, and the other by way of the Gulf of Mexico and the Mississippi River. To protect the fur trade along these routes from wandering Englishmen, they built a long line of forts from the St. Lawrence to the Gulf of Mexico: one at Quebec, one at Montreal, two south of Montreal, one on Lake Champlain, two on Lake Ontario, three on the upper Great Lakes, two on the lower Great Lakes, five in the upper Illinois country, three in the middle Mississippi region, and three in the lower Mississippi region. (Can you find these forts on the map on page 375?)

An English fort

Can you find the stockade? the blockhouses? Why have the trees
been cut down?

The English settlements were quite surrounded by
these forts. France claimed that the only part of the
New World which belonged to England was the narrow strip between the Appalachian Mountains and the
Atlantic Ocean.

The English Forts

On the other hand, the English colonies claimed the
land from "sea to sea"; that is, from the Atlantic to the
Pacific. They did not need to build so many forts as
the French had, because their settlements were closer together and because the mountains at their back protected
them better than many blockhouses could have done.
But they built several forts in the Hudson Bay region,

two on Lake Champlain, three in northern and western New York, and one in Maryland. (Can you find the English forts on the map on page 375?) The forts in western New York were reached by going up the Hudson River, up the Mohawk River, and then across to the Great Lakes.

The English also had a great advantage over the French because they were friends of the Iroquois. Sometimes they went with the Iroquois into French territory to trade, even though it was against the law of New France. One trading party went as far away as Mackinac and did a good business there, because they could sell goods for much less than the French.

Thus in some ways the French had the advantage, and in some ways the English.

The Forks of the Ohio

At the beginning of the eighteenth century the French did not intend to capture the English forts, nor did the English care to capture the French forts. But there was one region which they both wanted. The Ohio, — the "Beautiful River," as the French called it, — was the great highway into the interior. Whoever controlled it could control the trade of that vast country.

France had begun to see that her forts on the Mississippi and those on the St. Lawrence were too far apart. They should be connected by another line of forts, and that line should follow the Ohio River. And we know that the English had already formed the Ohio Company in order to get possession of the same region.

Both nations began to make plans for holding the land along this important river. On the map on page 433 you will see that two smaller rivers come together and form this larger one, the Ohio. The place where they join was called the Forks of the Ohio; it was the most important point on the river. Both English and French, then, turned their attention to "the Forks."

As soon as the party of surveyors returned to Canada after burying their lead plates, France sent men to build this connecting line of forts. They built one fort on Lake Erie, and another on a little river south of it, to protect the portage to the Ohio. (Find these two forts on the map on page 433.) A wagonroad was cut between the two. Then they captured an English trading post far up toward Lake Erie. The governor of Canada asked the king to send him ten thousand French farmers to settle the region; but the king was not greatly interested in this plan, and made no answer.

The governor would have sent men on to the Ohio at once, but there were not enough supplies, and winter was coming on. So they settled down in their forts south of Lake Erie. It is not hard to understand that this movement of the French toward the Ohio would cause trouble between the two nations.

Serving as Judge

I. First be sure that you can answer all these questions yourself. Then call on someone in the class to answer each one. You will have to decide whether or not the answers are right.

1. What two things was the French surveying party to do?

2. How did they take possession of the land?

3. Why did the English not have to build so many forts as the French?

4. Why did both nations want the Forks of the Ohio?

5. How did the French prepare to seize the Forks?

II. Call on someone to use in a sentence each of the words in the following list. You must decide whether or not the words are used correctly.

Name of Place	*Words*
1. Mohawk River	**3.** lead plates
2. Forks of the Ohio	**4.** blockhouses

The French people came down from Lake Erie to the Ohio River.

The English people went up the Hudson River, up the Mohawk River, and then to the Lakes.

Both sides built forts so that they might hold their lands.

Why is February 22 a holiday in the United States? Who was the "promising young Englishman" mentioned in the title of this story?

A PROMISING YOUNG ENGLISHMAN

We must now leave our story of the coming struggle between the French and the English long enough to learn about a young Englishman who was to play an important part in it. At the beginning of the struggle he was nineteen years old, over six feet tall, very strong, brown-haired and blue-eyed, and one of the best woodsmen in Virginia. His name was George Washington.

Washington's Family

It is interesting to know something about the family of a man whom we greatly admire. Many years before our story begins the Washingtons had come from England, where they had been farmers. Many Americans traveling in England today visit the old family home of the Washingtons there.

Two brothers of this family came out to settle in Virginia and took up large estates, which they left to their children and their children's children. The share which came to George Washington's father was five thousand acres. He was an important man in Virginia, a representative in the assembly. He owned iron mines and carried some of the iron to England in a vessel that he commanded himself.

392

He died, however, before George was twelve years old, and the boy was left to the care of his mother. She must have been a capable woman, for she was able to manage her family of five children and her large farms without help.

Washington's Youth

George Washington was born in the same year that the colony of Georgia was planned. His father died soon afterwards, so George was not sent to England as his older brothers had been. He was sent to a private school in Virginia, but the schoolmaster was not a very learned man. George received only a fair common-school education in reading, writing, arithmetic, and surveying. His handwriting was very regular and beautiful. His copy books may be seen today. They were very carefully kept. Some pages were full of such rules as: "Speak not when you should hold your peace." "Think before you speak." "Do not try to find out other people's concerns." "Do not drum with your fingers or feet when people are speaking." During all Washington's later life he kept his papers in the same careful way. His drawings of farms and his plans of battles later showed the same regard for order. He liked to *master* the things he had to do.

When he was only thirteen years old he liked to study the kinds of written work needed in business, such as notes and bills. You may think it strange that a boy should be interested in such matters, but his older brothers were business men, and George spent much of his time with them. Arithmetic was his favorite study.

Much that he learned was from his life out of doors rather than from books. He loved sports, especially riding and hunting. It was said that he could throw a stone farther than anyone else in Virginia, and that he sometimes formed the other schoolboys into companies and drilled them.

Some stories of his early life which are commonly told are not true stories. There is no reason to believe that he cut down his father's cherry tree with his hatchet, that he killed his mother's horse in trying to break it, or that he "couldn't tell a lie." Such stories are likely to grow up about the childhood of great men.

When George was fourteen years old he wanted to go to sea; but his uncle wrote a long letter against the plan, and his mother decided that he should stay in Virginia. He remained in school until he was sixteen, and by that time he had learned all that the master could teach him. He never went to college, but he believed strongly in the importance of college-training.

Learning by Living

At sixteen George left school. In those days a boy was considered almost a man at sixteen. After leaving school he went to live with his oldest brother, who had served in the war against Spain. This brother had a large estate which he had named "Mount Vernon."

George lived an outdoor life at Mount Vernon and was much in the company of older men. His brother, who was the chief manager of the Ohio Company, saw that trouble with France was coming. There was much talk of battles. Two old soldiers were brought to the plantation to teach the art of war and the use of the sword. George learned both.

One of his brother's best friends was a nobleman from England, a man past middle life, who had been trained in the best colleges of Europe. He was much interested in young George Washington and taught him the manners and the ideals of honor that were held in the Old World.

This nobleman possessed a vast estate of thousands of acres beyond the mountains. He knew that it should be surveyed in order to find out where the boundary lines were and to prevent other people from settling there.

George Washington had learned a little surveying in school and had taught himself a little more. Since few surveyors were to be found in Virginia in those days, the old nobleman gave the task to his young friend and sent with him, as a companion, another young man who was of about the same age as Washington.

A Surveyor in the Wilderness

The work of surveying in the wilderness and the mountains took the young men a month. They had to cross deep, swift rivers — the horses swimming and the men carrying the supplies over as best they could. Once their tent was blown away by the wind. At night they had to make their fires in the open woods. The flames once caught the straw on which they were sleeping and nearly burned them to death.

Washington wrote down the most interesting things that happened every day. He noted the beauty of the country and learned its rivers and its trails. He saw Indians and watched a war dance. Some of his accounts said: "Since I last wrote you I have not slept above three or four nights in a bed," and "For days at a time I have never had my clothes off." At last the work was done and the young men returned to Mount Vernon. The surveys were so well made that they have not been questioned from that day to this.

Washington's old friend was delighted; he at once had Washington made public surveyor. Other people wanted work done; and for three years he was kept busy in the wilderness. He bought a farm and paid for it by his own labor. He learned much about the Indians and the mountain country — knowledge which was to prove of great value to English troops within a few years.

The Head of his House

Then his oldest brother fell ill. This brother had never been well since the months spent in the rain and heat of the Spanish Main. The doctors thought that perhaps he might grow better in a warmer land, so he set out for an island in the West Indies, with George to take care of him.

The new life and the strange scenes were very interesting to young Washington, for this was the first time, and the last, that he was ever outside his own country. He took a terrible disease and was very ill for three weeks. Though he became well again his face was marked for life.

Washington as a surveyor
What is George Washington doing in the picture?

The brother did not grow better, and within a short time came home to die. After his death the care of his family and his large estate fell upon George. Then the brother's family also died, and Mount Vernon became his. He had become the head of his house.

Washington was no longer a boy, for although he was only nineteen years old he had to play the part of a man. The work on the estate was very heavy. He took excellent care of the place. When people saw how well he managed affairs they made him an officer of the Virginia troops and placed him in charge of eleven counties.

Some years afterwards he married Martha Washington, whose first husband had died leaving her with two children. The Washingtons lived happily at Mount Vernon for a short time, and then the call to serve his country broke up Washington's quiet life as a Virginia gentleman.

A Memory Test

Use the following questions to test how much you remember:

1. What do Washington's papers tell about the kind of work he liked to do?

2. What things did he learn by living with his brother?

3. What did the nobleman help to teach him?

4. How did Washington become the master of Mount Vernon?

5. Why did he leave his quiet life as a farmer?

A Missing-Word Test

Do you know the words that should fill these blanks? They were used in the story.

1. _____ _____ was very careful in his work.

2. He married _____ _____.

3. His estate was called _____ _____.

4. He was born in the same year that _____.

5. A man who measures off land is a _____.

George Washington knew a great deal about life in the forests.

He was patient, honest, and brave.

How would you travel from your home to the Ohio River? Would the journey be hard to make? Was it easier in Washington's time or harder? Why?

CARRYING A MESSAGE TO THE OHIO

We know that the French built two forts south of Lake Erie and would have gone on to the Ohio if their supplies had not given out. When winter came they settled down in their forts and waited for spring before making another advance.

The English traders and the friendly Indians lost no time in bringing the news back to the settlements. What should be done? The governor of Virginia was especially troubled. He was a member of the Ohio Company, and they were in danger of losing their money.

He sent a trader to find out whether the Indians were going to take the side of the English or the French and to learn the plans of the enemy. The trader advanced within a hundred and fifty miles of the French, but dared go no farther.

A Man of Courage Chosen

A man of greater courage was needed. The governor of Virginia began to search for one, and soon his attention was called to Washington. The young surveyor was by this time twenty-one; he knew the wilderness better than most Virginians, and was in charge of defending the northern frontier.

The governor therefore chose Washington to carry a message to the French, warning them to stay away from the Ohio. He knew that they would not leave, but his warning would show that England regarded the region of the Ohio as her own. The messenger might also be able to win the friendship of some of the Indians and to learn the strength of the French.

Washington set out on his journey the same day on which he was chosen. His party was small; the guide was an experienced woodsman. Slowly the little band with their pack horses pushed along through rain and snow for five hundred miles. Sometimes there was not even an Indian trail to follow. Every day Washington wrote down what they had seen and heard. When they reached the Forks of the Ohio, he saw at once that it was the best place in the whole country for a fort, and wrote that the English must have it at all costs.

At Logstown he stopped to find guides who knew the rest of the way, and to persuade the Indians to give up their friendship with the French. (Find Logstown on the map on page 409.) Many long speeches were made, and a few Indians agreed to go with him. They had little reason to love either the English or the French, though they could buy their goods more cheaply from the English. Usually they took the side which they thought would win.

At last the party reached the first fort. (On the map on page 433 find the two French forts south of Lake Erie.) The officers greeted them in a friendly manner, but told Washington that he would have to go on to the next fort if he wished to talk with the

Carrying a message to the French

Does this picture show Washington on his way to the fort or returning?

commander. They said plainly that the French would never leave the Ohio, and that though there were two Englishmen to every Frenchman in America, the English were too slow.

It was necessary to go on to the second fort, so the Virginians continued their journey, reaching it forty-one days after they had left home. The commander here also treated them in a kind and friendly way; but on reading the letter from the governor of Virginia, he said that he could do nothing about it. He would have to wait for orders from the governor of Canada. Meanwhile the French would hold the forts.

With this answer Washington had to be satisfied. He made a drawing of the fort and noticed very carefully how its cannon were placed. But he had trouble in persuading his Indians to leave; French liquor had won them over to the other side.

The Return

The first part of the return journey was made in a canoe, well stocked with supplies which the French commander had given the party. It was winter. Sometimes they all had to get out and carry the canoe around places where the water had frozen. At the first French fort the Indians left them.

From that point Washington and the woodsman traveled on foot, with their papers and food strapped to their backs. The weather was very cold, and they suffered greatly. Their Indian guide turned against them, and at one time fired his gun straight at them but missed. After that they got rid of him and went on alone.

When they reached a branch of the Ohio they found that they could not cross on the ice, as they had expected, because it was not frozen in the middle. But they managed with only their axes to make a raft, on which they tried to cross. When they were in the middle of the stream Washington was pushed off the raft by the floating ice, but by good fortune he saved himself by catching hold of one of the logs.

The two travelers passed the night on an island in the river, with no fire, and the woodsman's hands and feet were badly frozen. In the morning the ice was hard enough to bear their weight, so they reached the farther bank. They soon made a fire and warmed themselves.

By the time they arrived in the settlement their journey had taken eleven weeks. We can cover the same distance today in a few hours.

Washington gave his report to the governor, and the governor asked him to write it out. He worked all night, copying his notes. The next day the governor read the report to the assembly. It was printed in the few newspapers in the colonies, a copy was sent to all the governors, and it was read even in England. The young man of twenty-one had made his name known across the seas.

Virginia tries to seize the Forks

Washington's report had said that whoever held the Forks of the Ohio would control the river, and had advised building a fort there. (On the map on page 409 find the Forks of the Ohio.) The governor of Virginia was eager to do so. He sent a captain with soldiers to build such a fort, but it was taken by a much larger party of French, who sent the Englishmen back to Virginia and built a fort of their own instead. They called it Fort Duquesne (dŏŏ kān') in honor of the governor of Canada, and sent hundreds of troops there. (On the map on page 409 find Fort Duquesne.)

The assembly of Virginia was, as usual, quarreling with the governor and would vote no money for war. The Carolinas acted too slowly to be of any help. Some of the other colonies sent word that they doubted whether England had any claim to the land beyond the mountains; and the Northern colonies were too busy to pay any attention to the far-away Ohio.   Later we shall find out why.

The governor of Virginia at length decided to act alone.   He sent about three hundred men into the wilderness, with Washington as second in command, but it was already too late to get ahead of France.

Slowly the Virginians advanced.   They had to cut a path through the forest for the big guns and the wagons, and also to build bridges.   They could travel only from two to four miles a day.

Great Meadows

When they reached Great Meadows, a level, open place where the fur-traders used to rest their horses, they stopped.   Washington was by this time in command.   He knew that he was in great danger and that the French, with their larger numbers, could easily surround him.   He was very angry at the governor and the assembly for not sending him more troops and supplies, and wrote many letters telling them so.   Probably he should have given up and returned to Virginia, but instead he decided to try to reach the Ohio.   In the meantime he had begun to build a fort.

One dark, rainy night he learned that a small body of French was very near.   With forty men, walking one behind the other, he followed his Indian guides to the enemy's camp.   Just at sunrise they surprised the French, and in fifteen minutes all was over.   Only one Frenchman escaped.

Fort Necessity

Washington knew that the main body of the French would be upon him as soon as they heard of this. He quickly finished building his fort, but had no supplies and little ammunition, so he called it Fort Necessity. Besides his soldiers he had some forty or fifty Indian families to support. (On the map on page 409 find Fort Necessity.)

At last more troops arrived from Virginia, but they came too late. The assembly had been too slow. Washington tried to finish the road to the Ohio River; but his men were so worn out, either from the long journey from the settlements or from the hard work of building the fort, that they could not finish the road.

Word soon came that the French had begun to advance. At this the Indians quickly ran away. Washington and his men prepared to make their stand at Fort Necessity, which was in a bad location. The ground was low and was surrounded by little hills from which the French could fire down upon them. It soon began to rain, and the Virginians in the fort had to stand knee-deep in water.

The attack started in the morning and lasted all day. The English were worn out before the battle began; they had no food and little ammunition. The French were two to their one. In a few hours fifty or sixty men fell. To save those who were left, Washington surrendered.

He and his men were allowed to return home after promising that they would not come back to the Ohio for a year. The soldiers had to carry their food and their wounded companions on their backs, for all the horses had been killed. Thus the first expedition in which the young leader took part was a failure.

The Virginia assembly thanked the men who had made the attempt for them, but Washington felt very bad about it.

As a result of these battles England and France were at war. All the traders came in from beyond the mountains, and both sides settled down to a hard struggle.

Some Things to Explain

1. How did the English learn of the French plans?

2. Why was Washington chosen to carry the message?

3. What answer did the French commander give?

4. Why did the English not drive away the French while they were building Fort Duquesne?

5. What was the result of the struggle to control the Forks of the Ohio?

Choices to Make

Choose the right word from each group given below.

1. The man who sent Washington to the French was the

proprietor of Maryland   governor of Virginia
general of the army

2. The fort built at the Forks of the Ohio was

Fort Necessity   Fort Logstown   Fort Duquesne

Washington's journey showed that the French would not leave the Ohio.

War between France and England would surely come.

Which nation do you think won the first war? the second? the third? Write your answers on a piece of paper. After you have read the story, go back and see whether or not your answers were right.

THREE WARS BETWEEN THE FRENCH AND THE ENGLISH

We have found that the fur trade in the interior was the chief cause of war between England and France. A second cause was the wealth of the fishing grounds round the Gulf of St. Lawrence. Those waters belonged to France, but English vessels had been fishing there since the days of John Cabot. Fish and furs, then, were the main causes of four long wars between the two nations — wars which continued almost a century.

Which nation stood a better chance of winning? France had easier ways of traveling about in her territories, she had more Indian allies, and her king held all power in his own hands. When he said "Attack," the French armies attacked; when he said "Make a siege," they made a siege. All the French soldiers were paid by him. They were used to the wilderness and to war; the English were mainly farmers. Thus the French had four great advantages.

On the other hand, the number of Frenchmen in the New World was small, and they had to travel great distances in order to reach their forts. These forts had only enough supplies to last a short time.

The English had twenty men to every one of the French, and they were much nearer to their mother country than New France was to hers. England had so many ships that she could easily bring over supplies, and the Iroquois were friendly to her. Thus she also had four advantages.

But whenever the French attacked one of the thirteen English colonies, its governor could call out troops only from his own colony. The other twelve decided for themselves whether or not to help him; and it takes time to decide such matters.

Since each nation had certain advantages, it was hard to tell which would defeat the other in the long struggle for the continent.

On page 404 we read that the northern English colonies had not helped Virginia in her attempt to drive the French away from the Ohio. They had their hands full of Indian troubles, which had lasted for three quarters of a century, and the Ohio was too far away for them to be much concerned about it.

Indian Attacks on Outlying Settlements

While New France was building forts along the Ohio, the Great Lakes, and the Mississippi, she did not forget the English settlements along the coast. Wherever these settlements were near enough she struck at them too. At what points could she reach them most easily? The French themselves were so few in number that they could not lead an army against the settlements, but they had a great many Indian allies who would fight

HUDSON
BAY

C A N A D A

Quebec

Montreal · Lake
Champlain

(MAINE)

Island Fort

NEW YORK · N.H.
Hudson R. · MASS.

Logstown

Forks of the Ohio · × Fort Duquesne
× Fort
Necessity

A T L A N T I C   O C E A N

The great fishing island
The land northeast of
Maine taken from France

Early French and English Wars

for them. Along the New England frontier were many scattered farms which offered an easy mark for the Indians. These farms and the posts of the English traders were the places which the French could most easily attack.

Whenever war broke out in Europe between these two nations, it was soon followed in America by Indian attacks on the outlying settlements of the English. The English, however, could not get at the French cities on the St. Lawrence nor at the forts in the interior.

There were three wars between the English and the French, known in America as King William's War, Queen Anne's War, and King George's War. The following stories show how in each war the French and the Indians fell upon frontier farms.

Once a band of fur-traders and Indians from the French missions decided to attack a New York town in the middle of the winter. (On the map on page 409 find the part of New York nearest to New France.) They traveled on snowshoes, dragging their supplies after them on sleds and suffering severely from the cold. Late one afternoon they came in sight of the New York village, but waited until dark to surprise it; meanwhile they did not even dare to build fires to warm themselves.

In the middle of the night they came creeping up to the stockade. The gate was open. Silently they passed inside; soon every house was surrounded. Then the wild war whoop rang out, the doors were broken down with axes, and the people were killed as they rose from their beds. All the houses but two or three were set on fire, and the settlers' goods and horses were carried off into the wilderness.

Many other plans were laid to take the forts of the English colonists, for the French and the Indians did not like to make direct attacks. In a New Hampshire town two Indian women came to the fort one cold evening and asked if they might stay for the night. The English brought them inside and gave them a bed. Late in the night, when all were sleeping soundly, the Indian women quietly got up, opened the gate, and let in their friends who were waiting outside. The usual result followed. (On the map on page 409 find the part of New Hampshire nearest to New France.)

In Maine a group of Indians once appeared before a fort with a white flag and asked the English to come out and talk over the terms of peace. As the soldiers drew near the Indians seized axes hidden under their blankets and killed them all. (On the map on page 409 find the part of Maine nearest to New France.)

In another place, when an attack was made on a farm-house, a servant quickly hid the children under two large brass kettles. The Indians searched all around but did not find them.

In Massachusetts a woman was busy making soap one day when she heard a sudden noise, and found herself surrounded by Indians. She threw boiling soap over some of them, but the others captured her and dragged her into the forest. There a child was born to her, but it soon died for want of care. Half starved and worn out by carrying heavy loads, the poor woman was forced to walk all the way to Canada. A French family bought her from her Indian masters and treated her kindly. After several years her husband paid them a sum of money, and they allowed her to return to Massachusetts. (On the map on page 409 find the part of Massachusetts which was nearest to New France.)

So we might go on with story after story of the killing of men, women, and children in the fields and woods, and of attacks on homes while the men of the family were away at work. Do you wonder that the English grew to hate both the French and the Indians?

Sir William Johnson and the Iroquois

Matters would have been even worse if the Iroquois Indians had not taken the side of the English. For a long time, as we found in the story of the "Black Gowns," the Iroquois had been so strong that they had made even New France tremble. But the French governor, who was La Salle's friend, made peace with them, and afterwards the French were always trying to win them over as allies.

That the Iroquois remained friendly to the English was due to the work of Sir William Johnson, a landholder on the Mohawk River. He had come out to look after his uncle's land, bringing with him some fine sheep and horses. On his great estate he lived like a lord. He built up a great trade with the Iroquois, learned the languages of the different tribes, joined their games and dances, and married an Indian woman. In his house, "Johnson Hall," the Indians held many of their councils.

Indians attacking a frontier home

What do you suppose that the Indian chief and the white man are saying to each other? (From a painting by John Ward Dunsmore. Courtesy of the Title Guarantee and Trust Co., New York)

Sir William worked against the Jesuits and acted as the representative of the English in dealing with the tribes. He tried to prevent the English from selling liquor to the Indians, but with no success. They so loved and trusted him that they made him a member of the tribe and one of their chiefs. By his advice the Iroquois would not join the French. If they had, matters would have been even worse for the English.

During the early years of the war, Sir William Johnson led a force of Indians and colonists against the French forts on Lake Champlain. But he was not a soldier and the expedition failed.

England secures French Territory

Why did not the English pay the French back for their cruelties? These were some of the reasons. (1) By the time that the English soldiers could gather at the point of attack, the Indians and the French would be far away. (2) The English could not attack the frontier farmhouses of the French, for there were none. (3) The French towns were so few and so well protected that it was almost impossible to capture them.

The English, then, could not get at the French as easily as the French could get at them. One of the few places that they could reach was the land northeast of Maine. (Find the place on the map on page 409.) Massachusetts prepared to strike a blow there, even though the other colonies would not help her.

A fleet was gathered and the French colony was attacked from the sea. The conquest was very easy. The French officer surrendered and had to give up his fort and all that he had, even his silver forks and spoons. The English colonists returned to Boston in high spirits. At the close of the war (King William's) each side gave up what it had conquered, and thus all the efforts of Massachusetts came to nothing.

As soon as the next war (Queen Anne's) began, the Massachusetts colonists thought at once of the French colony east of Maine, and of how easily they had taken it before. A crowd of farmers, fishermen, and carpenters, who knew nothing about war, set out to capture it. Their ships had a hard time in entering the harbor through the narrow opening where the current ran

swiftly. One of them was wrecked. But the Massachusetts men landed. The town surrendered, and the
English won a section of French territory which was
never given up.

A second place where the English could easily attack the French was the large island in the Gulf of St.
Lawrence. (Find the island on the map on page 409.)
Since the time of the Cabots three hundred English
fishing ships had been there every year to fish in the
surrounding waters. They had a station on the island,
where they dried their fish. At the end of Queen Anne's
War this island was given up by France.

A third place which both nations wanted was the
fur-trading region around Hudson Bay. The English
already had trading posts there. They could ship goods
by sea all the way from England and could therefore
sell at a lower price than the French. Since they could
load their vessels for the return journey from wharves
at the very edge of the stockades, they could buy such
heavy skins and hides as those of the buffalo and deer.
France could not afford to deal in heavy skins, for her
merchants had to carry them long distances in canoes.

So the Indians had been coming from all the country
round about to Hudson Bay to sell furs to the English.
France had claimed this country as hers also, but had
secured less and less trade from it every year. Constant
attacks were made on the French by the English, and
on the English by the French. At the end of Queen
Anne's War the Hudson Bay country also was given
to the English. (On the map on page 409 find the
Hudson Bay country.)

Thus by the end of Queen Anne's War, England had won the *Hudson Bay country*, the *island in the Gulf of St. Lawrence*, and the *region northeast of Maine*.

Results of the First Three Wars

At the end of the first three wars the question as to who should own the continent had by no means been settled. England had won the land near Maine, the great fishing island, and the Hudson Bay region, but she had lost many men. France still held all the interior of the country.

You can understand now why the Northern colonies had had little time or thought for the Ohio. They had been too busy.

England was getting stronger and stronger at sea, and France was growing weaker. As the years went by command of the sea was to decide the wars in England's favor.

Are you Ready?

I. Are you ready to answer any question that your teacher may ask you about the story? Some of the most important questions are these:

1. What were the two chief causes of war between England and France?

2. In what four ways did France have the advantage? In what two ways did she not have it?

3. In what four ways did the English have the advantage? In what ways did they not have it?

4. What were three reasons why the English did not fight in the same way as the French?

5. What did the English gain in Queen Anne's War?

6. Did the first three wars decide who should control the continent?

II. You may make sentences of your own, using the following new words.   The class will decide whether your sentences are right.

Name of Person	Words
1. Sir William Johnson	**3.** stockade
Name of Place	**4.** war whoop
2. Canada	**5.** outlying settlements

The early wars with the French were for the possession of land around the St. Lawrence River.

It was hard to tell which side would win.

Do you know of any building or company named "Franklin"? Do you know of anything named in memory of Benjamin Franklin? This story will tell you why Americans honor him.

AMERICA'S FIRST MAN OF SCIENCE

Almost every American city has a Franklin street or a Franklin school or some other object named for Franklin. Why are they so called? Who was this man whom America delights to honor?

He was the youngest son in a Puritan family of seventeen children. His father's business was making candles and soap.

Early Years

Benjamin Franklin was born a quarter of a century before George Washington. He attended school only two years, but in spite of this he became the most learned American of his time.

One day, when he was a very small child, he was given some pennies, and set out to see what they would buy. Finding a pretty whistle in a shop, he at once put down all his money and hurried home with the toy. His family asked how much he had paid for it, and when he told them they all laughed. He had paid much more than the whistle was worth. Every time he blew his whistle one of the family laughed again. In later years, when he was tempted to act without thinking, he said to himself, "Don't pay too much for your whistle!"

Benjamin's father wanted him to become a minister, but he himself wanted to be a sailor. He did neither; for when he was only ten years old he had to leave school and work in his father's shop. But he never liked to make candles; he wanted to spend all his time in reading. He read over and over the few books which his father owned. He saved all his pennies to buy more books, and he borrowed many, which he tells us he returned "soon and clean." Often he read all night by the light of a candle.

The Young Printer

Franklin's father was afraid that the boy would run away to sea as one of his older brothers had done, so he tried to find work for him which he would like better. He decided to have Benjamin work for a brother who was a printer and who printed a newspaper. Benjamin was willing, and signed a paper promising that he would work for his brother nine years.

He liked printing, and soon learned to set type and mix ink. He tried to write poems. One of them was about the capture of the pirate Blackbeard. But his father did not like to have him write poetry, for he said that poets usually did not amount to much. Benjamin then wrote something for the newspaper; but he did not want to let his brother know that it was his own work, so he slipped what he had written under the door of the printing shop. When he heard some of his brother's friends praising what he had written and wondering who could have done it, you may imagine how proud he felt. Meanwhile he kept on reading everything that he could find.

All this time his brother had been paying a certain sum for Benjamin's board; but one day Benjamin said that if his brother would give him half that amount in money he would board himself. The brother was glad to save half the money, and Benjamin was able out of his half to board himself and also to buy some books. He ate no meat, but only vegetables.

Soon afterwards the brother found himself in trouble with the officers of the town of Boston because of some things he had printed about them. Once they sent him to prison, and again they ordered him to stop printing his newspaper. Nothing had been said about Benjamin, so Benjamin went on with the work and wrote and printed the paper himself.

But he and his brother did not get along well. They were all the time quarreling, and sometimes the brother beat Benjamin. At this, Benjamin left him; but he found he could get no other work in Boston, so he sold some of his books, and, with the money that he got for them, set out to seek his fortune.

Out in the World

Franklin sailed on a vessel going to New York. There was a great storm, but the ship stood it well, and in three days he reached New York.

No work was to be had there, so he set out for Philadelphia. He arrived there early one Sunday morning — hungry, cold, wet, and very lonely. In his pockets he

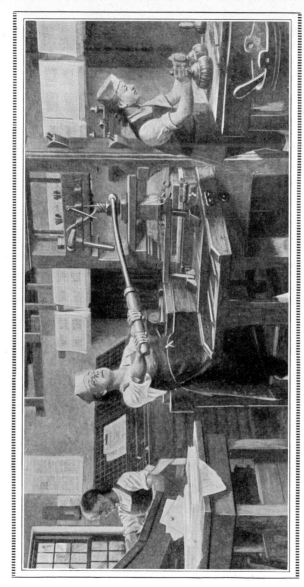

Franklin's printing shop

From a painting by Charles E. Mills

had some extra shirts and woolen stockings. He stopped at a baker's shop and bought three large rolls of bread, one of which he began to eat, carrying the others under his arm.

Thus he walked down the street.   A rosy-cheeked girl standing at the door of her father's house thought he looked very queer and laughed at him. Some time afterwards she was glad to marry the queer-looking boy, who became one of America's greatest men.

There were only two printing shops in Philadelphia. Franklin, who was a very good printer, found work in one of them and stayed there several months. Then a friend from Boston brought him to the attention of the governor of Pennsylvania.

The governor advised Franklin to set up in business for himself. The boy had no money, so the governor wrote to ask the boy's father in Boston to furnish a shop for him. But the older Franklin thought that Benjamin was too young to set up for himself. When he was twenty-one he might try.

In England

At this the governor himself offered to lend the money, and advised the young printer to go to London to buy his press. Franklin was only too glad to follow such advice. The day for sailing came; Franklin went on board ship; but no money had yet been sent by the governor. A servant, however, told Franklin to go on with the voyage, and letters and money would be given to the captain for him.

Franklin and a friend who went with him did as they were directed, but when they landed in England they found that the governor had not done as he had promised. They were alone in a strange country, without any money.

Franklin soon found work in a printing office in London, where he became known as the "water American," because he drank only water. He lived next door to a bookstore and was soon able to borrow all the books that he could read.

He had a very good time in London, he met a number of well-educated men, and he even did a little writing. But he saved no money. After a time an offer came for him to open a swimming school, for he was a very fine swimmer. He needed money, and he almost accepted the offer. But fortunately he went to a merchant friend for advice, and the merchant not only advised against the swimming school but offered to send him back to Philadelphia and to give him a place there in his business. This offer settled the matter in Franklin's mind, and he decided to go home.

Back in Philadelphia

When he returned to Philadelphia he was twenty. Eagerly he began his new work; but soon the merchant fell ill and died. Franklin also was very ill.

After this he went back to printing, and found work with the very printer that he had served before. For two years he worked for this man and then was able to borrow money to set up a shop of his own.

As there was not enough printing to keep him busy, he began to run a newspaper also. He put into it much more news than could be found in other newspapers. He printed advertisements, which was then a new idea, and he wrote about questions in which the people of Philadelphia were interested. Postriders carried his paper to all the country round about.

In trying to pay back the money that he had borrowed he worked far into the night and lived very simply. The girl who had seen him with the rolls of bread became his wife and helped him in many ways. She kept a shop in which were sold soap, paper, tea, and coffee. Together they carried out one of Franklin's favorite ideas: "Work and save."

Franklin continued his reading and formed friendships with other young men who were, like himself, great readers. They joined together in a club which lasted for forty years.

What Franklin did for his City

One of Franklin's chief purposes in life was to do good. He was a man of hard common sense, and saw many ways in which he could help to make life better and happier for the people of his city.

One way was by helping to start a public library, so that other boys would not have as hard a time as he had had to get books. They could borrow as many as they wanted to read. Another way was by founding a college which many years later became the University of Pennsylvania.

Benjamin Franklin's book shop

Which one is Franklin?

Franklin also turned his attention to the night watch, or police, that were supposed to protect the city from dark until dawn. Instead of watching people's property they sometimes robbed strangers and citizens who had to travel at night. Franklin put them out and hired men who were paid out of the public taxes and who had to do their duty.

He helped to found a hospital, and his club formed one of the first fire-fighting companies in America. Before that, whenever there was a fire, people had come running from all directions to put it out, but no one was in charge, and no plan was followed. But this fire company knew just what to do and did it.

He persuaded the city to pave some of its streets and to have street lights. He hired people to sweep the streets, and when the citizens saw how clean they were, a regular street-cleaning force was employed by the city.

Franklin was a member of the assembly. He was the first postmaster of Pennsylvania, and afterwards postmaster-general of all the colonies. It is wonderful how any one man could possibly have been interested in so many different matters and could have done so much.

Poor Richard's Almanac

Have you ever seen an almanac? Franklin printed one each year. It contained lists of the days and months, lists of kings, the days for holding courts and fairs, and the changes in the moon. It told about such matters as how to make a fence, how to fertilize a field, and how people lived in other parts of the world.

He called it *Poor Richard's Almanac*.   He called himself Poor Richard.   He put many wise sayings into his almanac, such as,

> One today is worth two tomorrows.
> Lost time is never found again.
> A small leak will sink a great ship.
> If you would have your business done, go; if not, send.

Ten thousand copies of this almanac were sold every year. They went into the home of so many farmers and shopkeepers in all the country that Franklin has been called the schoolmaster of a nation.

Franklin's Inventions and Discoveries

Every day Franklin spent an hour or two reading in the library, and made himself one of the wisest men of his time.   He believed in bathing often and in having fresh air in sleeping rooms at a time when most Americans believed that such things would make them ill.

He invented a stove which is even yet called the Franklin stove.   It warmed the whole room much better than the old-fashioned fireplace had done, and yet it saved fuel.

Franklin's favorite study was the study of electricity, on which the men of science in Europe had been working for some time.   At last he sold his newspaper, his printing house, and his almanac so that he might have more time for study.

He was sure that lightning is electricity.   To prove this he made a kite which had a silk string, and fastened

© Detroit Publishing Company

Franklin and his kite

What did Franklin prove with his kite and his key? (From a painting by Charles E. Mills)

a key to the end of the string. The kite had a pointed wire to catch the electricity from the clouds. One day during a June thundershower Franklin went out into the fields, sent up his kite, and waited. As the lightning grew brighter the silk threads stood away from each other, and at last he got an electric spark from his key. He was sure he had proved his point. He then advised people to use lightning rods for their houses.

His discoveries made his name known to every learned man in Europe. He was the first American whom they all respected for his knowledge.

To Help You to Study

Did you get the most important points in the story? If you can answer the following questions, you did.

1. Why did Franklin's father think he would like printing?

2. Why did Franklin leave Philadelphia and go to England?

3. How did he happen to return to America?

4. What were some of the things he did for the city of Philadelphia?

5. Why was Franklin called the schoolmaster of a nation?

6. What did he prove with his kite?

Making up Riddles

For a long time now you have been filling in blanks with new words. This time you may write your sentences, using the following words. Then write your sentences again, leaving blanks where the new words should be. Give your sentences to someone in another class, and see if he can fill in the blanks correctly.

Name of Person	*Words*
1. Benjamin Franklin	2. *Poor Richard's Almanac*

Franklin became a learned man.

He made many inventions.

Does the name of this war mean that the French were fighting the Indians or that, together, they were fighting another nation? The story will tell you.

THE FRENCH AND INDIAN WAR BEGINS

The battles fought in America as part of the fourth great war between England and France are known as the French and Indian War.

When England and France saw that this great war was upon them, France, which kept up the greatest army in Europe, sent many of her soldiers to Canada. England, which had the greatest fleet, sent it to guard the enemy's coast, so that no more French ships loaded with soldiers might leave for America.

England also sent soldiers to the colonies. Those in Virginia were under the command of General Braddock. He was an old man, rough, narrow-minded, but brave as a lion. He had been a good officer in the wars at home, but knew nothing about Indian fighting. It did not seem possible to him that his well-drilled soldiers could learn anything from colonial troops, and he was sure that the Indians would be no match for men who had fought on the great battlefields of Europe.

General Braddock landed in Virginia in February, expecting to take only three or four days for the conquest of Fort Duquesne, and then to march on to Lake Erie. Instead, it was May before he even began to cross the mountains. Months earlier the colonists had been ordered to gather supplies of food and ammunition, but nothing had been done. The general stormed and raged, but he could not hurry them. One hundred and fifty wagons were needed; only twenty-five were ready. Franklin came down to Virginia to find out what was being done, and Braddock persuaded him to undertake the task of securing the wagons. He succeeded, and the general wrote home of the matter as "the first example of ability I have seen in all these colonies."

Washington was invited to join the British forces as Braddock's *aide*. This gave him a fine chance to learn the rules of war as practiced in Europe. All the British officers at once set to work training the colonial troops to "make them as much like soldiers as possible." But after everything else was ready they had to wait a month for their cannon.

The March on Fort Duquesne

In May the regiments started to cross the mountains. Some were British, some were Virginians, and a few Indians served as scouts. They went by the route that Washington had taken several years earlier — a long, roundabout trail over rough country.

Braddock had been sent to do an impossible thing. He had neither enough men nor enough supplies, and he was facing a different kind of war from any that English generals had ever met.

The road was not wide enough for wagons; three hundred men with axes had to go before to clear the way. In eight days they went only thirty miles. In the meantime the French had plenty of time to send more soldiers and supplies to Fort Duquesne.

Braddock sent some of his troops ahead; then came the wagons and supplies; then more troops to protect the end of the line. Scattered soldiers marched some distance out on each side, and the Indian scouts ranged still farther out in the forest. (On the map on page 433 find Braddock's route.)

When the expedition arrived at a low place through which they had to pass, the French and the Indians attacked from higher ground and drove them down into the hollow. At once the Virginians scattered and began to shoot from behind trees and rocks. The British troops stood their ground; they all raised their guns at once as they had been trained to do; they heard the signal to fire. But at what? No enemy could be seen — nothing but smoke rising into the air from all around them. After the battle was over one of the English soldiers said that he had not been able to see one Indian or one Frenchman during the entire time. But the red coats of the English soldiers were a fine mark for the enemy.

Bullets kept raining down upon the Englishmen. Some of the troops tried to hide behind logs, but Braddock drove them back into the open with his sword, calling them cowards. He himself had no fear. He rode here and there in full sight of the enemy, making no attempt to protect himself. Four horses were shot under him, and at last he himself fell. Then his troops retreated. One cannot blame them. Washington, who had had two horses shot under him and had received

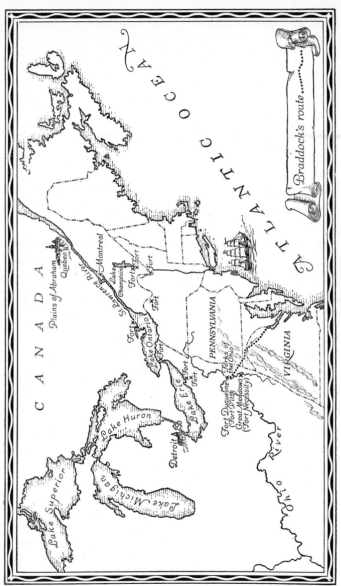

The French and Indian War

four bullets through his coat, tried to draw the scattered soldiers together during the retreat, but he could not. Even those at the end of the line, who had not been in the battle, caught the fear of the others. All night they fled back through the woods to the nearest fort in Maryland. Washington angrily said that they "ran as sheep before hunting dogs."

Braddock died on the way back, saying, "Another time we shall know better how to deal with them." He was buried in the road, and men and horses marched over his grave so that the Indians might not be able to find it.

The British had been completely beaten. Most of the officers and three fourths of the fifteen hundred men had been lost. All the ammunition and supplies had been left on the field. The French had suffered little.

Result of the Defeat

As a result nearly all the Indians in the West went over to the French. During the rest of the war they constantly attacked the southern frontier, traveling over the very road which Braddock had cut to the Ohio. Their villages were full of English prisoners. The pioneers suffered terribly.

Washington had no chance to take part in the great events which happened afterwards in the North. For three years he had to spend all his time trying to defend three hundred and fifty miles of frontier with his few soldiers. The assembly of Virginia would give little help because it was quarreling with the governor;

Braddock's defeat

Do you see two American soldiers?

Pennsylvania would do nothing, partly because the Quakers did not believe in fighting and partly because they were quarreling with the Penn family about their taxes.

All that Washington could do was to build a few block-houses at the points of greatest danger, such as the gaps and passes through the mountains. He left a small band of soldiers in each, and thus did his best to protect the settlements. For this reason, Washington did not take part in the most stirring events of the French and Indian War. But his work saved the South from the Indians.

Fortune Changes

During the first three years of the war the French kept their forts on Lakes Erie and Ontario and secured the English forts on Lake Champlain and in western New York. We have already learned what happened to Braddock's men who tried to take Fort Duquesne.

The British had failed everywhere during the first three years.

The cause of the British failure was that no one person was in charge. Many plans had been made by different people, but they were not carried out. But when things had reached their worst, a great man came into power in England and took matters into his own hands. His name was William Pitt.

In spite of Braddock's expedition, war had not yet been declared between France and England. Though there was open fighting in America, the two nations were supposed to be at peace.

Pitt declared war with France. He saw that what happened in America was very important, and he began at once to hurry troops across the ocean. But the colonial assemblies were very slow to vote money enough for supplies.

Pitt saw that the points to attack first were the forts on Lakes Ontario and Erie. If those could be taken, then the French could not send supplies to Fort Duquesne, and it too would fall. After that he could attack Quebec. (Find these forts on the map on page 433.)

The French governor at this time had to call in some soldiers from Lakes Erie and Ontario to help to defend

Quebec. The English immediately sent an expedition against the forts and captured them, together with many supplies and much ammunition. The French and the Indians retreated to Detroit. The British shot the forts to pieces with the cannon that had been taken. There was no longer any danger of their giving help to Quebec. The victory on Lake Ontario was the first real victory for the English. It was soon followed by many others.

French soldiers from Lake Champlain were also needed in Canada, so they blew up and burned their own forts and marched away. There was no longer any danger from the Lake Champlain region. (See the map.)

In the meantime three English leaders, one of whom was Washington, advanced for the third time against Fort Duquesne. They went by way of Pennsylvania. They would travel a short distance, build a blockhouse, leave some soldiers in it, then advance again and build another blockhouse. This time there should be no such defeat as that of Braddock.

The loss of the forts on the Great Lakes made it impossible for Canada to send help to Fort Duquesne. The French saw that they could not possibly defend the fort against an attack, so they blew it up, burned it, and escaped down the river to New Orleans.

When the English arrived they found only ruins. They put up a stockade and began to build a new fort in the same place that the old one had been. They called it Fort Pitt in honor of the great English statesman. Today we call the city that grew up there Pittsburgh.

The only important points that the French had left were those on the St. Lawrence River.

Testing your Neighbor

I. First test yourself by answering these questions. Prove that your answers are right by turning back in the story. Then ask the questions of your neighbor.

1. Why did it take General Braddock so long to start over the mountains?

2. Why did his soldiers have no chance of winning?

3. Who held the forts on Lake Champlain and Lakes Erie and Ontario at the end of the third year of war?

4. Who changed the British plans after the third year?

5. Why did the English attack the forts on Lake Ontario first?

6. What happened to the French forts on the Lakes and on the Ohio?

II. Ask your neighbor to finish these sentences. You must decide whether the sentences are correct.

1. General Braddock was the general who

2. Fort Duquesne was

3. Fort Pitt was

4. An aide is

5. Pittsburgh is

6. A regiment is

7. To retreat means

The last war in America between the English and the French was called the French and Indian War.

This war was fought to obtain possession of the Ohio River and of Quebec.

Is a battle called great just because many men lost their lives in it? This story will tell you about a great battle which decided that the English language should be the national language of our country.

ONE OF THE GREATEST BATTLES IN THE HISTORY OF THE WORLD

The strongest city that the French held was Quebec. As long as they could keep it, they could control the valley of the St. Lawrence. Pitt's attention was therefore turned next to Quebec. (Find Quebec on the map on page 433.)

During the first three wars several attempts had been made to capture Quebec, but none had been successful.

The Two Generals

Before going on with the story of the battle, let us hear something about the two generals, both of whom were soon to meet death, but at the same time to win fame that will not die. The French leader was General Montcalm. He was a learned man, but so small that when the Indians first saw him they had said: "We are surprised to find the great father such a little man. It is only when we look into his eyes that we know he is great." He belonged to a noble family. He loved his books and his farm, but he had also made himself well known as a soldier. So he was chosen to lead the army in Canada.

It was Montcalm who took the forts on Lake Champlain from the British. He worked very hard on such expeditions — sometimes as much as twenty hours a day — and looked after everything himself, even to telling how the soldiers' bread was to be baked.

In his attempt to make Canada ready for war he met difficulties and troubles. He did not like the Indians. He thought them wicked and cruel, and so they were, but the governor of Canada insisted on using them. All about him he saw the officers of the government stealing and cheating the colony. They stole the presents that the king meant to give to the Indians, and sold them instead. They took the supplies sent over for the soldiers and used them. The people were suffering from hunger while the officers were spending huge sums which should have built up the country. Montcalm and a few other honest men could do nothing except to write the king what was happening.

Without enough soldiers and without supplies, Montcalm could look forward only to certain defeat. At first he thought of asking to be sent back; but after Fort Duquesne and the island fort had fallen, he saw what was coming and decided to stand by Canada in her hour of need.

Wolfe, the English general, was a tall thin man whose health was so poor that he had to spend much of his time in bed. He had been in the king's service ever since he was fifteen years old. When the command of the army was given to him, many of the people of England were surprised, but they soon learned to trust him above all the other generals.

The Battle of Quebec

The city of Quebec is built on a rock two hundred feet high, with the great St. Lawrence River, a mile wide at that point, rolling below it. On top of the rock great walls surrounded the city, and cannon were placed on hills close by. The gates were closed every night.

Wolfe himself did not believe the city could be taken. But, though Wolfe did not know it, the French were in no condition for battle. Montcalm had more men than the British, but he had few trained soldiers. They would not be able to stand up in battle against the well-drilled British troops. No help could be expected from France, for the English navy controlled the sea. There was not even enough food in the city, for the farmers had been away fighting all summer instead of raising crops.

Every able-bodied man in the colony and every boy who could fire a gun had been called to the army. Montcalm's plan was to hold Quebec until the hard northern winter should force the English to give up the attack. He wrote, "I shall do everything to save this colony, or die."

Word soon came that the British fleet had sailed from the island fort and was coming up the river. The French had doubted whether ships of such size could pass through strange waters full of islands, rocks, currents, and shallow places, but on they came within sight of the city. Fire ships sent down upon them did little harm.

The British fleet stopped while Wolfe studied what to do. On the other bank of the river he placed guns which fired cannon balls across and into the city and knocked many houses to pieces. His soldiers burned the farm buildings and drove away the people of the surrounding country. But how could he take the city?

September came. Whatever was done would have to be done quickly, for the fleet must return to England before the river began to freeze. The only plan of attack that Wolfe could think of was to land at the foot of the cliff at night and climb up by a path that he had noticed. There were guards all along the top; but as the French had to watch fifteen or twenty miles of cliff, there could not be many at any one place.

Just at this time the governor of Canada removed part of the guard back into the city, although Montcalm objected strongly. Wolfe's chance had come. He had been ill in bed, and knew that he must soon die, but he had begged the doctor to "patch him up" long enough to let him take Quebec.

He rose from his bed and in the middle of the night set out with his men in small boats. Believing that he was not to live through the battle, he gave to one of his officers a small picture of the girl he was to have married and asked him to return it to her.

Silently they floated down the river. French guards called out to them to learn who they were, but they answered: "Supplies. Hush! the English will hear you." Wolfe in a low voice told his companions about a great poem which he had learned. One line was "The paths of glory lead but to the grave." "Gentlemen," said he, "I would rather have written those lines than take Quebec."

A view of Quebec
Can you see where the English must have climbed up?

Just before dawn they landed at the foot of the cliff and silently climbed upward. Capturing the guard at the top was easy. By the time that it was light five thousand British soldiers were in line on the great plains outside the walls of Quebec — the Plains of Abraham.

All this time the fleet below the city had been firing its cannon and making as if to attack from another direction, so that Montcalm's attention might be drawn away from the landing.

Matters had been going badly in Quebec. The city lay in ruins from the work of the British cannon, no one had enough to eat, almost all the cattle and horses had been killed, and the Canadian soldiers were deserting by hundreds.   Wolfe wrote of them, "Montcalm is at the head of a great number of bad soldiers and I am at the head of a small number of good ones."   For three months Montcalm had not had his clothes off, but slept ready for action at any minute.

When word was brought to him that the British troops stood ready for battle on the Plains of Abraham, he quickly gathered together the four thousand men whom the governor could spare from the city and made an attack. His four thousand men, many of whom had never before been in battle, were no match for five thousand British regulars.   The French line soon broke and retreated to the city.   The battle was over in fifteen minutes.

General Wolfe had led the charge.   He was shot three times, so badly that his friends did not even send for a doctor.   As he was lying on the ground he heard the cry "They run."   "Who run?" he asked suddenly, like a man coming out of a sleep.   "The enemy, sir," was the answer.   "Now, God be praised," he said, "I shall die in peace," and, turning from his friends, he died.

General Montcalm, directing the battle on his big black horse, had also been shot through the body, but managed to reach the city.   As he lay suffering he asked how much longer he had to live.   "Perhaps twelve hours," the doctor replied.   "I am happy that I shall not live to see the surrender of Quebec," said Montcalm.

The governor of Canada left Quebec and went quickly up the river to Montreal.   Wolfe's troops entered the city and raised the British flag; and a British flag waves there to this day.   From Quebec the English followed the fleeing governor up the river and took Montreal also.

On the Plains of Abraham there stands a tall stone bearing on one side the name of Wolfe and on the other the name of Montcalm. The carving on the stone says that death gave them the same grave and that history gives them the same glory.

Thus France lost her empire in the New World. Great Britain won; and English speech, English customs, and English ways of thinking spread over most of North America. Our whole continent today bears the marks of English life.

A Memory Test

1. Why did the English want Quebec?

2. Why did General Montcalm have a hard time to carry out his plans?

3. What three difficulties did the French in Quebec have?

4. What was General Wolfe's plan of attack?

5. Why were the British able to win the battle?

6. Why was the battle of Quebec one of the greatest battles in the world's history?

Making up Riddles

Should you like to make up your own sentences again, leaving blanks in place of these names?

Names of Persons	Name of Place
1. General Wolfe	3. Plains of Abraham
2. General Montcalm	

The English wanted to take Quebec because it was the strongest place along the St. Lawrence River.

Would it have made any difference to you and me if the French had won in this war instead of the English?

THE END OF FRANCE IN NORTH AMERICA

Though the fall of Quebec ended the war, it was three years before the treaty of peace was signed. During those years the French officers and soldiers and many of the nobles of Canada went back to France. They did not want to become subjects of the king of England.

The priests, farmers, and woodsmen remained, and promised to be loyal to England. They were allowed to keep their lands and their own religion. Even today many people of eastern Canada speak French, though all around them their neighbors are English; their cities and streets have French names; and they keep up many of their old French customs.

The Treaty

France was heavily in debt and could not afford to keep up the war any longer. So she chose some of her ablest men, and England chose some of her ablest, and together they sat down to decide how peace could be made. France had been defeated in the war, so it was clear that she would have to give up some lands. But what lands?

England was not certain whether she would rather have Canada and its fur trade or one of the islands in

North America in 1763

the West Indies which had a rich sugar trade. Neither nation had any idea of the real value of Canada; they thought only of its furs. But England at last decided to keep it, and France signed a treaty of peace.

By the terms of the treaty France gave to England all her land east of the Mississippi River except two little islands in the Gulf of St. Lawrence to serve as a shelter for the French fishermen and to dry fish. But no forts were to be built on those islands. (On the map on page 447 find the lands left to the French.)

At the same time Spain, which had been helping France, gave Florida to Great Britain in order to get back some of her own islands that the British had taken. (On the map on page 447 find the British territory in North America.)

France gave Spain, to pay for her help, all the land that France had owned west of the Mississippi. Spain was not eager to have this land, but after two years she accepted it. (On the map on page 447 find the Spanish lands in North America.) All these points were written down in a paper called a *treaty*. The treaty of peace was signed in the year 1763. The men from France signed it in the name of the French government, and the men from England signed it in the name of the British government.

Results

France had met with a severe loss. Of her once proud empire extending from the St. Lawrence to the Mississippi, she had left only two little islands. She had once had a great navy. Now she had left not one warship. Never since has she built up a great navy.

England had control of the sea and had become, with Spain, owner of North America.

What was the effect of the war on the English colonies? They no longer needed the mother country to protect them from the French and the Indians. How long would they accept British rule when they no longer needed British help? We shall see.

During the war Great Britain had spent great sums of money. She was almost as deeply in debt as France. She thought that the colonists ought to help her to pay that debt, because they were the people who would use the new lands. What did the colonies think about it? We shall find out in our next unit.

Getting Ready

It is almost time for you to take the test on all of Unit IV. These questions will help you to get ready.

1. How long after the battle of Quebec was the treaty of peace signed?

2. Who decided what should be written down in the treaty?

3. What did France give to England? to Spain?

4. What did Spain give to England?

5. Name two effects that the wars had on France; name two effects that they had on England.

6. What did these wars show the English colonists?

Reminders

These words should remind you of facts you read in the story. Give one fact about each group of words.

Name of Place

1. land east of the Mississippi River

Date

2. 1763 — end of the French and English wars.

Words

3. treaty of peace.

In the peace treaty of 1763 France gave up all her claims to land east of the Mississippi, except two small islands for fishing.

England was then the strongest nation in North America.

Unit Five

How the English Colonies came to separate themselves from the Mother Country

||||||||||||||||||||||||||||||||||||||||||||||||||||||||||||||||||||||||||||||||||||||||||||||||||||||||||||||||||||||||||||||||||||||||||||

TITLES OF STORIES

Unit Five

*How the English Colonies came to separate
themselves from the Mother Country*

What does anyone mean when he says "I pay taxes"?
For what is tax money used? What do we mean by the
"mother country"? This story will tell you how the
colonies and their mother country quarreled about taxes.

WHY THE COLONIES AND THE MOTHER COUNTRY COULD NOT AGREE

Until the French and Indian War, England had paid
little attention to the colonies. She had sent out governors, had given land, and had sometimes given money,
but on the whole she had left them alone.

The Effect of Distance

Three thousand miles of ocean divided Englishmen
in America from Englishmen in England. The voyage
took two months or more. The colonists could not wait

for the mother country to help them when they were in trouble. They had to take care of themselves, and they became so used to thinking and planning for themselves that they no longer wanted to be directed by any far-away power.

Colonial Trade Laws

People of the eighteenth century believed that colonies were made for the benefit of the mother country. According to their idea, America had been settled in order that she might send to England raw iron, lumber, and wood. Out of these goods the British manufacturers would make axes and hatchets, masts and furniture, which the colonies would buy back again. Such a plan was supposed to help both parties. The *colonies were to supply the raw materials*, and the *mother country was to manufacture* those materials into goods.

In order to carry out the plan, laws were made about colonial shipping, about colonial trade, and about colonial manufacturing.

The law in regard to *shipping* said that goods could not be sent out of the colonies or brought into them except in British vessels. The Dutch did not like this law at all. But the colonists were themselves British, and so having to use British ships did not harm them much. In fact, some of them made large sums of money by building new ships. This law did not cause much trouble.

The laws in regard to *trade* provided that the colonists should sell certain of their goods only to Great Britain. Tobacco, rice, furs, and material for building

John Hancock's house in Boston

ships could not be sold anywhere in Europe except in British ports. The colonists did not like this law, because they could get more money for their goods from other countries than they could get from England.

Then too they had to buy most of their goods from England. They were not allowed to buy raisins and wine directly from Spain, or silk from China, or coffee from the West Indies. Such goods had first to pass through English ports and pay a tax, and then they were allowed to come into the colonies. Those goods which could come directly into the colonies had to pay a heavy tax.

Such laws may not seem fair to us. We might think that the colonists ought to have been allowed to buy their goods from any country which could sell cheaply. Yet all the countries of Europe had the same kinds of laws; in fact, the United States today makes much the same kind of trade laws for its own colonies.

These laws would have ruined New England and the middle colonies if they had been obeyed. But, as we read on page 453, England had left the colonies alone for a long time and had paid little attention to whether or not they were obeying the laws. So the colonies quietly continued to trade with other countries. A ship would come into a harbor at night, and its goods would be taken ashore secretly in small boats. Such secret trading, which the law did not permit, was called *smuggling*.

The law about *manufacture* provided that the colonists should not make for themselves goods which Englishmen in the Old World made and wanted to sell to them. For example, they must not make beaver hats, nor rolled iron, nor steel, because British manufacturers had such goods for sale. But how could they buy British goods without money to pay for them, and how could they get money to pay for them if they were not allowed to sell their lumber and fish and tobacco and rice where they could get a good price for them?

These laws about shipping, trade, and manufacture had been on the books for more than a hundred years, but had never been put into force strictly.

Tightening up the Laws

When England began to plan how to pay her war debt and how to support the troops in America, it was decided that the colonists themselves should pay for the

troops. They were well-to-do and could afford it.   It
would not be necessary to make new laws to raise the
money if only the laws already made were put into
force.   So England sent ships to America to see that
trading vessels should carry only the kinds of goods that
the laws allowed.   Officers were sent to look over all the
goods as they were landed.   Soldiers were sent to search
in colonial barns and houses for goods which had been
smuggled.   England treated the colonies as if they were
children, not stopping to think that the children had
grown up.

The tightening up of the old laws made the colonists
very angry; they had been let alone for such a long
time.   They did not question the right of the mother
country to lay a tax on goods brought in at the ports,
but they did not think that soldiers should be allowed
to search their homes.   They said they did not want
British troops to defend them, and they kept on
smuggling as they had done before.

A Direct Tax

The ships, officers, and soldiers that were needed to
collect the port taxes cost so much that little was left to
pay the troops.   So the king's men tried a different
plan.   The English Parliament passed a law that all
newspapers, bills, notes, letters, — almost all papers
used in business in the colonies, — must have on them
stamps which were made and sold by the British government.   The money raised from the sale of these
stamps was to be used to govern and protect the colo-

nies. The king's men knew that this tax would be easy to gather, and they thought that the colonists would not object much to it. They asked Franklin if he could think of a plan which would work any better, but he could not. The *Stamp Act* became a law in 1765. It was called a *direct tax* because each citizen paid it directly to the king's officers.

To the king's surprise the anger of the colonists at the laws taxing goods at their ports was as nothing compared to their rage at the Stamp Act. It was not the amount of the tax that they objected to, but the fact that it was a tax which they had not agreed to and which their representatives had no part in making. The assemblies in the different colonies had often laid such taxes on their own people, and the colonists believed that they were the only ones who had the right to do so. They did not want the English Parliament to lay a tax upon them directly.

What a storm was raised! Newspapers came out with black borders as if for a death. Straw men were made to represent the men who sold the stamps, and were burned in public squares. The stores which had stamps for sale were set on fire. Samuel Adams in the North and Patrick Henry in the South made fierce speeches against the act.

A meeting, or congress, of representatives from different colonies sent a message to the king, asking him to remove the tax. Merchants in the colonies agreed not to buy any English goods until a change should be made ; and a society called the Sons of Liberty declared that they would continue to use papers without stamps. Many

Franklin before one of the Houses of Parliament

From a painting by Charles E. Mills

people even in England believed that Parliament had gone beyond its rights. Soon the Stamp Tax was removed. The colonists were full of joy and thanked George III, the king of England. They felt that the trouble was over.

Nobody talked about independence yet. What they wanted was to be ruled only by their own colonial assemblies, not by the English Parliament.

Back to Taxes at the Ports

Instead of the Stamp Act, the king's men went back to the plan of taxing goods at the ports. The goods that were taxed this time were glass, paper, paints, and tea. The colonists did not object to the plan itself; but they were not willing that the money thus raised should be used to pay the king's officers in America — his governors and his judges. If they were to pay for these officers, they wanted to have something to say about choosing them.

Again the merchants in the colonies agreed not to buy English goods until the law was changed. Women agreed to drink no more tea so long as there was a tax upon it. Again the colonies wrote letters to one another, promising to buy nothing from Great Britain. British merchants soon lost so much of their trade that they too wanted the tax removed. After a time glass, paper, and paints were allowed to come in free. The only tax that remained was that on tea. This was kept by England to show that she had a right to tax the colonies. But though the tax was small the colonists steadily refused to pay it.

For two years nothing important happened.   The tax was continued; the people refused to buy; and tea was smuggled in whenever it was possible.   Most people believed that the trouble was over.

The Quarrel about Representation

Now, while matters between England and the colonies are quiet, let us go back and find out why the colonists believed the English Parliament had no right to tax them.   On page 459 is a picture of the English Parliament.   These men were Englishmen.   They met in London and made the laws for Great Britain.

For more than five hundred years these men had been the only people who had the right to lay taxes in the mother country.   The great question was, Did the English Parliament have the right to tax the colonies also?

England said to the colonies, "You *are represented* in Parliament and therefore Parliament can tax you." (Children in the grades in school will not understand why England believed this until they study history in the high school.)   The colonists at first thought that if they could send men from America to be members of Parliament, they would be satisfied.   Look at the picture on page 459.   Do you think that a few men from America would be able to have their way when all the rest of the members wanted things done differently?

At last the colonists said, "We *are not represented* in Parliament; we do not even want to be; and therefore Parliament must not tax us."

You can see that England held one idea about representation and that the colonies held another idea. Neither one understood the other, and neither one would give in.

The Beginning of the End

The king had sent troops to America even before the Stamp Act was passed, and the colonists did not like to have them there. So the soldiers and the townspeople had a great many quarrels. Boys threw snowballs at the soldiers; and once the soldiers fired on a crowd in Boston, killing six Americans. Each side grew more and more angry at the other.

Then England changed the way in which tea was to be sold. The colonists still objected. Ships loaded with tea began to arrive in their harbors. What were they to do? In some cities they allowed it to land, but stored it away, and no one would buy it. In others the ships were made to return to England without landing.

In Boston a great meeting was called to decide what should be done, for the governor would not allow the colonists to send the ships back. They talked until it grew dark. Samuel Adams, who was probably the first American to believe that independence would come out of this trouble, then rose and said, "This meeting can do no more to save the country."

At this signal some fifty men dressed as Indians ran to the wharf, rowed out to the ships, and began to break open the boxes of tea, throwing both boxes and tea into the harbor. For two hours they worked — so quietly that the people on shore could hear only the sound of

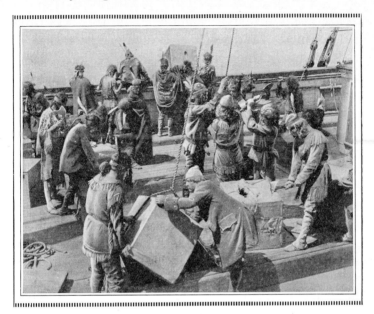

The Boston Tea Party

What are they going to do with these boxes? (From "The Eve of the Revolution," one of The Chronicles of America Photoplays. Copyright, Yale University Press)

their axes, but no voices. The next morning tea was scattered along the beach for miles. Seventy-five thousand dollars' worth had been destroyed. This was called the Boston Tea Party.

When the king learned of it he was very angry. Even men who had been friends of the colonists thought they had done wrong and that they should only have refused to buy the tea. Boston was punished. Her harbor was closed. No vessels were allowed to come in or go out until the tea was paid for.

The result was great suffering. No work was to be had, for most of the people of Boston had been engaged in shipping. Many almost starved. More British soldiers were sent over to see that the punishment was strictly carried out.

Other Colonies take up Boston's Cause

Quickly other colonies came to the aid of Boston. They sent flour, wheat, corn, and rice, using wagons because no boats could get into the harbor. They sent whole flocks of sheep. They also called a meeting, or congress, at Philadelphia to decide what they should do to stop the trouble. The representatives came from twelve different colonies, and the meeting was called the First Continental Congress. John Adams was there, and Samuel Adams, and Patrick Henry, and George Washington, and many other great men. At last this was a meeting which could speak for all the American colonists. Patrick Henry said: "There are no more differences between Virginians, New Yorkers, and New Englanders. I am not a Virginian, but an American."

They drew up a list of what they thought were their rights and sent letters to the king and to the British Parliament. They agreed to buy nothing from England and sell nothing to her until the trouble was settled.

The next year another meeting was held, called the Second Continental Congress. No answer had been received from the letters that had been sent, but blood had been shed in America, and war had begun.

What was the Trouble?

When we try to set down the causes of the Revolution in a few words, no single act or happening can be mentioned. We might sum up the matter thus: England felt that the colonies wanted the *rights* of Englishmen, but were not willing to do the *duties* of Englishmen. Thus she blamed them for the trouble.

The colonies were willing to remain British, but they wanted the right to govern themselves completely, even to deciding on their own taxes. Great Britain answered this demand by saying, "Then you would not be a part of the British Empire at all."

The real problem, then, was this: *How may a colony govern itself completely, and yet remain part of a larger nation?* Neither side could solve the problem. It was not solved until the United States found a way fourteen years later.

Finding your Score

If you can answer all these questions, your score is 8. Look back in the story for help if you need to. If you cannot find the answer to one question, your score is 7; if you cannot find the answer to two questions, your score is 6; and so on. What is *your* score?

1. What did people in the eighteenth century think that colonies should send to the mother country? that the mother country should send to the colonies?

2. What laws were made about shipping? about trade? about manufacture?

3. How did the colonists keep from obeying the trade laws?

4. What is a direct tax? Why did they object to it?

5. Why did the colonists object when the king tried again to collect taxes at the ports?

6. How did England blame the colonies for the trouble?

7. What did the colonists say they wanted?

8. What problem could neither side solve?

A Matching Game

In the column at the right you will find words which describe the words in the column at the left. Copy the words *in the right-hand column*. Put the figure 1 before those which describe Samuel Adams (No. 1 in the left-hand column); put the figure 2 before those which describe Patrick Henry; and so on.

1. Samuel Adams	money paid to the government
2. Patrick Henry	the king of England during the Revolution
3. George III	the group of men who represented all the colonies
4. 1765	a leader in the Boston Tea Party
5. tax	the great war which changed our form of government
6. Revolution	when the Stamp Act was passed
7. Continental Congress	a great speaker in the South

The mother country thought that the colonies were made for her benefit.

The colonies did not want England to interfere with their trade.

They wanted to govern themselves completely.

Have you ever heard of Paul Revere's ride? Perhaps your teacher will read Longfellow's poem about it to your class. This story will help you to understand it.

THE WAR BEGINS IN NEW ENGLAND

No sooner had King George III closed the port of Boston than the country round about began to prepare for trouble. Towns stored arms and ammunition in barns and empty houses. Boys and men drilled every night on the village green. Some of them were "minutemen"; that is, men ready to march to war at a minute's notice.

Colonists who remained loyal to the king became known as *Tories*. Often they were badly treated by the other colonists. The New England men who were ready to fight England were known as *Yankees*. The song "Yankee Doodle" was sung by the British soldiers to make fun of them.

Lexington and Concord, 1775

The British general in Boston was told that arms and ammunition were being gathered at Concord, a village about eighteen miles away. Secretly he sent orders for a small body of troops to go out and destroy them. The soldiers gathered at night by the waterside and set out on the march.

In some way the colonists learned of this plan. Paul Revere rode on horseback through the dark, over one of the roads, while others took other roads, warning the farmers and townspeople of the coming of the British. The soldiers soon found out from the sound of guns and bells and from signal bonfires that their purpose was known, and they sent back to Boston for help.

Samuel Adams and another leader of the Revolution were known to be staying at Lexington, a village on the way to Concord. The king's troops had been ordered first to seize these two leaders and then to advance to Concord and destroy the ammunition.

Very early in the morning they arrived in Lexington, where they were met by a group of country people with guns in their hands. The farmers did not look at all like soldiers, but they knew how to shoot. Some of them had fought in the old French wars.

The British officer commanded them to lay down their guns and return to their homes. He was not obeyed. Someone fired a shot — whether it was an American or a British soldier is not clear. It does not matter. War had begun.

Firing continued for a few minutes on both sides. Eight Americans were killed or died from their wounds. The others moved silently away. The two leaders whom the British had been sent to seize were not to be found.

The troops then marched on to Concord, six miles farther, where they set fire to the village courthouse and destroyed what ammunition and supplies had not been carried away. At the Concord bridge they met a large number of minutemen who had gathered from all the country round about. A sharp fight followed. One of

Gathering the army together

What do you suppose the messenger is saying? (From a painting by
John Ward Dunsmore)

our poets has said that at Concord was fired the "shot
heard round the world." What he meant was that the
battle of Concord was fought by a people determined to
govern themselves, and that before long other countries
all over the world would do the same.

The Return to Boston

By this time the British troops were very tired.
They had marched eighteen miles from Boston, with no
breakfast and no dinner, and had fought two battles.
The commanding officer allowed them to rest a little
after the fight at the bridge was over; then they started
on the march back to Lexington.

All the way a sharp fire was poured upon them from behind trees, rocks, and stone walls. Minutemen had been gathering all the morning. The fire upon the British was so heavy that they could not even stop to pick up their wounded.

At noon they reached Lexington, where, to their great joy, they found the second body of troops that had been sent out to help them. It was high time, for they were hungry and worn out. Their ammunition was gone, and many were wounded. They dropped down on the ground, "their tongues hanging out like dogs after a chase."

They could rest only a short time, for they still had to march twelve miles back to Boston. And again from behind every hill, fence, house, barn, and stone wall came the fire of the colonists. "The Americans seemed to drop from the clouds," the British said.

It was after dark when they reached Boston. The expedition had been a failure, and the whole force had narrowly escaped being captured. (Find Lexington, Concord, and Boston on the map on page 471.)

The Siege of Boston

The news flew to the other colonies. Within twenty days even far-away Georgia had heard of the fight. An army began to gather outside of Boston. What an army! Some were boys, and some were old men. Some had left their plows standing in the fields in which they had been working when the news came. Each man supplied his own gun and his clothing. None of them had uniforms.

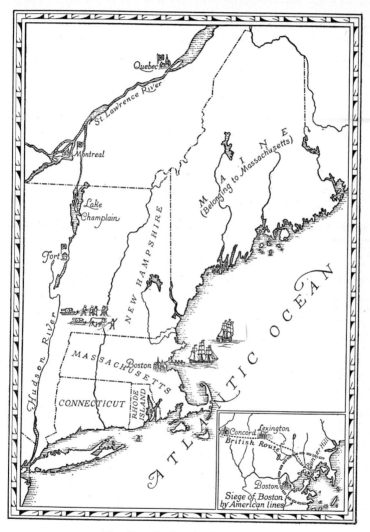

The Revolution in the North

There were not enough houses or tents for all to sleep in, nor enough kettles to cook their food, nor enough blankets to keep them warm. There was no leader to command them, and no plan of war. Yet this army spread in a great circle around Boston and let no supplies reach the British troops who were shut up within the town. Many of the Yankees had already left Boston and were living in villages close by.

The Fort on Lake Champlain

A danger greatly to be feared was that the British might come down from Canada to New York and thus cut the colonies in two. To prevent such a movement, a company of colonists called "Green Mountain Boys," with a few others, set out for the region around Lake Champlain without asking permission from anybody. Early one morning they reached the British fort and dashed in, to the great surprise of the soldiers on guard, who had not yet heard of Lexington and Concord. The commander, only half awake and not yet dressed, was ordered to surrender.

More than a hundred cannon and a large amount of powder and balls were taken. Later we shall learn how these were used.

In the same year Washington sent expeditions to take Quebec and Montreal, but they failed. Canada would not join the Revolution.

Bunker Hill

Around Boston rise a number of hills. On one of them, called Bunker Hill, the British decided to place cannon to protect the town. But the Americans were ahead of them; and quietly one dark night they seized a hill to the east of Bunker Hill. All through the night a thousand men worked with spades, throwing up a wall of earth, and by morning it was six feet high. Though they were within gunshot of five British ships they had not been heard. (Find Bunker Hill on the map on page 471.)

When the British general saw this fort in the morning, he knew that he must attack it at once or it would fire upon Boston. He could have gone around and approached the Americans from behind, but he believed his soldiers could defeat them anyway. Therefore he attacked directly from the front.

The British troops marched out heavily loaded with packs containing three days' food. Though suffering from the heat, they began steadily to climb the hill. The American officer, whose men had very little powder, ordered, "Do not fire until you can see the whites of their eyes."

When the British had advanced far up the hill, all at once a sudden fire burst forth upon them. Those in the front ranks fell. The others faced the guns for some moments and then retreated.

But at the bottom of the hill they drew themselves together and came on again. The "crack shots" among the colonists each selected an officer in a red coat and brought him down. With true British courage, however, the soldiers stood their ground as best they could, and the second time they were successful. The Americans were quite worn out with digging all night and fighting all day. They had powder enough for only one more round. So they fired and then had to retreat; and the redcoats gained the hill.

It was a victory for the British, but their losses were very heavy. All that night wagons were busy bringing their dead and wounded into Boston. The Americans had not lost nearly so many, and they had learned that they could stand up in battle against the king's best soldiers. This gave them courage to go on.

Washington made Commander in Chief

When the Congress in Philadelphia learned that war had already begun, they had to choose a leader for the army. There was one man who, above all others, seemed fitted for this place. George Washington was made commander in chief. He was in doubt as to whether or not he could fill the place, but he promised to do his best. Without this "best" of his it seems that the Revolution could not possibly have succeeded.

When the new commander reached his army he saw what a task lay before him. He had to bring order out of the mixed crowd of men and tents scattered about the hills. He had to drill the men. He had to plan for feeding numbers of men, for supplying them with clothing and places to sleep, and for finding doctors to care for the wounded. He had to persuade Congress to raise money enough to pay the men for their time.

The British leaving Boston

Can you see the wall of earth built by the Americans? (From an
old engraving)

For months he did not have enough powder even to
fire on the troops in Boston. At the end of the year
most of the soldiers said that their time was up, and
that they were going home. He had to persuade as
many as he could to stay in the army.

It was a good thing for the Americans that the British
did not make an attack at that time. But the British
general delayed, hoping even yet that war might not be
necessary.

Meanwhile the people in Boston were suffering.
There was little food to be had anywhere. Doors and
church towers were torn down and burned to keep the
people warm. So many died that at last the church
bells were no longer rung for them.

The winter dragged on. Washington could not attack; and as long as the British in Boston could get supplies from England by sea, they could not be driven away. But at last the worst of the winter was over, and cannon and ammunition from the captured fort on Lake Champlain were dragged on sleds to Boston. Then Washington could attack.

One dark night the Americans advanced to the hills south of Boston. Eight hundred men with wagons and spades went ahead, then twelve hundred men with oxcarts and lumber, and then the heavy guns. All night they dug and built, and in the morning the British found American cannon pointing down toward the city. (On the map on page 471, find the line which shows the siege of Boston.)

The British ships in the harbor sent word that they could not stay without danger of being blown to pieces. There was nothing for the British army to do but to leave Boston. This they did, taking many of the Tories with them and leaving behind a great store of cannon, powder, balls, and other supplies, which they could not carry away.

The war in *New England* (east of the Hudson) was over. Boston was now in the hands of the Americans and remained so during the rest of the war.

Getting Ready

1. Who were the Tories?

2. Why were the British soldiers sent to Concord? Why were they sent to Lexington?

3. Who took the forts on Lake Champlain? Why?

4. What did the battle of Bunker Hill teach the Americans?

5. Why did Washington not attack Boston at once?

6. Why did the British at last leave Boston?

A Test on Missing Words

Write the words which should be placed in the blanks below. Show the list to your teacher.

1. The people in the mother country were called _____.

2. The first battle of the Revolution was fought at _____.

3. The first great battle was the battle of _____ _____.

4. The shot "heard round the world" was fired at _____.

5. The war began in the year _____.

6. All the colonies east of the Hudson River together were called _____ _____.

7. An American who took the side of Great Britain was called a _____.

8. A native of the New England colonies was called a _____.

9. The song _____ _____ was sung to make fun of the Americans.

England punished Massachusetts, so the rest of the colonies helped Massachusetts.

The colonists drove the British out of Boston.

In the North the Americans were successful.

What is meant by "the cause"? What does the title of the story tell about the Revolution in the middle colonies? Should you like to know why there was more danger there than in New England?

DANGER TO THE CAUSE IN THE MIDDLE COLONIES

The Declaration of Independence Signed

When the British army left Boston, Washington knew that they would attack some other colony, and would probably attack by sea. At what point would they strike next? He believed it would be New York; for if New York could be taken, Massachusetts and Virginia, the two leaders of the Revolution, would be separated.

Therefore Washington hurried down to the mouth of the Hudson, his army moving more slowly after him. In the meantime Congress was signing the Declaration of Independence, about which we shall read later.

The Battles for New York

The Americans were too few to defend New York, for the British might land almost anywhere on the islands or the mainland near the mouth of the Hudson. But preparations were made to receive them. Forts were hastily stocked with supplies, and walls of earth were thrown up on the hills which overlooked the city.

478

Nathan Hale

What do you think Nathan Hale has been saying? (From a painting
by Stanley M. Arthurs)

On came the great British force in seven hundred
ships. Two brothers were in command; one in command of the army, and the other in command of the
navy. Neither of these commanders was in favor of
war; both hoped to come to terms without fighting.
Washington did not know how many men the British

had or what their plans were. When he asked for someone to find out for him, a young schoolmaster from Connecticut, Nathan Hale, offered to go. Although young Hale knew he was risking his life, he entered the British lines and found out their numbers and some of their plans. When he was almost ready to leave he was discovered, tried, and sentenced to death. Just before he was hanged, he said, "I only regret that I have but one life to give for my country."

For two days after the British landed, Washington did not have time to sleep. He was busy everywhere. In the first battle on Long Island he lost heavily; if the British had pushed on quickly they probably could have taken his entire army. But they did not. While they waited he gathered every kind of boat that he could lay his hands upon one night, put Massachusetts fishermen in charge of them, and before morning had moved his ten thousand men to a safe place on the mainland.

Again the British commanders lost time by offering peace; but they did not promise the Americans the right to decide their own taxes, so the offer was firmly refused.

After the British had taken Long Island the city lay open to them. Many of the citizens left and, taking what goods they could carry, moved north into the country. The Tories, of course, stayed. They offered their houses for the soldiers to stay in and gave them splendid dinners.

The British took possession of the city, and there they remained for seven years, until the war was over and their soldiers were called home.

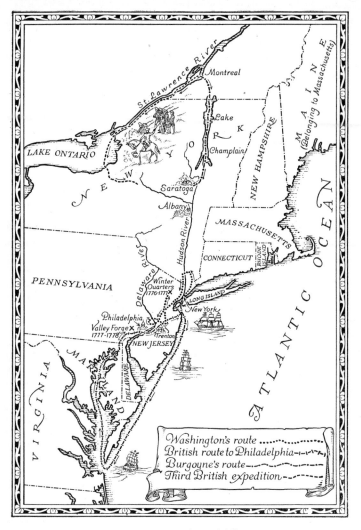

The Revolution in the middle states

Washington had to fall back to the higher land north of New York. One of the most important points in the whole country had been lost; and if the British should sail up the Hudson they could carry out their plan of cutting the colonies in two. Washington wanted to prevent this at all costs. But the only thing which saved the Americans was that the British moved slowly.

The ill fortune which began with the loss of New York continued. Two great forts that guarded the Hudson were taken, and with them most of the supplies of blankets, guns, and powder for the American army (or the Continental army, as it was then called). This loss was worse than the loss of a battle. More British troops arrived, and Washington had to cross the river into New Jersey. He ordered one of his trusted generals to come after him, but the general did not obey. (On the map on page 481, show the route that Washington took.)

The Retreat across New Jersey: the Darkest Hour of the Revolution

Matters quickly went from bad to worse. The British were following the Americans so closely that as the last of one army was marching out of a town, the first of the other might be seen entering it. There were six British soldiers for one American; so it was clear that Washington could not stand and give battle. He had expected to be joined by large numbers of men in New Jersey, but less than a hundred appeared. Many of his soldiers became discouraged and deserted; at times he had only three thousand to face eighteen thousand of the enemy. Congress, not understanding his difficulties, found fault with the way he was managing affairs. At this time England made another peace offer, which many of the colonists wanted to accept.

Washington's men were forced across the Delaware River; and if it had not been for his wisdom in seizing all the boats up and down both sides of the river for many miles, his army and the city of Philadelphia would probably have been taken.

It was December, and on New Year's Day the time of most of the Continental soldiers would be ended. They said that they were going home. It looked as if within a few weeks the commander in chief would be left without an army.

This was the most discouraging time of the war. Washington wrote to his brother, "I think the game is pretty near up." Some of the British generals packed their bags and sent them to the ships, believing that the fighting was over. (On the map, p. 481, find the place where Washington was forced to cross the Delaware.)

Things take a Turn for the Better

Washington now took a bold step. He knew that the British general had gone back to New York for Christmas, leaving in the nearest town some German troops whom King George III had hired to fight for him. They had no interest in the war in America, and at Christmas they would probably be thinking of their far-away homes rather than of winning battles.

Washington decided to go back across the Delaware and attack them. Christmas night came, stormy and bitterly cold. The river was running swiftly and was full of floating ice. It seemed impossible for an army with its heavy guns to cross in rowboats. The other American generals said it could not be done.

But Washington was determined. That night he chose twenty-five hundred soldiers, put his boats again in the care of Massachusetts fishermen, and within ten hours every man and all his cannon were safely over.

By early morning they were once more on the New Jersey side. A march of nine miles through the storm was still necessary. Some of the men marched barefoot, leaving bloody tracks in the snow. They reached the town at about eight o'clock, surprised the Germans completely, and took many prisoners.

This victory meant much to the Americans. They took courage, and many of those who had said that they were going home promised to remain in the army six weeks longer. The British began to think that conquering the colonies might take a little more time.

After this victory Washington fell back a few miles. The British commander, General Cornwallis, who had hurried back from New York, set out to attack him. By the time he came in sight of the American troops it was late afternoon, so he put off fighting until the following day. He said he was sure that he could "bag the old fox" this time.

All night long fires burned in the American camp; men could be seen throwing up a wall of earth, and the sound of their voices was plainly heard by the British

George Washington

From a painting by James Peale

guards. But when morning came Cornwallis found only the wall of earth and empty fields beyond it. The "old fox" had quietly drawn off his soldiers by a back road, had led them around behind the British lines, and had cut off the British supply trains from New York. A second victory had been won.

The Americans had by that time been fighting or marching for eighteen hours and were worn out; so Washington moved northward into the hills and settled down into winter quarters. So long as he remained there, New Jersey was not a safe place for the British. They would have to return to New York. (On the map on page 481, find Washington's route after he came back across the Delaware.)

The Continental army had been saved. Fighting would begin again in the spring. Washington's wisdom and promptness had won a success that filled the Americans with hope. What might have happened if he had failed in New Jersey?

What happened in the Spring

Philadelphia was the next most important point in the middle colonies. It was the largest American city and the place where Congress met. The British now held New York, but they felt that they must take Philadelphia also. Many Tories lived there, and it was thought that they would be glad to help. The British general felt sure that if he took Philadelphia too the Revolution would be over, and Washington would be forced to ask for peace.

The Americans seemed to have little chance of holding Philadelphia. The British fleet could land an army anywhere they chose along the coast. They had plenty of money, and their soldiers had to remain with the army for years at a time.

Washington never had enough money, he had no ships, and his men usually served for either six weeks or three months. Some of them served for six months or even nine months, but that was considered a very long term. Congress was slow to act, and often was not able to raise money or to gather troops, even when it tried.

But the British had their troubles too. They were three thousand miles away from home; all their food, clothing, blankets, and ammunition had to be carried across the ocean in ships. To carry supplies so far took a long time and cost a great deal of money. The British soldiers did not know the country as the Americans did, and many times they let Washington and his men slip through their fingers. Then too some of their own citizens in England were not in favor of war against brother Englishmen in America. Some of their greatest leaders said so very plainly.

The Advance on Philadelphia

Washington was eager to keep the British army so busy around New York and Philadelphia that it could not move up the Hudson. He was willing to suffer defeats, if necessary, so long as he kept the British away from the North.

So he was glad when he learned that they were on their way to Philadelphia. He would delay them as much as he could; and even if they took Philadelphia they would not have time that year to turn north and sail up the Hudson.

He met them at a little stream on the way to Philadelphia, and though he could not beat them he delayed them. The city at last was taken, and Congress had to leave. The British troops made themselves very much at home in the richest town of all the colonies. Many townspeople were glad to sell their products for good British gold instead of the worthless paper money of the United States. (On the map on page 481, find the route of the British from New York to Philadelphia.)

After a time the British general received orders from London to return to New York and advance up the Hudson River to help another general who was coming down from Canada. But he dared not move, for Washington kept him busy by attacking again and again.

When fall came it was too late to give help in the North. The force coming down from Canada had already been met by another part of the American army and had been forced to surrender. Matters had worked out as Washington had hoped they would.

Now, while the British are holding both Philadelphia and New York in the middle states and seem to have defeated Washington, let us turn to the story of this expedition which had been forced to surrender to the Americans in the North.

Cornwallis entering Philadelphia

From a painting by H. A. Ogden

The British Plan to cut the Colonies in Two

Up to this time the British had lost a few small battles, but had received no great defeat. They had lost the Northern states, but in the middle states they seemed much more powerful than the Americans. They believed that they could hurry the war to a close if they could separate New England from the rest of the colonies. It would be like cutting the head away from the body.

There were three parts to their plan. One British army was to sail up the Hudson from New York. Another was to come down from Canada by way of Lake Champlain and meet the first army near Albany. A third army was to go by way of the St. Lawrence River and Lake Ontario to the Mohawk River, and join the others at the Hudson. The British were no doubt very proud of their plan and felt sure that it would succeed. (On page 481, find the three parts of this plan.)

But it did not work out as they had planned. The general of the New York forces did not receive his orders in time and, as we know, went to Philadelphia, where he settled down for the winter. One important part of the plan, then, failed before the others were begun.

Burgoyne's Expedition

Now we will follow the British army which was ordered to come down from Canada by way of Lake Champlain. General Burgoyne was in command. He had seven thousand men and hundreds of Indians. He advanced very easily as far as Lake Champlain, and after a little delay took the forts there.

Then leaving his ships, he began to march overland to the Hudson. But the Americans had burned all the bridges on the way and had cut down great trees across the roads. In many places there were no roads; the British army had to struggle through the wilderness, dragging after them their heavy cannon and their supply wagons. In twenty-four days they advanced only twenty-six miles, and during that time they had to build forty bridges.

It took so long to make the journey that their supplies began to fail. The wheat, flour, and meat for seven thousand men had to be brought all the way from England, so we know that they could not get more for a long time. Canada had nothing to give them except hay. The Americans had driven off all the cattle and burned all the crops in the country through which they had to pass. In the wilderness no supplies of any kind were to be found.

Every time that Burgoyne sent troops to the settlements of Vermont and New York to get food, the farmers would hastily gather a force and drive them back. Still the British struggled on.

Burgoyne looked longingly toward the Hudson for help, but we know that none was coming. (On the map on page 481, find Burgoyne's route.)

His Indians deserted him because he tried to keep them from killing the country people and stealing their property. Many of his own men also began to slip away into the woods.

The Third Expedition

What had happened in the meantime to the third expedition? It had sailed up the St. Lawrence, crossed Lake Ontario, and was advancing by land to the Mohawk River. At least half this force were Indians. When the Americans learned of its coming, a small force was sent to meet it. The road led over a narrow bridge through a swamp, and there the two forces met.

The battle that followed was the most bloody of the war. Slipping and sliding in the mud, pushing each other from the bridge into the swamp, and falling into the dark water as they grappled one another, both sides fought fiercely. A heavy rain began to fall and wet their powder. Then only axes and knives could be used, and the battle grew more terrible than ever.

At a place a little farther west an American general was badly wounded. He could not stand, but he calmly sat down under a tree and directed the battle by shouting his orders. A few days later he died from his wounds.

At a fort a short distance away the American flag, which had just been chosen by Congress, was used for the first time in battle. It was made of a white shirt, a blue coat, and some red strips from a woman's dress.

At last news was brought to the British that a great force of Americans was advancing under another general. So the British forces retreated. Their third expedition had failed. (On the map on page 481, find the route of this expedition.)

Washington and Lafayette at Valley Forge
From a painting by John Ward Dunsmore

Saratoga, 1777

Burgoyne was thus left alone, surrounded on all sides by American forces. Both the expeditions which were to have helped him had failed. He also wanted to retreat, but his orders from England left no choice but to go on to the Hudson.

His men were deserting daily, his food was almost gone, and he was surrounded by American troops who seemed to spring up out of the ground. Soon they numbered four to his one.

Several times he tried to attack, but was not successful. Finally, at Saratoga, in the fall of 1777 he had to surrender. England lost ten thousand men and suffered her first great defeat of the war. The British plan had failed. Another of the greatest battles in the history of the world was ended. (On the map on page 481, find Saratoga.)

Valley Forge

To Washington, standing guard over the British army in Philadelphia, the news from Saratoga brought courage to hold out. Winter came, and he led his army to Valley Forge, where he could keep watch over Philadelphia. (Find Valley Forge on the map on page 481.)

The weather was terribly cold. For shelter the soldiers had to cut down trees and make huts for themselves. The horses starved because there was no food for them, and men had to pull the wagons and sleds.

There was not enough clothing or shoes for all, and again as they marched through the snow they left

bloody tracks. There were no blankets, and in some of
the huts not even sheets. No medicines were to be had;
the sick lay on the frozen ground without beds or even
straw. There was no soap. Once the soldiers had no
bread for three days. It was fortunate that armies in
those days did not have the custom of fighting battles
in the winter.

The pay of the men was sometimes two or three
years past due. United States paper money was worth
almost nothing. Washington said that it took a wagonload of money to pay for a wagonload of goods. At
times a paper dollar was really worth about two cents.
The country people would not sell their pigs and cattle
and hay to Washington for this paper money, but were
glad to sell them for British gold.

One of the members of Congress who tried to raise
money for the army was Robert Morris, a rich citizen
of Philadelphia. He often went about from house to
house, borrowing to pay the soldiers. He spent his own
fortune, passed several years in prison for debt, and
died a poor man; but he is remembered as one who
did much to win the war.

In Valley Forge men deserted every day, and when
their time was up many officers would not stay in the
army. We cannot blame them. Our only wonder is
that *any* remained at all. But they did.

Congress found fault with Washington because he
did not fight more battles. Some of his own officers
plotted against him and tried to have the command
taken from him. It was under such discouraging con-
ditions as these that his true greatness showed forth.

Yet in the midst of his troubles he found many friends who were true to him. His secretary, young Alexander Hamilton, was a great help; so was the noble Frenchman Lafayette, who had left home, family, and wealth to fight for the freedom of the states. A German officer who had served in the finest army in Europe spent the whole winter drilling the army and teaching them how to use their guns.

All felt that if they could live through the winter they might hope for better things in the spring.

Effects of the Battle of Saratoga

In France the news of the battle of Saratoga was received with great interest. Very early in the war Congress had sent representatives to different countries, asking for help, and France had not known what to do. She wanted to see England defeated, for England had been her enemy and might be so again. But she did not want to fight England alone. So she helped America quietly by giving guns and powder and sometimes lending gold to pay the soldiers.

But America now needed more help than could be given in that way. So Congress asked Benjamin Franklin to go to France and try to persuade the French king to help them openly. Franklin, then a man seventy years old, consented to make the hard voyage and to do what he could.

The battle of Saratoga made the French more ready to help. The colonies then seemed to have a fair chance of winning. So a treaty of trade and commerce was signed between France and the United States of America, and France declared that she considered the United States a nation and no longer a group of English colonies. Then the two nations signed another treaty in which they agreed to fight together to the end, the only treaty of its kind that the United States ever signed.

Very soon afterwards France sent to America armies, supplies, and, more important than anything else, a part of her fleet. Before that time Washington had many times been forced to stand and watch the British moving their armies from place to place by sea. He had not been able to prevent them, for he had no ships. But now, with the French fleet to help, the American army would be much more powerful.

In a very short time England had to fight not only the colonies and France but also, in Europe, Spain, and Holland. So she could send few forces to continue the struggle in America.

End of the War in the Middle Colonies

When word reached America that the French were coming, the British in Philadelphia were much concerned. Most of their supplies had to be brought in by sea, and the French fleet might easily cut them off.

Then too, if the British tried to hold both New York and Philadelphia, their army would be divided. Either part might be surrounded and attacked. They decided, therefore, to give up Philadelphia and to gather all their troops in New York. This they did, and remained in New York during the rest of the war.

Washington entered Philadelphia as soon as the British had left; and Congress moved back. They felt that they were safe again. Then for several years Washington's chief task was to keep the British shut up in New York. He did not dare to leave them and go south to help his generals in Georgia and Carolina, but had to pretend that he was ready to attack at any time.

Choosing Partners

First prove to yourself that you can answer these questions. Turn back in the story to be sure that you are right. Then perhaps your teacher will let you choose a partner and ask the questions of him.

1. Why did Washington not fight the British army instead of retreating across New Jersey?

2. What were four difficulties met by the American army? four difficulties met by the British?

3. How did the British plan to cut the colonies in two?

4. Why is the battle of Saratoga called one of the world's most important battles?

5. Why did France decide to help the United States?

6. Why did the British give up Philadelphia?

Testing your Partner

Be sure that you yourself can use all the words on page 498 in sentences. Then hear the sentences your partner has prepared. If he makes a mistake, prove to him from the story that he is wrong.

Names of Persons	*Date*
1. Lafayette	8. 1777, battle of Saratoga
2. General Burgoyne	
3. Robert Morris	
4. Nathan Hale	

Names of Places	*Words*
5. Saratoga	9. retreat
6. Valley Forge	10. surrender
7. Albany	

The British held New York throughout the war.

Burgoyne could not cut the colonies in two.

Washington's army suffered a great deal.

It was very hard to find money enough to buy supplies for the army.

France helped the colonies when she knew that the British had failed at Saratoga.

What part of the United States was called the North-west? Your teacher will show it to you on the map. This story tells how our soldiers had to wade through icy water, sometimes up to their necks, in order to capture the enemy's forts in the Northwest.

HOW THE NORTHWEST WAS WON

At the time of the Revolution the British troops were holding the forts in the West which had formerly belonged to the French. There were only five of any size; each consisted of a blockhouse in which were a few British soldiers, and a village in which the settlers were chiefly French farmers and traders.

The British did not try to settle the land beyond the mountains; in fact, King George III wanted to keep the colonists shut up in the narrow plains along the seacoast. But we have already learned that pioneers had advanced into the wilderness to settle Kentucky and Tennessee, and that Virginia had sent Washington to warn the French away from the Ohio. The colonists seemed determined to spread toward the west, no matter what the English king thought about it.

The Revolution begins beyond the Mountains

When the Revolution began, the British soldiers at Detroit, Mackinac, and the forts in the Illinois country did not know what to do. There were no Americans near enough for them to attack, and they dared not leave their posts to join the British army in New York. How, then, could they take any part in the war?

The only way was to make use of the Indians. So the British gave guns and ammunition to the savages and sent them out against the backwoods settlements. To prove that they had killed white people, they used to carry scalps back to Detroit, where the British general paid for them — as much for the scalp of a woman as for a man's.

The settlers in Kentucky suffered severely; for a time all attempts to settle the West stopped. The settlers also tried to get help from the Indians, but they had less money for presents than the British, and the Indians wanted pay for everything they did. Then too the Indians did not like the people who had cut down their trees and made farms in their hunting grounds. So most of them took the side of the British.

The Plan of George Rogers Clark

One of the pioneers in Kentucky who had spent years defending the settlements against Indian attacks was George Rogers Clark. Clark was a young man of twenty-five, tall and strong, with red hair and sparkling bright eyes. Like Washington, he was a hunter and a surveyor. He thought to himself: "Why wait here in Kentucky until the Indians come to attack us? We know they are being sent out from the forts in Detroit and the Illinois country. Why not make an expedition against those forts and put an end to our troubles? Let us march against them."

He sent out two young men to see how well the forts were protected. These men came back and reported that the forts were weak. The idea that the war could be carried so far west had never entered the heads of the British officers. The French in the villages around the forts had no love for the British and would probably give them little help in battle.

Clark decided to carry out his plan. But where could he get troops and money? Not in Kentucky, which was already fighting for its life. Perhaps Virginia would help. So he went back to Virginia by way of Boone's Wilderness Road, and overtook on the way a party of discouraged settlers who were going back to find greater safety.

The governor of Virginia, Patrick Henry, listened to the plan and thought it was a good one; but he could give only a little money and the permission to raise troops. The expedition had to be kept a secret in order to surprise the forts, so the troops were raised as if for service in Kentucky. It took all winter to secure one hundred and fifty men.

The Expedition against the Illinois Country

At last the expedition started. The men went down a branch of the Ohio River in flatboats, stopped for supplies at Fort Pitt, "the gateway of the West," and soon reached the falls.

There Clark learned of the treaty that France had made with the United States. His hopes rose high; for he believed that now the French townspeople around the forts would join him all the more willingly.

At the falls of the Ohio he told his men the real object of the expedition. Some of them lost courage and went back to Virginia; some remained where they were and founded a city; the rest, picked men who could bear great hardships, floated on with Clark down the river.

When they neared the Mississippi, they left the river and struck out for one hundred and twenty miles overland so that no one could see them coming. Six days they traveled through the woods and across the plains, and on the evening of the Fourth of July came in sight of the first fort, or blockhouse, surrounded by a town with two long narrow streets knee-deep in mud. The fort contained two or three times as many men as Clark had; but most of them were French, and they probably would not fight for their English masters. (On the map on page 503 find George Rogers Clark's route.)

The only hope of success lay in surprising the town. After dark the Americans quietly crossed the river. Some dogs barked, but the British paid no attention to the warning. Soon the village was surrounded.

An old story, which may not be true, says that the townspeople were having a dance that night. The music rose merrily, and all the young men and women were gayly tripping about, when suddenly a tall leather-clothed figure leaning on a gun appeared at the door.

At first no one noticed him. Then an Indian who had been watching the dance jumped to his feet with a war whoop. At once the music stopped, and all was excitement. Clark told the people to go on with the dance, but added, "You are now under the power of the United States, not of the British."

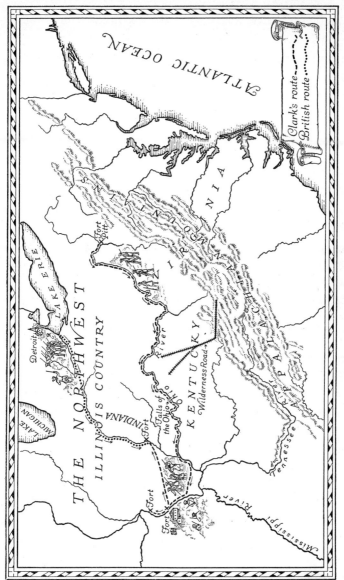

The winning of the Northwest

The truth probably is that the Virginians surrounded the town and, finding a gate open, entered and captured the fort with hardly a struggle. The villagers were ordered to stay within doors during the night, and in the morning they were told that Clark would not harm them if they would promise to obey the United States Congress. They were glad to promise anything, for they had heard terrible tales about the "Big Knives," as the Americans were called.

Clark spent the winter in the fort. It was not long before both Indians and French learned to respect him. Many of his men went home when their time was up, and he filled their places with young Frenchmen.

When the village priest found out that his church was not to be harmed, he himself traveled to another fort, in what is now Indiana, and persuaded the villagers there to pull down the English flag and run up the Stars and Stripes in its place. Clark had so few men that he could spare only one officer and one soldier to take charge of this second fort, so easily won.

A third fort, a little farther up the Mississippi, had meanwhile been taken by a few men on horseback. Thus without firing a shot or shedding a drop of blood, a great part of the West had been won. But, to hold it, Clark had to depend entirely on himself and his hundred followers.

Taking the Indiana Country

When the British general in Detroit learned of the loss of his forts, he at once made plans to get them back. He prepared a great force of five hundred men, with boats, guns, ammunition, supplies, cattle, and cannon. These he moved to the Indiana country, and after a hard journey reached the nearest of the forts which Clark had taken. The fort with its officer and its one soldier surrendered. There was nothing else to do.

As it was now December the British officer decided to delay the attack on the other two forts until spring. He sent most of his soldiers back to Detroit. The French townspeople cared little whether they were under the British or the Americans, and the general from Detroit won them over as easily as the priest had won them over to Clark.

Clark's two forts in the Illinois country were then in a very dangerous position. He knew that they would be attacked in the spring by a large British force, and that he could not get any more men from Virginia. He knew too that he could not depend on the French towns-people to help him.

So he struck a bold blow. Instead of waiting to be attacked in the spring, he decided to attack first in the winter. He got together a hundred and seventy men, some of whom were backwoodsmen and some French, and in February set out for the Indiana country. (On the map on page 503 trace his route to the Indiana country.)

A large flatboat called *The Willing* was supplied with four guns and was sent around by way of the Mississippi and Ohio rivers. Clark and his men set out overland on a march of sixteen days to the Indiana fort, which was now held by British troops.

For the first week the journey was not hard, except when they had to cross rivers. Clark always marched in front of his troops and laughed and sang to keep up their spirits. They shot some buffaloes for food and sat around warm camp fires at night.

The second week they tramped over low swampy ground where rivers were running full with the spring floods.

All day long they had to wade through icy water, sometimes up to their knees, sometimes to their waists. They could find no food anywhere. At night they lay on the cold wet ground, without even the shelter of tents. In the morning their clothing was covered with ice, and they broke the thin ice as they waded along.

They dared not make fires for fear the British would see the light and so learn of their coming. Day after day Clark and his followers plodded on. Some of the French wanted to go back, but the Americans marched steadily on.

The last day was the worst. The water came up to the shoulders of the men. All held their guns and ammunition over their heads to keep them dry.

By this time some were so weak that they fell down into the water and could not rise again. Canoes paddled swiftly about, trying to save them. As they crossed the last river Clark led the way, leaving twenty-five men at the end of the line to shoot any who might try to turn back. When at last they reached higher ground, many fell forward on their faces, not able to move.

The fort was then in plain sight. An Indian canoe with some corn and buffalo meat was captured. This gave the men a little food. A Frenchman hunting ducks was taken prisoner; from him they learned that

Clark's expedition
The men are on their way to Indiana

the British knew nothing of their coming. They also learned that a large number of Indians had lately joined the British in the fort.

When Clark heard how many men the British general had, he gave up the plan of surprising the fort and used his wits to think of some other plan. He wrote a letter to the French townspeople saying that he was advancing with a great army and warning all friends of the British to seek shelter in the fort. All who stayed shut up in their own houses would not be harmed. He felt sure that the French villagers would not fight for the British. They did not even warn the British, but, instead, gave the Americans the first full meal which they had had in six days.

Then Clark marched his men back and forth many times through the woods, to make it seem that he had a large army. The Indians who had been with the British ran off, afraid to join the fight. A few who returned to the fort with scalps were surprised and killed, and the townspeople saw their bodies thrown into the river.

In the battle that followed, the French took no part on either side. Clark at last made the fort surrender, though the British had cannon, and he had only rifles. The terms of surrender were hard, because this was the general who had bought scalps. He was sent to Virginia as a prisoner.

Clark's wish was to go on and take Detroit, but with so few men that was impossible. He did, however, capture a party coming from Detroit with a large amount of supplies. These he divided among his men.

Results of Clark's Work

During all the rest of the Revolution the Americans were able to hold the forts which Clark had taken and to keep the Indians quiet. Congress, three weeks after his last victory, laid claim to all the Northwest. Settlement advanced rapidly in Kentucky and Tennessee.

When the Revolution was over and the treaty of peace was signed, Clark's men still had the Western forts. So the Western lands were given to the United States by the treaty. The further settling of the West was thus made possible.

Some Things to Explain

1. What was George Rogers Clark's plan to protect Kentucky?

2. What did Clark tell the people at the first fort he captured?

3. Why did not the British general take all the forts after he took one?

4. Why was Clark in danger during the winter?

5. What did he say in his letter to the townspeople at the fort in Indiana?

6. What result of Clark's work showed in the treaty of peace?

Choose One

From the following groups of words choose those which will make a true statement. Write them in a list.

1. The American who conquered the British forts north of the Ohio was

General Burgoyne   **George Rogers Clark**
Samuel Adams

2. His conquests gave the United States the

interior   Southeast   Northwest

3. A group of men who go upon a journey into strange lands for a particular purpose make an

expedition   exposition   exhibition

George Rogers Clark took some British forts in the back country north of the Ohio River.

Later the United States laid claim to all this land.

What is the difference between a warship and a merchant ship? What is a navy? At the beginning of the Revolution did the American colonies have a navy? How could they do any fighting at sea without one?

FIGHTING AT SEA

Before the Revolution the colonies had no navy. They depended on British men-of-war. But in New England and New York there were a great many fishing and trading ships. It is easy to mount guns on merchant vessels and thus to change them for a time into warships. Very early in the war the colonists had done this very thing.

Privateers

Such vessels, sent out to seize supply ships and trading vessels of the enemy, were called *privateers*. They were not part of the regular navy, and did not fight men-of-war if they could help it.

Any rich merchant might buy a ship and get letters from Congress or from Franklin, giving him permission to attack the trading fleet of the enemy. He might arm his merchant ship with cannon, hire officers and a crew, and send the ship out to do as much damage as possible. Franklin's letters ordered the privateers not to burn coast towns unless they had a good reason, and even then to give notice so that the women and children, the sick and the old, might first be taken away.

These privateers attacked British merchant ships chiefly in the West Indies and along the North American coast. They would slip out to sea and search about for the enemy, stationing a sailor high up on the mast to look for a sail. Almost every day one or two could be seen after they reached the *high seas*, three miles away from land.

The privateer would give chase as soon as a vessel was sighted; if she found it too large to attack, or if it showed the flag of a friendly nation, she would turn back.

If it proved to be a British merchant ship, and not too large, she would attack it. A sharp fight would follow, and the merchant vessel, which usually carried fewer guns than the privateer, would have to surrender. The crew of the privateer would seize the British captain, with all his papers, and keep his men below the decks as prisoners. A small crew would then take charge of the captured ship, which was called a "prize," and would sail her quickly to the nearest friendly port. There they would bring her crew before a court; and her load — molasses, rum, sugar, or army supplies — would be sold. Sometimes the ship itself was sold, and sometimes it was fitted out as another privateer. The "prize money" was divided among the crew.

We do not wonder that service with privateers was preferred to service with the regular navy or with the army. There was always a chance for prize money, and the risk was less.

The exact number of such vessels is not known, but it must have been very large. During the war more

than six hundred prizes were captured. British merchant ships did not try to make long voyages except in
fleets, with men-of-war to protect them.

But as the war went on, the privateers met with less
success. The British men-of-war sailed up and down
the American coast, seizing any ship that dared come
out and burning port towns. At last the attempt to
send goods by sea, even from one colony to another,
became so dangerous that it was not made. For while
the American privateers took six hundred merchant
ships, the British took nine hundred American vessels.

The use of privateers, then, did not bring success to
either side.

The American Navy

It soon became clear that privateers alone were not
enough. A regular navy was needed to protect the
coasts and the merchant vessels of the United States
and, if possible, to prevent British supply ships from
reaching the British armies in America. If ships bringing guns and ammunition from England could have been
kept away from the British army in New York, the city
would soon have been in the hands of the Americans.

Even before the Declaration of Independence was
signed, Congress had begun to build a navy. But it
was slow work, because many of the best shipbuilders
were away privateering, and none of the colonists knew
how to make cannon.

Congress did not have enough money to build large
ships, but on the advice of John Paul Jones they ordered
small fast-sailing vessels. The first United States fleet

consisted of eight ships, only one of which carried as many as twenty-four guns. They were manned largely by American sailors.

Besides the United States navy, all the states but two built navies of their own to defend their coasts.

During the entire war there were only forty-one ships in the United States navy, and most of these were either captured or were destroyed by their own crews to prevent them from falling into the hands of the enemy. When the end came, only six were in service at sea. The American navy had not played a great part in the winning of the war.

John Paul Jones

The American sailors, however, were brave men. The greatest of them all was John Paul Jones. He was born in Scotland, his name then being John Paul. When only twelve years old he found work on a ship, and sailed the seas for many years. On one voyage the captain and all but five of the crew died of yellow fever, but John Paul brought the ship home. Afterwards he became master of a merchant vessel.

One of his brothers had settled in Virginia and had taken the name of Jones. When this brother died he left his plantation to John Paul on condition that he also should take the name Jones. Thus John Paul became John Paul Jones.

Two years before the Revolution he settled in Virginia and took charge of his plantation. But as soon as war broke out he offered his services to Congress.

He advised them to send ships into the waters around Europe, so that the nations of Europe might see the new American flag and be forced to think of the new nation. Congress gave him a vessel, and with it he took a British man-of-war, the first that the British ever lost to a smaller ship.

The year after France decided to help the United States, he was given command of a little fleet of five vessels, most of them built in France and manned by Frenchmen. They set out from a port in Europe, but at sea they scattered. Jones's own ship was called by a French name that meant "Poor Richard," in honor of Franklin's *Poor Richard's Almanac*. It was made out of a merchant vessel, with holes cut in the sides for the guns.

First Jones sailed to the British coast that he had known as a boy, and there he attacked some of the towns. One of the towns laid a line of logs and chains across the harbor to keep him out, but he took the forts on the hills and set fire to the ships in the harbor.

The Most Famous Sea Fight of the Revolution

Sailing farther south with two of his little fleet, he saw a fleet of forty-one British merchant ships protected by two men-of-war. Here was his great chance.

Leaving his smaller ship to attack the smaller man-of-war, the *Poor Richard* made for the large one. The fight began about seven o'clock at night and lasted for more than three hours. Some of the American cannon were so old that they burst the first time they were

© Carlton T. Chapman

The *Poor Richard's* greatest fight

Which is the American ship? (Courtesy of the City Art Museum of St. Louis)

fired, killing a dozen of their own men. The British fire was very hot, and soon the *Poor Richard* was leaking in many places.

Jones then ran his ship directly into the other. "Have you hauled down your flag?" shouted the British commander. "I have not yet begun to fight," said Jones.

The ships lay so close together that the mouths of their cannon touched. Jones fastened them together and began shooting. Soon the *Richard* had only three guns left. Her decks were covered with the dead and wounded; she was on fire; and she had five feet of water in her hold. It was "a scene dreadful beyond the reach of language."

Both vessels were almost torn to pieces. The British commander was left almost alone on deck. His ship had been on fire ten times. When the Americans boarded, he had to surrender. All the wounded were carried over to the British vessel, and in a short time the *Poor Richard* sank.

This victory made the people of Europe begin for the first time to respect the Americans as sailors. It showed what the United States could do if it had a navy.

Jones spent most of the rest of his life in France and Russia; but after his death his body was brought back and buried at Annapolis, where the United States has a great school to train officers for the navy.

How the French Fleet saved the Day

One of the French commanders, shortly after coming to this country, said to Washington, "Nothing can be gained without control at sea." Washington, remembering the times when he had been obliged to stand and watch British troops being carried from one port to another, agreed with all his heart.

One of the chief advantages expected from the French treaty was that the French fleet might be able to hold the British fleet in check. But for some years the French fleet did little. Fear of its coming drove the British out of Philadelphia and back to New York, but the French admiral was afraid he could not get his great ships into New York harbor, and he did not try.

A battle was begun off Rhode Island, but a storm blew the ships away and scattered them. After that the French commander sailed to the West Indies.

For a long time nothing happened; but at last came the right moment for the fleet to strike. In Virginia the British general Cornwallis had brought all his army to a narrow neck of land, expecting British ships to come and take his soldiers on board.

Instead of that a French fleet of twenty-eight great ships carrying twenty thousand men sailed in and surrounded him. A little later nineteen British ships came down from New York. A great battle followed, but the British could do nothing against a force so much larger than theirs. For the first time during the war the British had lost control of the sea. In the midst of the fight twelve more French ships from Rhode Island were added to the fleet. It was impossible even to continue fighting. The British vessels had to retreat.

Cornwallis had no hope of getting help. He was surrounded by the French ships and the American army, and surrendered. The war was over. The French navy had played an important part in winning peace.

Picking out the Most Important Facts

You need not try to remember everything that was told in the story. These questions will help you to pick out the most important facts:

1. Why did the Americans use privateers when the war first broke out?

2. For what three purposes was a regular navy needed?

3. What effect did John Paul Jones's victories at sea have?

4. What was one great advantage expected from the treaty with France?

5. What was the right moment for the French fleet to strike?

6. Why could the British ships not help General Cornwallis?

Completing Sentences

In the story you learned facts that will help you to complete the following sentences. Give your sentences before the class. If yours are right, perhaps your teacher will let you call on the next person to give his.

1. John Paul Jones was

2. Annapolis is

3. By the "high seas" we mean

4. A privateer is

The American navy was very small.

Much of the fighting at sea was done for the Americans by the French.

John Paul Jones was a great American hero.

Which nation won the Revolutionary War? How do you know? Should you like to read about how the British were at last forced to surrender?

THE WAR ENDS IN THE SOUTH

During the first four years of the war the British met with no great successes. In the New England states they had been driven out of Boston and held only one or two coast towns. In the middle states they held New York, which gave them a chance to reach the interior of the country by going up the Hudson, but this they had not been able to do.

They decided at last to turn to the South, where many Tories lived who would help them. The American troops from New England could not come so far as that, they thought, and Washington and his army would be a thousand miles away. At the same time the British continued to hold New York. They knew that so long as they kept that city Washington would have to stay there to watch them. He would not dare to let them get control of the Hudson River. Therefore they would have a free hand in the South.

Conquest of Georgia and South Carolina

Georgia was at that time the weakest of the states and had the fewest people. The British plan was to march through Georgia and the Carolinas upward toward Virginia, which was one of the richest states and a leader in the war.   After conquering the states to the south, they thought Virginia could be easily taken.   Their plan very nearly succeeded.

The war in the South was fiercer and more cruel than in the North or in the middle states, though not so many great battles were fought.   There were many sudden attacks at night and much hard riding.   Captured soldiers were crowded together in dreadful prison ships, and some were killed even after they had surrendered.

As some of the Southerners were Tories, and others were in favor of the Revolution, there were sad scenes of neighbors fighting against one another.   Whichever side was for the moment in control burned the houses of the other, drove their women and children out of doors, and killed their cattle.   Merchants would not buy from those who belonged to the other side, nor sell to them, and there was much hard feeling.

Georgia was easily taken.   Forts were placed at important places in the interior, and many Tories joined the British army.   A French fleet and an American army tried to win back some of the coast towns, but did not succeed.   (On the map on page 521, find the route of the British through Georgia and South Carolina.)

After Georgia was conquered, the Carolinas were next.   Their most important city, Charleston, had been in American hands since the beginning of the war ;   but when it was surrounded by the British, there were few who came to its defense.   The country people were afraid that if they left their homes to fight, all their slaves would run away.   So the large American force in Charleston had to surrender, and at the end of the first

The Revolution in the South

year of the war in that section not a trace of the American army was left in all the South. A man in London wrote, "We look on America as at our feet."

By the end of the first year of fighting in the South, both Georgia and South Carolina had been conquered and the only American army in that section had been taken.

Congress saw that help was needed at once, and ordered Washington to send part of the army to the Carolinas.

He did so; and near Charleston, where the road comes in from the north, the American general in charge of the expedition, with three thousand men, met Cornwallis with two thousand British. The Americans were ill from their long march without proper food, for they had had only green apples, peaches, and corn that was not ripe. In the battle that followed they were completely beaten. One thousand were killed, one thousand were taken prisoners, and the rest were chased twenty miles. They lost nearly all their guns.

For the second time inside of three months the American army was swept out of the South. It was the darkest hour of the Revolution in that region.

Here and there, on the frontier of the regions held by the British, small companies of brave men continued to attack and to worry the army of Cornwallis. Sometimes as few as twenty, sometimes as many as seventy, but seldom more than that, would fire upon the British from swamps and forests. Some were armed with guns, some with swords made out of saws. They would hide for a while, then come suddenly out and capture British supply wagons, or set prisoners free, or stop riders carrying important messages; and whenever a large force of the enemy came out to search for them they would scatter and could not be found. They were called "swamp foxes."

The Attempt on North Carolina

With no American army to stop them, the British advanced into North Carolina. Cornwallis marched directly north with part of his army, while he sent another part to the west to gather in the Tories who were willing to fight for the king. As this second division marched toward the mountains they began to feel that they were being surrounded by farmers and backwoodsmen. They stopped and took up a strong position on the side of a steep mountain called King's Mountain; but the backwoodsmen, waiting only long enough to tie their horses, began to climb after them. Dashing from tree to tree and from rock to rock, Indian fashion, they trapped the British. They killed four hundred of them and took seven hundred prisoners. Then the members of the backwoods army went home.

This battle of King's Mountain was the first American victory in the South. The result gave the Americans a little hope at a time when hope and courage were greatly needed. Cornwallis retreated to South Carolina, and North Carolina was saved. (On the map on page 521, find Cornwallis's route through North Carolina.)

Discouraging Times in the South

By the end of the year 1780 it seemed that the war could not continue and that Great Britain would surely win. No important American victories had been won for three years. Washington himself had almost given up hope, and his letters were bitter. Neither Congress nor the assemblies of the states would support the army. Instead of laying taxes, they printed paper money which was almost worthless. It took $150 to buy a bushel of corn, $12 for a pound of butter, $90 for a pound of tea, $10 for a pound of sugar, $1575 for a barrel of flour, and $2000 for a suit of clothes. Because this paper money was sent out by the Continental Congress, the words "not worth a continental" were used when one meant to say "worth nothing at all."

The army suffered almost as badly as at Valley Forge. Four months' pay of a private soldier would not buy one bushel of wheat for his family; and a month's pay of an officer would not buy grain for his horse, and even this amount was sometimes fifteen months overdue.

It is not surprising that men would not join the army, nor that one or two hundred every month went over to the enemy. The really surprising thing is that any remained. Without the help of France the war could not have gone on.

But things were happening in Europe which were to have a great effect on the war in America. We have seen that not only France declared war against England, but also Spain and the Netherlands. The rest of

Europe was not friendly to her. From 1780 on, England had her hands full at home. Hope came, then, from across the seas rather than from the efforts of the people at home.

Greene sets the Carolinas and Georgia Free

Washington was afraid that if a blow were not struck soon, the Revolution would go to pieces. He sent his best general, Nathanael Greene, to see what could be done in the South. Greene had no army, and there was none to give him. He found the South in a dreadful condition, but he at once set to work building up a force. He needed men, clothing, food, guns, ammunition, wagons — everything. For months he could not give battle, but had to hide and retreat. He spent most of his time in persuading men to join him and in drilling them, but now and then he would attack a supply train and worry Cornwallis, as the "swamp foxes" had done before.

Cornwallis sent troops to clear out this small army. One of Greene's generals met him in battle, having fresh soldiers most of whom had never before been under fire. He placed these men with their backs to a broad river so that they could not retreat if they wanted to. They did not want to. They fought like old soldiers and won the victory. The worst days in the South were now over.

Greene then retreated through North Carolina, drawing Cornwallis after him into a rough country where few people lived. What he wanted was to get Cornwallis far away from his supplies, while he himself was all the time adding the farmers of the countryside to his army.

He would not stand and fight, as Cornwallis wanted to do, but he wore out the British and saved his own army.

At last Cornwallis had nothing for his soldiers to eat, and so had to go back to the coast, where he could get supplies from the fleet. Greene's plan had worked as he intended, and the interior of North Carolina was once more saved. (On the map on page 521, find the route of the Americans. Find Cornwallis's route to the coast.)

Cornwallis did not want to remain on the coast after he had his supplies. Where should he strike next? He advanced into Virginia, one of the largest and richest of the states. Greene decided that Virginia could take care of itself, so he left Cornwallis and marched back to free Georgia and the Carolinas. The British had thought these states were conquered once for all. What was their surprise and anger, then, to find that in a short time all their interior posts were taken and that only the seaport towns were left to them. Their work of the last two years was undone.

Cornwallis in Virginia

Virginia was defended by Lafayette. "That boy cannot escape me," Cornwallis said. It was true that Lafayette had few troops — so few that he wrote, "I am not strong enough even to be beaten." But he slipped through Cornwallis's fingers and dashed about from river to river and mountain to mountain, his army all the time growing larger by the addition of the farmers. In time he thought enough men would join him so that he might offer battle.

Cornwallis again went back to the coast and took up a position at Yorktown, where he could get supplies by sea. Lafayette followed and surrounded him on the land side, but Cornwallis did not care for that. He expected help from the British fleet which was at New York, and asked the British commander there to send it down. (On the map on page 521 find Yorktown.)

But the British commander in New York had been so closely guarded by Washington that he did not dare to send help to anyone.

All this time a large French army was camping in Rhode Island, waiting for more troops from France that never came.

Washington's Great Opportunity

Just at this moment word was brought to Washington, patiently watching New York, that a large French fleet from the West Indies would come up to help him for a few months. It was the chance for which he had been waiting ever since the war began. For a short time he would have control of the sea.

He would have chosen New York as the point of attack, but the French admiral sent word that he was coming to Chesapeake Bay. So Washington quickly changed his plans. He asked the French army in Rhode Island to join him, and together the two armies moved down the Hudson. The commander at New York thought they were surely going to attack him, but instead they turned and crossed New Jersey. How different from the terrible retreat across New Jersey five years before!

Where were they going? The British did not know.
Even the French and American armies did not know
until they reached Philadelphia. Then they understood that they were on their way to Yorktown. "Washington is going to catch Cornwallis in his mousetrap,"
they said. (On the map on page 521 find the route of
the Americans.)

Washington could not get ships enough to carry the
armies from Philadelphia to Virginia, so most of the
soldiers had to march overland. Lafayette's own
brother-in-law, a great noble of France, marched all the
long distance (seven hundred and fifty-six miles) from
Rhode Island to Yorktown.

On the way Washington stopped for a few hours at
his home at Mount Vernon, which he had not seen since
the day so long ago when he had set out as a member
from Virginia to the Second Continental Congress.

The two armies, American and French, reached
Yorktown and joined Lafayette in surrounding Cornwallis on the land side. In our last story we read how
twenty-eight French ships, the greatest fleet that had
ever gathered in American waters, closed in upon
Cornwallis from the sea and completed the circle.

The British fought bravely and well, but their cause
was lost. Shells dropped on the town day and night.
Houses were full of holes, and windows were broken.
Many of the British soldiers were sick and in the
hospital.

At last, just four years after the battle of Saratoga,
Cornwallis gave up. For the second time an entire
British army surrendered. The American troops,

The armies at Yorktown, 1781

ragged and worn, lined up on one side, and the French in their bright uniforms, on the other, and the British marched out between them. The band played "The World turned Upside Down."

When the news was received in the different states, bonfires were lighted, prayers were offered in the churches, and special days of thanksgiving appointed.

The war had really ended, but some fighting went on for another year, especially in the South. There were no great battles; the country was tired of war and only waited for the treaty of peace. It was 1783 before the last British soldier left New York.

The Treaty of Peace, 1783

America sent John Adams and some others to join Franklin in Paris and decide on the terms of the peace. There they met the British representatives. For several months each side tried to gain advantages over the other.

France asked nothing from the colonies in return for her help, though she had spent much money.

Great Britain at last agreed that the United States should be independent, and that they should have all the land from the Mississippi River to the Atlantic and from the Great Lakes and the St. Lawrence River to Florida and the Gulf of Mexico. The treaty was signed in 1783.

The British Empire had been broken; but the new nation, though independent, was still English in language, in customs, and in ways of thinking.

"*Prove It*"

Are you ready to play the game given below? Prove to yourself that you are ready by answering these questions:

1. For what two reasons did the British turn to the South?

2. Why did General Washington not take his army south?

3. Why did the war in the South move so slowly?

4. What did General Greene have to do first in the South?

5. Why did General Cornwallis take up a position at Yorktown?

6. What was agreed in the treaty of peace?

A Choosing Game

Here is a list of words. From the list choose the right word or words to complete each sentence below:

Cornwallis	Paris	1783
Nathanael Greene	Yorktown	"swamp foxes"

1. The great battle which ended the Revolution was _____.

2. The treaty of peace was signed in the city of _____.

3. It was signed in the year _____.

4. The American general who freed the South from the British soldiers was _____ _____.

5. The few soldiers who kept the Revolution alive in the South during the darkest days were known as _ _ _ _ _ _ _ _ _ _ _ _ _ .

6. The British general who had to surrender because his fleet could not help him was _ _ _ _ _ _ _ .

Most of the fighting in the South was done by small American forces.

The British general was shut up in Yorktown.

The French fleet would not let any more British troops come in to help him.

Cornwallis surrendered, and the war was over.

Why do we celebrate the Fourth of July every year?
Why should we always remember July 4, 1776? What
nation is meant in the title of our story?

THE BIRTH OF A NATION

At the beginning of the Revolution the colonists were
fighting for their rights as Englishmen. They did not
wish to separate from the mother country, where many
of them had been born and their fathers and grand-
fathers before them. The Second Continental Congress
in the summer of 1775, even after the battles of Lexington and Concord, declared that the colonies were not
fighting for independence. Most of the men who owned
a great deal of property were against war altogether,
for war always destroys property.

John Adams, however, had for a long time favored
independence; and early in the year 1776 George
Washington came to the same view. By that time he
and his army had come to believe that the trouble between England and America could only be cured by
separating. Many others were beginning to feel the
same way.

Why People began to change their Minds

There were several reasons for the feeling that the
colonies ought to be independent:

1. Whenever two nations go to war they always learn
to hate each other, no matter how they may have felt

before. Some have sons or brothers killed by the enemy; some have their houses burned before their eyes, and their cattle and crops taken to feed the troops who burned them. England and the colonies did not hate each other at the beginning of the war, but they soon learned to do so.

2. In the years of quarreling before the war, many letters had been written to the king, asking him to make right what the colonists thought were wrongs. He refused even to read the last of the letters and, as Samuel Adams said, "answered by armies and fleets." The colonists came to believe that they could never secure their rights by simply asking for them.

3. Independence would be a great advantage in securing help from other countries in Europe. If the colonists remained subjects of King George III, they would have no more right to ask France for help in war than the city of London would. But if they should declare themselves to be a new nation, the new nation would have a right to ask other nations for help.

4. When the Americans heard that the king had sent for German troops to fight against them, many who had not been willing to leave him before decided that they would no longer be ruled by him.

5. A little paper called *Common Sense* was printed and widely read throughout the colonies. It put into words what many people had been thinking and made them think still harder. It declared that independence was necessary, that the king was unfair, and that America would get along better by itself. This made the colonists still more ready to separate from England.

Steps toward Independence

Slowly one colony after another made a new state government for itself, but no one of these could act alone. A Declaration of Independence must be made by the Continental Congress, to which all had sent representatives.

The Continental Congress held its meetings in Philadelphia, in a building which we today call Independence Hall. Everyone knew that the representatives from New England and from Virginia were eager to separate from Great Britain. The other Southern colonies would probably follow, but there was doubt about the middle colonies.

Virginia took the lead. In June, 1776, she directed one of her representatives to say to Congress that "these United Colonies are and of right ought to be free and independent states." What a stir that short speech made! It meant, if the colonies voted for it, a long, hard war. It meant that every man who voted for it would probably be hanged as a traitor if he should fall into the hands of the British. Surely the representatives should think well before they voted for a thing like that.

Some of them did not know whether or not the colonies from which they came would want them to vote for it. They were given three weeks in which to find out. In order to save time a committee was appointed to draw up a paper stating just what the Declaration of Independence should say. Then, when Congress voted on it three weeks later, they would not have to wait for it to be written out.

John Adams, Benjamin Franklin, Thomas Jefferson, and two others were appointed as the committee. John Adams said to Jefferson, one of the youngest men in Congress: "You can write ten times better than I can. You do it." Jefferson replied, "I will do as well as I can." So Jefferson wrote the Declaration, and Adams and Franklin made a few changes in it afterwards.

The three weeks were up in July, and Congress again considered the question of separating. John Adams made a great speech in favor of independence, and a few made speeches against it.

Representatives from some of the Southern states did not like all that was in the Declaration, but they felt that they must agree. "We must all hang together," cried John Hancock, the president of Congress. "Yes, we must indeed all hang together," said Franklin, "or we shall all hang separately."

At first nine colonies were in favor of independence and four were not, but at last all thirteen colonies voted for it. The Declaration of Independence was passed on July 4, 1776. No longer were there thirteen colonies; there were thirteen *states*. No longer were the people British subjects; they were Americans. The bell in the great hall of the building was rung to let all the people know that a new nation, the United States of America, had been born. Today we call that bell the Liberty Bell. It still hangs in Philadelphia, and people come from far and near to see it.

Other bells rang in other cities, cannon were fired, and bonfires were lighted. The Declaration of Independence was read to the army. It was written in

Signing the Declaration of Independence
Why are so many men present? (Courtesy of the Philadelphia
Historical Society)

French and sent to France, so that her people might
know that we had become an independent nation.

In New York the lead statue of King George III was
pulled down and melted into bullets. No longer could
any American say in this quarrel, "I am neither on one
side nor the other." If he was not in favor of the
Declaration he was a Tory, and Tories were not wanted.

The paper drawn up by Thomas Jefferson was written out carefully and signed by John Hancock as president of Congress. Perhaps your teacher can show you a
copy of his bold writing, which, he said, "King George
could read without glasses." After Hancock, the other

The first public reading of the Declaration of Independence,
Philadelphia

From a painting by Clyde O. De Land

representatives signed their names. Some whom we know are Samuel Adams, John Adams, Robert Morris, Benjamin Franklin, and Thomas Jefferson.

How Well do you Read?

1. At the beginning, what were the colonists fighting for?

2. Why could not each state declare itself independent?

3. What group of people would have to decide on independence? Why?

4. Why did the representatives have to think carefully before voting?

5. How did the people of the nation learn about the Declaration of Independence?

Using New Words

This time you may give your own sentences, using the new words below:

Name of Person	Date
1. John Hancock	**3.** July 4, 1776, Declaration of Independence

Name of Place	Words
2. Independence Hall	**4.** Declaration of Independence
	5. Fourth of July
	6. state **7.** independent

At first the colonies were fighting for their rights as Englishmen.

Later they decided to make a nation of their own.

The history of the *United States* begins with the Declaration of Independence.

Do all nations have the same kind of government? Why do we think that ours is a good one? Should you like to find out how our present government was formed?

A GOOD GOVERNMENT AT LAST

After the war was over, every wise man in the United States knew that the old government, called the Articles of Confederation, under which the states were united during the war, would serve no longer. The government was breaking down. Already the weaknesses of the old government had been shown, and two meetings had been held to try to patch them up. But in order to make any change the consent of all thirteen states must be had, and it was hard to get all of them to agree. There was always at least one state which would not consent to changes. Thus the years dragged on, and matters went from bad to worse.

The Great Meeting

At last, after the Articles of Confederation had been tried for six years, a great meeting was held in Independence Hall, Philadelphia, to see what could be done about making a better government.

Washington, the man of action, was made president of the meeting. He sat in a large high-backed chair on a platform, and his ideas were listened to carefully. Franklin was by this time eighty-one years old. He wrote out his speeches, and they were read to the meeting by a younger man. It was decided to write a new plan of government, which was to be called the *Constitution of the United States.*

The leader in the work was young James Madison, who knew more about government than any other man present. He did so much of the writing of the new plan of government that he was called the Father of the Constitution. Another young man, who had served as Washington's secretary during the Revolution, was Alexander Hamilton. We shall hear of him again.

For more than four months of a very hot summer these men thought, talked, and planned to make the best possible government. Their meetings were secret, so that the country might not know how hard it was for them to agree.

Making the Constitution

The greatest problem that the members had to face was the question of *how the states could be left to govern themselves* and yet at the same time *join together in a United States government* that should have power enough to get its work done.

The problem was settled by dividing the powers. Some were given to the states themselves and some to the United States as a whole. They were all written down clearly, so that there could be no mistake.

Among the powers given to the United States Congress were (1) the power to coin money, (2) the power to lay and collect taxes, (3) the power to raise an army, (4) the power to declare war and make peace, and (5) the power to govern trade. This time not only was the United States given these rights, but it also could *force* people to obey. No longer did it have to *ask* the states not to tax each other's products; it *took charge* of all trade between them. No longer did it have to ask the states for soldiers; it could raise its own army. No longer did it have to ask the states for money; it could collect money for itself. Thus the greatest weakness of the old plan of government, called the Articles of Confederation, was changed in the new constitution.

The Constitution also said that there should be a president of the United States and there should be United States courts.

How Differences of Opinion were Managed

You must not suppose that the fifty-five members who were present at one time or other at the meetings agreed on all questions. Sometimes they did not. Many times when one member could not make the rest agree to his ideas, he went home, declaring that his state would not accept the new government.

Their greatest dispute was between the states which had a large number of people, such as Massachusetts, Pennsylvania, Virginia, and the Carolinas, and the states which had fewer people, such as Connecticut, New Jersey, Delaware, Maryland, and New York. The question on which they could not agree was about the number of representatives that each should send to the United States Congress.

The large states believed that there should be one representative for a certain number of people. The

The men who made the Constitution

From a painting which hangs in the Wisconsin State Capitol

more people that there were in any state, the more representatives that state should have. Rhode Island might have only one representative, and Massachusetts might have six or seven because Massachusetts had so many more people.

The small states believed that every state should have the same number of representatives, no matter how many or how few people lived in each. They thought that New Hampshire should have as many as Virginia, and that Delaware should have as many as Pennsylvania.

For two months they quarreled over this. Neither side would give in; both grew excited and angry. It seemed as if they could never agree. But all of them had been so discouraged over the failure of the old government, called the Articles of Confederation, that they felt they must not go home without something better to offer. So they stayed and worked on. At last somebody thought of a plan. They agreed that Congress should meet in two different rooms, or houses, instead of in one, as they had always met before. In one house of Congress the representatives should be chosen according to the number of people, to please the larger states. In the other house each state should have the same number of representatives, to please the smaller states.

So each side gained part of what it wanted and gave up part for the sake of union. Such an agreement is called a *compromise*. The agreement about representation has been called "the Great Compromise."

There were other differences of opinion which were settled in the same way — by compromises between the different states or sections of the country. One representative wrote that he "did not believe a single member was perfectly satisfied, but it was the best they could ever agree upon." Each one gave up something for the good of all.

At last the Constitution was copied on a long roll of paper, and the members signed their names.

1789 — the Constitution goes into Effect

The worst of the trouble might seem to be over when the representatives of the states had signed the Constitution, but the states themselves still had to agree to it.

No state could understand why it had not received all that it wanted; but after much arguing and explaining, all thirteen of the states agreed to the new government. It went into effect in 1789. New York was chosen as the capital of the nation for the time being, and George Washington was elected the first *president of the United States*.

Today the Constitution is looked upon as one of the greatest papers in the history of the world. An English statesman called it "the most wonderful work ever struck off at a given time by the brain and purpose of man."

A Memory Test

You need not try to remember all the facts told in the story, but it is necessary that you understand the most important of them. The following questions will help you to select the principal facts:

1. Why was it hard to change the Articles of Confederation?

2. What was the hardest thing to settle in making the Constitution of the United States?

3. How was it settled?

4. What were the two groups of states which could not agree?

5. What opinion did each hold about representation?

6. How was this difficulty settled?

Which do you Choose?

Choose from each group the year or the words which make the sentence true:

1. The Constitution of the United States went into effect in   1776   1783   1789

2. The government under which we are now living is the

Constitution of the United States
Articles of Confederation
Declaration of Independence

3. The first president of the United States was

Benjamin Franklin   George Washington
John Hancock

The Constitution provided for a much stronger government.

We still have the same government in the United States today.

George Washington was elected the first president.

To the Boys and Girls who have read This Book

||||||||||||||||||||||||||||||||||||||||||||||||||||||||||||||||||||||||||||||||||||||||||||||||||||||||||||||||||||||||||||||||

You have now read all the stories in *The Beginnings of the American People and Nation.* You found that America was discovered because people in Europe were trying to find an all-sea route to Asia, and you found that the history of America has been greatly influenced by Europe ever since.

You know why we speak the English language here in the United States, and you have read how it happened that the colonies came to make themselves an independent nation.

During your reading you learned the names of a number of important persons in our history. Many times you will hear grown people talking about these persons, and you will be glad that you can understand the conversation.

You have learned the location of many places where great events happened, and you have learned a few dates. When you are old men and women you will still remember some of them. You have learned the meaning of many words which you will find used very often in newspapers and books.

But these are not all the stories which make up American history. At the time of the last story in this book (the one about the Constitution), you remember that the United States extended westward only as far as the Mississippi River.   Today it reaches from the Atlantic Ocean to the Pacific Ocean.

At the time that the Constitution was adopted, the United States was a poor weak nation with a new and untried government.   Today it is one of the strongest and richest nations in the world.   Then men traveled on horseback, sent messages by the post, burned candles, and wove cloth to make their own clothes.   Today we travel by railway and airplane, send messages by telephone and radio, light our homes with electricity, and buy everything we need at great stores.

You will like to know how such great changes in our ways of living came about.   The history book which you will read next year will tell you.   Its name is *The Growth of the American People and Nation*.   If you have liked the stories in this book, you will like to read those also.   They were written to tell boys and girls more about the history of our country.

Appendix

Content Organization — Teachers' Guide

NOTE. To assist teachers in finding for each story the technique as given in the author's *Teaching American History in the Middle Grades of the Elementary School,* the following outline has been drawn up. The pages in the teachers' book (T. A. H.) appear in the first column, and those in the children's text relating to the same story, in the second column.

Unit I

Why Men wanted to reach the Countries of the Far East

	T. A. H.	THIS BOOK
I. Marco Polo told the people about China.	55–57	7–18
II. Men who went on the Crusades learned to like new things to eat and wear.	57–62	19–28
III. Some went in ships and some on the backs of camels.	62–66	29–38
IV. Prince Henry wanted to go all the way by sea. His country sent Dias and Da Gama.	66–69	39–50
V. Men learned to use things that made travel easier.	73–76	51–58
1. Compass.		
2. Improvements in shipbuilding.		
3. Influence of the printing press.		
VI. Columbus's great idea was to go west and sail clear around the world.	77–81	59–71

Unit II

How the Nations tried to get Wealth from the New World

I. The Spanish.		
1. Columbus found land which he thought was India.	93–96	75–88
2. Magellan proved that it was a new world.	96–100	89–99

549

	T. A. H.	THIS BOOK
3. Cortez conquered the natives.	103–105	100–114
4. De Soto explored the land far from the sea.	106–109	115–125
II. The English.		
1. John Cabot discovered North America.	113–117	126–133
2. Francis Drake sailed around the world but found no rich lands like Spain's.	120–123	134–145
3. Walter Raleigh tried to build towns but failed.	124–127	146–155
III. The French and the Dutch.		
1. Cartier found a great river leading into the country.	130–133	156–163
2. Champlain built towns and made friends with the Indians.	134–136	164–172
3. Henry Hudson found a great river.	144–148	173–182

Unit III

Why English People came to live in the New World

I. Some people came to earn a better living.		
1. Virginia was the first English colony.		
a. John Smith helped the colony in the beginning.	166–169	185–201
b. After a while it grew and prospered.	169–172	202–209
2. How the people in the South lived.	172–176	210–226
a. Houses and furniture.		
b. Food.		
c. Clothing.		
d. Work.		
e. Churches and schools.		
f. Amusements and social life.		
g. Punishments.		
h. Travel.		

Unit V

How the English Colonies came to separate themselves from the Mother Country

Index and Pronouncing Vocabulary

ılılılılılılılılılılılılılılılılılılılılılılılılılılılılılılılılılılılılılılılılılılılılılılılılılılılılı

KEY. făt, fāte, necklâce, ärm, àsk, sofạ; mĕt, mēte, ĕnough, hẽr, novẹl; ĭt, īce; nŏt, nōte, ôbey, hôrse, anchọr; ūse, ûnite, fûr, stirrụp; fŏŏt, fōōd; oi as in oil; ou as in out; iṉk; bathe; natûre.